Architecture, Film, and the In-between

Architecture, Film, and the In-between

Spatio-Cinematic Betwixt

EDITED BY

Vahid Vahdat and James F. Kerestes

intellect

Bristol, UK / Chicago, USA

First published in the UK in 2023 by
Intellect, The Mill, Parnall Road, Fishponds, Bristol, BS16 3JG, UK

First published in the USA in 2023 by
Intellect, The University of Chicago Press, 1427 E. 60th Street,
Chicago, IL 60637, USA

A catalogue record for this book is available from the British Library.

Copy editor: MPS Limited
Cover designer: Vahid Vahdat & James F. Kerestes
Production manager: Debora Nicosia
Typesetter: MPS Limited

Hardback ISBN 978-1-78938-737-7
Paperback ISBN 978-1-78938-965-4
ePDF ISBN 978-1-78938-738-4
ePUB ISBN 978-1-78938-739-1

Printed and bound by CMP.

To find out about all our publications, please visit our website. There you can subscribe to our e-newsletter, browse or download our current catalogue and buy any titles that are in print.

www.intellectbooks.com

This is a peer-reviewed publication.

Contents

Figures

Acknowledgments

The editors wish to thank, first and foremost, our contributors. The creative lens through which each author has approached the topic has enriched the book beyond our imagination. We also offer our gratitude to Mark Foster Gage for his provocative foreword. Many thanks to Neil Denari and Greg Lynn for supporting the project in its search for resources. We are grateful to the care and dedication that the publication team at Intellect (Jelena Stanovnik, Debora Nicosia, James Campbell, and others) have put into this volume. The publication of this book would not have been possible without Ball State University's Aspire Internal Grant Program.

Foreword

Mark Foster Gage

Years ago, Peter Eisenman generously wrote the afterword to the first monograph on my work. In it, to paraphrase, he describes the loss of modernist subjectivity as a monolithic backdrop against which new architectural ideas could be seen. Eisenman was noting, as is even clearer today, that there no longer exists any monolithic ideological force in architecture that can be subverted as an act of resistance to uniformity—the very strategy on which so many architecture careers of the past half-century, including Eisenman's, were based. While the initial reactions to, for instance Denise Scott Brown and Robert Venturi's House for Vanna Venturi, Michael Graves's Portland Building, or Peter Eisenman's Wexner center, were frequently apoplectic, today such projects would warrant little, if any, reaction—or even attention. There is simply no formal language, no style, no programmatic arrangement, no selection of materials, and no process of construction that could today be considered taboo, radical, or even interesting enough to compel notice. The worry here is that the lack of any monolithic ideological consensus to react against, combined with the disciplinary wariness of seeing weirder and weirder images on social media masquerading as architecture, has left architecture in a state of innovation exhaustion. This is a defining conundrum for contemporary architecture that it is getting increasingly harder to not only matter but also to even be seen.

This book, *Architecture, Film, and the In-between: Spatio-Cinematic Betwixt*, offers a new kind of solution to the aforementioned problem. While framed from an aerial view as an exploration into the liminal spaces that exist between architecture and cinema, most of the individual texts also suggest there are new forms of invention to be found not in resisting monolithic ideologies or desperately participating in the proliferation of increasingly weirder shape-making for social media, but rather through simply looking more carefully into the less visible, hidden gaps between things that have been here all along. This includes new areas of inquiry into not only disciplinary liminality between architecture and cinema but also research into more specific betwixt spaces operating internally to certain movies, film sets, technologies, materials, philosophical positions, and re-readings of architecture's inherited lore. In this book, we find new areas of stretchy dramatic tension, ranging from the formally tortured poche spaces of the 1987 film *Hellraiser*, to the atmospherically pressurized viewing mechanics of Miesian monoliths, to the philosophical taffying of an object's qualities away from the object itself in the service of aesthetics.

In-betweenness, liminality, and betwixtness are all states that require the existence of at least two entities, otherwise there would be nothing to be in-between, liminal within, or betwixt. These entities might be physical, disciplinary, or conceptual—but they need to be *entities in full* for there to be any identifiable space between them. As the authors address, much attention has been given to the influence of Deleuze on architectural theory over the past quarter century, perhaps most notably in his idea that everything is in a state of becoming rather than existing. I would argue that this book heralds a new era for architectural theory in which entities can exist in-full, and our ability to understanding them, and the spaces between them, is contingent on this fullness rather than on their states of change or continuities of becoming. It is only in this new arrangement where architectural theory addresses entities-in-full that seeing in-between spaces is even possible.

Perhaps that is why a book like this exists now in a way that it simply would not have two decades ago—as architectural theory has shifted from the constancy of change and becoming to the stability of objects and entities, therefore allowing the spaces between them to more clearly exist. Of course, this is a very simple reading of this subject, but I think it is enough of an observation to warrant the following simple claim—that as architecture relied on a discourse of becoming, there was no entity-stability and could therefore be no stable in-between-ness. The rise of stable entities in architectural theory, largely ushered into the field by philosophers Graham Harman and Timothy Morton, has allowed us to see once again the in-between as a stable location of inquiry.

In re-attuning our eyes to stability and the in-between conceptually, we, as this book illustrates, can now begin to notice finer resolutions of in-betweenness visually. This book is largely about these observations and about finding new creative material for architectural conjecture in the darker, overlooked, remote-snatching crevices between the sofa cushions of now stable entities—whether they be disciplines such as architecture and cinema, or related positions more internal to philosophy, theory, physical objects, or material effects—all of which are addressed in a forward-looking, (and fully existing), book.

As an academic book that addresses cinema, this compendium is full of erudite and often beautiful observations about numerous intellectually celebrated films. Within this context, I will risk the academic suicide of referring to a Marvel blockbuster. Not long ago, while mildly suffering with the Omicron variant of the coronavirus and in a "show hole" with seemingly nothing to watch, I found myself binge-watching the Disney+ show *Hawkeye* (2021) —a spinoff from the massively successful *Avengers* franchise. One does not typically enter the Marvel universe for cinematic innovation beyond special effects, however the show presented me with a surprising and delicious metaphysical puzzle. In the show, the titular character Hawkeye (played by Jeremy Renner) finds himself sitting in a Broadway theater with his kids watching a live musical titled "Rogers: The Musical," which itself is a hilariously bad adaptation of the first *Avengers* movie from 2012 which Jeremy Renner, as Hawkeye, was featured in—which itself is an adaptation of a 50 year-old Avengers comic book which was conceived of and drawn on the fourteenth floor of the Empire State building where Marvel Comics was then based—a building which was saved by the Avengers, and about eight blocks from the location of the musical, where the character Hawkeye (Jeremy Renner) was watching his fictional life from ten years prior unfold to musical fanfare. This is confusing, let me try to rephrase: I was in my Manhattan apartment looking out over the very neighborhood that the Avengers saved from annihilation in 2012 (thank you Avengers), and also watching my TV where a character that was part of this life-saving action, Hawkeye (Jeremy Renner), was himself watching a musical about himself, played by another actor, saving Manhattan—the plot of which was all based on a decade-old movie that Hawkeye (Jeremy Renner) was in, which was all based on a half-century old comic book, created and drawn in New York City, where fictional characters with no actors had saved my neighborhood, which I was now looking out the window at.

I am probably not in a minority in that I am not one to watch Marvel movies to prompt intellection, but the metaphysical Spatio-Cinematic Betwixt conundrum that this created left me thinking for hours. I am still not sure I have it figured out. The point of this excursus is that neither the materials for thought nor innovation are always found in the places we are used to looking, and sometimes they are deeply embedded betwixt the entities we take for granted—in this case a seemingly mediocre superhero TV show that through a sophisticated Ouroboros of physical reality and cinematic fiction stretched through a comic book's origins in New York City, into a movie, through a musical, into a television show, and back into my apartment overlooking New York City—the physical origin of that same comic book that prompted the movie that ... and so on ...

In reading this book, I found myself confronting similar mind-shifting prompts that demanded further thought, all coming from material that I had thought I was already quite familiar with, whether work by Mies or the movie *Hellraiser* (1987), which I rented on Video Home System (VHS) with friends at least ten times after it was released in the late 1980s. This is a form of joy, to realize that newness is not only present in the giant leaps of Space X rockets to Mars, proposals for sustainable floating Islands, or the world's most radically shaped museum—but that it is often found betwixt the entities of contemporary life. This book is a field guide to such moments, especially as they emerge from the subjects of architecture, space, and cinema.

In an architectural climate that often devalues creative innovation and is increasingly content to regress into infantilizing arrow-laden diagrams or kitschy pastel neo-neo-neo-postmodernism (or is it just two neo's?), this book is a welcome compendium that reminds us that sometimes the greatest sources of disciplinary innovations are not the bright shiny things on the horizon, but the smaller observations of the darker, overlooked nooks that are surprisingly, as this book suggests, much closer, and much more interesting than we ever thought possible. This is an important book for those who have hope for a future of architecture as a creative rather than servile endeavor. Densely packed with unexpected insights ranging from the holy-sounding "luminiferous" surfaces in Giuliana Bruno's writings about the work of Tobias Putrih, to the purely evil poché spaces of liminal torture found in *Hellraiser* as identified by Kerestes, this book reveals new source material vitally nourishing to those who think architecture has a future dependent on creative research, observation, and speculation. It is rare to find an architecture book that takes us not only from shiny luminiferous membranes of heavens to the sinister spaces of hell but also manages to work in intriguing new insights into everything from the work of Mies, Scorsese, and Varda, to new ideas about affect, aesthetics, and the very nature of perception and reality—while still having room to address the Mazda CX-5 of a celebrated philosopher. Bravo to the editors.

Introduction

I had a neighbor, and whenever he would knock on my wall, I knew he wanted me to turn my music down, and that made me angry because I like loud music. So, when he knocked on the wall I'd mess with his head. I'd say: "Go around! I cannot open the wall. I don't know if you have a doorknob on the other side, but over here there's nothing. It's just flat."[1]

—Mitch Hedberg

In the humorless spirit of scholarly seriousness, let us "neutralize" this joke, as Graham Harman might suggest (see Chapter 9), and descend it from the artistic to the literal, by committing the sin of expanding an already brilliantly minimal joke. When discussing the joke, we the editors realized that we both imagined the setting in a situation between comic strip, architecture, and film. Maybe our architectural training is to blame here, as a section appears of an apartment, with two frames: in one, Mitch jamming out to his loud music while an annoyed neighbor tries helplessly to "go around" in the other frame.

The space between frames of a comic strip is called the gutter. This "unceremonious" architectural terminology, according to the prominent comic scholar Scott McCloud, signifies "that space between the panels [...] here in the limbo of the gutter, human imagination takes two separate images and transforms them into a single idea."[2]

It functions somewhat like the act of montage in a film but also has the framing quality of the camera. This dual function is shared by the combination of a wall and its openings in architecture. Walls cut our continuous experience of space, while openings frame our view. In the way we imagined this particular joke, the gutter replaces the wall; in other words, the wall assumes the role of the gutter, without exposing its inside materiality. A dematerialized wall that is thinned out to its two flat sides of "nothingness" and perhaps an ill-placed doorknob.

Counting out the similarities between the comic gutter and the filmic montage is a rather nonsensical effort a century after the infamous sequence diagrams by Sergei Eisenstein, the Soviet film director and one of the first to theorize montage.

Architects would of course enjoy attributing these innovative comic-strip-like drawings that would determine Eisenstein's montage decisions to his architectural training—and they probably have a point.

The parallels between the framing quality of architectural openings and the camera have also been well theorized, including by Beatriz Colomina.[3] A classic example of the merging of the two frames is in Alfred Hitchcock's 1954 *Rear Window*.[4] Juhani Pallasmaa has provided a brilliant analysis of how the windows of different apartments facing the film's protagonist function as a screen that—much like films—share visual mini-narratives with the spectator.[5] The mini-narratives of the different apartments in *Rear Window* however are also partially withdrawn from the viewer because of their walls (see Juhani's visual analysis in Chapter 1). The viewer here actively takes part in imagining the story that the wall cuts out.

The modern Miesian, all-glass curtain wall would probably not satisfy Hitchcock's desire for suspense. Quite like how a literal description of a joke would ruin its humor, the tasteless transparency of the curtain wall gives too much away. Jacques Tati's critique of modern architecture in his 1967 *Playtime* involves a similar scene, where Monsieur Hulot watches the lives of two families through their windows.[6] This time, the curtain-wall windows have consumed the entirety of the façade so their blunt transparency would leave no room for suspense. And between the two apartments, stands a dematerialized wall that is thinned out to a flat surface of "almost nothingness."

The erasure of the wall thickness to draw attention to the spaces on its adjacent sides should not upset architects too much. After all is this not exactly what we do with our hatches in architectural drawing conventions (of plans and sections)? Is this not the very definition of poché—privileging space at the expense of the hidden material and infrastructural complexities within a wall?

Again, as architects, we would prefer to think that our sectional thinking/drawing has found its way to cinematography and contributed to its ever-evolving language. Wes Anderson's infamous panning through the cross-section of the enormous model of a research vessel in his 2004 *The Life Aquatic with Steve Zissou*[7] (which is also reintroduced several times in his 2021 film *The French Dispatch*)[8] is a vivid example of how the intersection of architecture and film can generate creative moments. Earlier examples include Buster Keaton's 1921 *The High Sign*[9] and Lloyd Bacon's 1933 *Footlight Parade*.[10] Other attempts, including the memorable movement of the camera through the walls in David Fincher's 2002 *Panic Room*[11] (or the overhead scene of the apartment complex in Steven Spielberg's 2002 *Minority Report*)[12] seemed to showcase their technical achievements in rendering a realistic view of the poché.

But this bothersome architectural element, when enhanced with filmic prosthetic, can reemerge as a new bionic being. The filmic capacity to expand time through slow motion (as Michael Young will discuss in Chapter 7) can similarly expand space. The neglected, crossed-out depth of a wall no longer needs to shy away into an almost-nothing flatness of a surface—it can expand through the magic of movies to occupy space, and with it, stories. Chapters 3 and 4 discuss how the cinematically emptied out pochés can become pregnant with horror or fantasy.

The poché here stands as a metaphor (again to use from Graham Harman's lexicon in Chapter 9) for the "betwixt"—the central theme of this book. The concept of "betwixt," as developed in the late 1960s by British cultural anthropologist Victor Turner, allowed him to formulate his theory of "liminality," a framework to analyze rites of passage within sociocultural systems. The limen in this context simultaneously refers to a transitional phase that separates the initiand from a previous status, as well as the spaces within which the transition occurs.

With the flattening of the poché (again, a metaphor) in modernist architecture, one might argue that betwixt conditions also vanished. Discussions about John Lautner's cineramic spaces and the screen-like quality of the envelope in the architecture of Mies Van der Rohe in Chapters 2 and 5 partially confirms (and complicates) this notion. Can this almost-nothing poché that denies any betwixt condition for the interior/exterior duality also lead to or reflect the split subjectivities of its contemporary users?

Looking back at the last CIAM Congress in 1959, this lecture by Van Eyck can be rather illuminating:

> Take an example: the world of the house with me inside and you outside, or vice versa. There's also the world of the street—the city—with you inside and me outside or vice versa [...]. Two worlds clashing, no transition. The individual on the one side and the collective on the other. It's terrifying. Between the two, society as general throws lots of barriers, whilst architects in particular are so poor in spirit that they provide doors two inches thick [...] flat surface in a flat surface—of glass often as not [...] between such fantastic phenomena—hair-raising, brutal—like a guillotine. Every time we pass through a door like that, we are split in two—but we don't take notice anymore and simply walk on, halved.[13]

Does this halved subjectivity explain the interest in the cinematically expanded pochés, where animated mice hide from clumsy blue cats, unsupervised children slide through purposeless pipes, besuited spies crawl inside unconvincingly sturdy ducts, and over-pierced villains patiently wait for their annoyingly unassuming, stereotypically blonde victims?

Or maybe aside from the flattened poché and the expanded poché, there is a third possibility that can help in further explaining our condition—the negative poche. How else can it be explained that the interior space of the vacation house in David Koepp's 2020 *You Should Have Left* is larger than its exterior?[14] Negative poché operates like a black hole that sucks all the in-between conditions plus its expected adjacencies. Maybe it is because of the negative poché that the office of the hotel manager in Stanley Kubrick's 1980 *The Shining*,[15] located between rooms and corridors, can still have a window to outside.

Negative poché enables a teleportational experience, similar to how the magic circle in David Lynch's (1989) *Twin Peaks*[16] becomes a short-circuit of space (see more about the magic circle in Chapter 8). It is a "Sling Ring" (to borrow from Marvel's *Doctor Strange* franchise)[17] that has the ability to create a dimensional gateway to travel throughout the multiverse. The multiverse, investigated in Chapter 14, can thus be considered a repository of endless negative poché—a minus infinity, in which the cinearchitecture of George Nolfi's 2011 *The Adjustment Bureau*,[18] finds a more immersive experience (for a definition/discussion of cinearchitecture, see Chapter 6).

The phenomenological reality of the negative poché is not unfamiliar to modern subjects, who experience a delayed version in subway routes and air travel—through which two stations, cities, continents, and localities are stitched together at the expense of all that lies in-between. John Ford captures this condition perfectly in his 1956 *The Searchers*,[19] where the cozy interior domesticity of a house and the intimate relations it creates, by a fireplace or the dining table, is juxtaposed next to the overwhelming vastness of the western landscapes. As if in the absence of any betwixt space (a road perhaps, a neighbor, let alone a neighborhood, a city), the flimsy narrow porch can somehow bear the weight of the infinite wilderness that surrounds it.

Yes, the negative poché is a metaphor of all spatial conditions that defy hierarchical relations and thereby position spatial objects onto a flat ontological plane (see Chapters 2 and 10). It is also a signifier of negative liminalities—the transitionless passage of the initiand outside its sociocultural system and into one that does not acknowledge its previous status. But it is nevertheless a real condition (as contemporary definitions of reality in Chapters 9 and 10 would attest) and needs theorization.

Reactions to negative liminalities may include a range of strategies, from rethinking the screen (see Chapter 12), reintroducing social critique (see Chapter 6), or seeking ontological hybrids (see Chapter 13)—but they all involve the gutter, the poché, the betwixt, the liminal, the interstitial. The "interstitial space" is according to Žižek, "[the] proper place of utopian dreaming." His own dream, "of a house composed only of secondary spaces and places of passage—stairs, corridors, toilets, store-rooms, kitchen—with no living room or bedroom,"[20] while impressively architectural, is not as utopian as one would expect. It is like a comic strip composed of only gutters, a subway ride without a destination, an endless liminality—the labyrinth (see Chapter 4).[21] A rethinking of our liminal conditions would however involve redefining the passage. A poché that is flat on the one side and has a doorknob on the other is an architecture of halved subjectivities. A proper door would have solved the confusion (and ruined the joke). Maybe that explains Van Eyck's obsession with the reality of the door:

> What [...] is the greater reality of the door? Well, perhaps it is the localized setting for a wonderful human gesture: Conscious entry and departure [...] something that frames your coming and going, for it is a vital experience not only for those that do so but also for those encountered or left behind. A door is a place made for an occasion that is repeated millions of times in a lifetime *between* the first entry and the last exit [emphasis added].[22]

This introduction is perhaps a door—a brutally thin existence between the words that come next and the meanings that would later find home in the minds of its readership. It does not intend to frame the content, but rather hopes to "frame your coming and going." It does not claim to offer some illusion of coherence and singularity to the fragmented body of text that follows, but rather hopes to be a neutral space, or a white box, as Eva Perez De Vega discusses in Chapter 11, that houses different creative ways to examine screen, space, and the in-between.

The films discussed in the book, often from the familiar Western cannon, are excuses to celebrate the multiplicity of ways our authors approach the liminal space between architecture and film—through existential experience (Chapter 1), post-phenomenological thinking (Chapter 2), layered interiorities (Chapter 3), horrific transitions (Chapter 4), exhibitionary domesticities (Chapter 5), socio-political cinearchitecture (Chapter 6), cinematic temporalities (Chapter 7), ritualized spaces (Chapter 8), sensual realities (Chapter 9), fake architectures (Chapter 10), (dis)embodied spaces (Chapter 11), projective environments (Chapter 12), fictive ecologies (Chapter 13), and spatio-visual framings (Chapter 14). We will keep the door open, hopefully for another white box in the future, that this time through an exhibition of non-canon, non-Western films further enriches the discussion.

This section started with overexplaining a joke and ended with under-interpreting a dream, and *between* the two an attempt to set the tone for what you will encounter in this book. We consider the book like an anthology series, and while we would like to imagine that you would binge watch it in the thematic order of the book, we are aware that the actual reading experience is often more like an impatient viewer with a TV controller in their hands, switching between channels, and using their agency to re-gutter the content. The door is now open, and between the last word of this sentence and the next one you will read lies a fluid poché of thoughts that we hope this book would enrich.

NOTES

1. John Wenzel, *Mock Stars Indie Comedy and the Dangerously Funny* (Golden, CO: Speck Press, 2008), 13.
2. McCloud Scott, *Understanding Comics: The Invisible Art* (New York, NY: Harper Perennial, 2010), 66.
3. Beatriz Colomina, *Privacy and Publicity: Modern Architecture as Mass Media* (Cambridge, MA: MIT Press, 1996).
4. *Rear Window* (1954), director Alfred Hitchcock.
5. Juhani Pallasmaa, *The Architecture of Image: Existential Space in Cinema* (Helsinki: Rakennustieto, 2001).
6. *Playtime* (1967), director Jacques Tati.
7. *The Life Aquatic with Steve Zissou* (2004), director Wes Anderson.
8. *The French Dispatch* (2021), director Wes Anderson.
9. *The High Sign* (1921), directors Edward F. Cline and Buster Keaton.
10. *Footlight Parade* (1933), director Lloyd Bacon.
11. *Panic Room* (2002), director David Fincher.
12. *Minority Report* (2002), director Steven Spielberg.
13. Cited in Unwin Simon. *Analysing Architecture* (London: Routledge, 2009), 225. Also see Aldo van Eyck, Vincent Ligtelijn, and Francis Strauven. *The Child, the City and the Artist: An Essay on Architecture: The In-Between Realm* (Amsterdam: Sun Publishers, 2008).
14. *You Should Have Left* (2020), director David Koepp.
15. *The Shining* (1980), director Stanley Kubrick.
16. *Twin Peaks* (1989), director David Lynch.
17. *Doctor Strange* (2016), director Scott Derrickson.
18. *The Adjustment Bureau* (2011), director George Nolfi.
19. *The Searchers* (1956), director John Ford.
20. Žižek Slavoj. "Architectural Parallax: Spandrels and Other Phenomena of Class Struggle." *How to Read Lacan*. Accessed January 4, 2022. https://www.lacan.com/essays/?page_id=218.
21. But if we accept Graham Harman's logic that the opposite to beautiful is the ordinary and not the ugliness (see Chapter 9) and extend it to utopian thinking, then this dystopian dream can be seen as an inspiring strategy in its rapture with the ordinary.
22. Cited in Unwin. *Analysing Architecture* (2009).

REFERENCES

Anderson, Wes, director. *The French Dispatch*. Century City, CA: Searchlight Pictures, 2021.

Anderson, Wes, director. *The Life Aquatic with Steve Zissou*. Burbank, CA: Buena Vista Pictures, 2004.

Bacon, Lloyd, director. *Footlight Parade*. Burbank, CA: Warner Bros., 1933.

Cline, Edward F. and Buster Keaton, directors. *The High Sign*. Los Angeles, CA: Metro Pictures, 1921.

Colomina, Beatriz. *Privacy and Publicity: Modern Architecture as Mass Media*. Cambridge, MA: MIT Press, 1996.

Derrickson, Scott, director. *Doctor Strange*. Burbank, CA: Walt Disney Pictures, 2016.

van Eyck, Aldo, Vincent Ligtelijn, and Francis Strauven. *The Child, the City and the Artist: An Essay on Architecture: The In-Between Realm*. Amsterdam: Sun Publishers, 2008.

Fincher, David, director. *Panic Room*. Culver City, CA: Sony Pictures Releasing, 2002.

Ford, John, director. *The Searchers*. Burbank, CA: Warner Bros., 1956.

Hitchcock, Alfred, director. *Rear Window*. Los Angeles, CA: Paramount Pictures, 1954.

Koepp, David, director. *You Should Have Left*. Universal City, CA: Universal Pictures, 2020.

Kubrick, Stanley, director. *The Shining*. Burbank, CA: Warner Bros., 1980.

Lynch, David, director. *Twin Peaks*. Santa Monica, CA: CBS Television Distribution, 1990–1992, 2017.

McCloud, Scott. *Understanding Comics: [The Invisible Art]*. New York, NY: Harper Perennial, 2010.

Nolfi, George, director. *The Adjustment Bureau*. Universal City, CA: Universal Pictures, 2011.

Pallasmaa, Juhani. *The Architecture of Image: Existential Space in Cinema*. Helsinki: Rakennustieto, 2001.

Spielberg, Steven, director. *Minority Report*. Los Angeles, CA: 20th Century Fox, 2002.

Tati, Jacques, director. *Playtime*. Italy: Specta Films & Jolly Film, 1967.

Unwin, Simon. *Analysing Architecture*. London: Routledge, 2009.

Wenzel, John. *Mock Stars Indie Comedy and the Dangerously Funny*. Golden, CO: Speck Press, 2008.

Žižek, Slavoj. "Architectural Parallax: Spandrels and Other Phenomena of Class Struggle." *How to Read Lacan*. Accessed January 4, 2022. https://www.lacan.com/essays/?page_id=218.

1

Veracity of Experience

Juhani Pallasmaa

Nothing is real until it was experienced.[1]

—John Keats (1795–1821)

In its abstract spatial and temporal structure, music has been historically regarded as the art form closest to architecture. "Architecture is frozen music," as Friedrich Schelling and Johann Wolfgang von Goethe declared.[2] A shared Pythagorean harmonic ground has also connected these two arts, although today's professionalistically oriented architecture has regrettably become uninterested in harmonics or the philosophical grounding of building. The art of dance has, likewise, its parallels with architecture, as the organization of spaces, scales, atmospheres, movements, views, and emotions in architecture can be seen as an architectural choreography—a score for complex physical, perceptual, and emotional movements and acts. Although architecture is usually understood as static material structures, the very use of a building, as well as its experiential dynamics, turn it into a network of actions; it invites, enables, and prohibits. As a consequence, buildings could be regarded as verbs rather than nouns.

However, of all the art forms, cinema, "the seventh art," is closest to architecture, not solely through their similar space–time structures but also because both articulate and express existential experiences. As already the Greek philosophers understood, everything in human life is always placed, and both cinema and architecture create experiential places.[3] The two arts project and mediate experiential situations of life by means of projecting and structuring scenes and situations of lived life, either real or imagined. Even our dreams take place in spaces, settings, and rooms, and they evolve with a cinematic progression and montage. Our consciousness of being projects the sense of reality and place, which both art forms maintain and mediate.

Art as experience

Buildings are usually regarded as aesthetically conceived and perceived spatial and material constructions, which are experienced primarily through vision, while cinema is understood to be an art of projected and illusory visual imageries. Yet, neither the physical nor the illusory object or space is the mental reality of the work. Artistic works are not essentially objects; they are human experiences and emotions. Instead of being autonomous and closed significations of the work or its author, artistic entities are relational and mediating experiences, and their meanings are about the world and its human existential encounter. "They make us experience how the world touches us," as Maurice Merleau-Ponty describes the experiential impact of Paul Cézanne's paintings.[4] Behind their utility and apparent reason, buildings do the same; they mediate our contact and interaction with the world. This encounter gives rise to multi-sensory and cross-sensory experiences. The essential interaction of the senses tends to be lost through the common association of different art forms with specific senses, "visual," "sonic," or "plastic" arts, for example.

Regarding art not as an object but an experience is the lesson of John Dewey's significant book *Art as Experience* (1934). He emphasizes the seminal interaction of the senses.

> In seeing a picture, it is not true that visual qualities are as such, or consciously, central, and other qualities arranged about them in an accessory or associated fashion. Nothing could be further from the truth [...] when we perceive, by means of the eyes as causal aids, the liquidity of water, the coldness of ice, the solidity of rocks, the bareness of trees in winter, it is certain that other qualities than those of the eye are conspicuous and controlling in perception [...]. This bearing has many aspects. One of them is the inherent tendency of sense to expand, to come into intimate relations with other things than itself, and thus to take on form because of its own movement instead of passively waiting to have form imposed on it. Any sensuous quality tends, because of its organic connections, to spread and fuse.[5]

This inherent sensory interaction further reinforces the affinity of cinema and the art of building. In his essay *The Work of Art in the Age of Mechanical Reproduction*, Walter Benjamin deliberates on the connections between architecture and cinema. The philosopher suggests that, regardless of their apparent visuality, these two art forms are essentially tactile arts. In his view, architecture and cinema are communicated primarily through the haptic realm in opposition to the pure visuality of painting.[6] Benjamin's idea suggests that while the physically passive situation of viewing a film turns the viewer into a bodyless observer, the illusory cinematic space and the implied motions give the viewer back their body, as the experiential haptic and motor space provides powerful kinesthetic stimuli. A film is experienced by the muscles and skin as much as by the eyes. The philosopher regards the cinematic reality basically as a sensory experience, anticipating thus Dewey's view. Both architecture and cinema imply a kinesthetic manner of experiencing space, and the images entering one's consciousness and memory are embodied and haptic sensations, not merely retinal pictures.

Art as mediation

Maurice Merleau-Ponty argues that an artistic work directs our sensory attention away from itself to the world. "We come to see not the work of art, but the world according to the work," he suggests.[7] This view implies that the meanings of a work of art are outside the work itself—every piece of art refers to or is about something else than itself as a physical object or act. In the case of architecture, the inherent contextual relationality arises from its contextuality and choreography of action, attention, experience, and emotion—it relates the dweller to the larger spatial context, as well as to the continuum of time. "Our house is our corner of the world [...] it is our first universe, a real cosmos in every sense of the word [...]. It is an instrument with which to confront the cosmos," as Gaston Bachelard writes.[8] Thus, the "windowness" of a window, for example, is not the opening in the wall or its frame, but the experiential connection it opens to the world and for light to enter. The window enables the dweller to enjoy the distant mountain top, or the blossoming apple tree in the garden; it connects the near and the far, and articulates and celebrates the passage of light. Architecture is usually understood as the art of space, but it structures and articulates equally importantly our experience and sense of time. "Architecture is not only about domesticating space," philosopher Karsten Harries writes, "it is also a deep defense against the terror of time. The language of beauty is essentially the language of timeless reality."[9] The interplay of the dimensions of space and time suggests the space–time continuum of modern physics that has also been projected on the artistic and architectural realms since the first decades of the last century, especially in Cubism and Functionalist architecture. In his canonical treatise *Space, Time and Architecture*, Sigfried Giedion, the most influential historian of modern architecture, quotes a statement from the mathematician, Hermann Minkowsky: "Henceforth, space alone or time alone is doomed to fade into a mere shadow: only a union of both will preserve their existence."[10]

This fusion of the two dimensions became a doctrine in the theories of modernity. In my view, however, a concept of physics may not be directly applicable in the experiential reality of the arts; space and time articulate our experiences of the world, but the two dimensions maintain their experientially separate identities in the human lifeworld and arts. Architecture articulates our experiences of time; it preserves, speeds up or slows down the experience of time. Cinema is similarly an art of space, situation, and time; these dimensions are organized in accordance with a "poetic logic" rather than theories of physics. Cinematic time can be accelerated, slowed down, stopped, or reversed. Andrei Tarkovsky named the poetic dimension as the most significant in cinema: "There is only one way of cinematic thinking—poetic."[11] He clarifies his point in another context: "When I speak of poetry, I am not thinking of it as a genre. Poetry is an awareness of the world, a particular way of relating to reality."[12]

Also, architecture obtains its experiential and emotive qualities from poetic images, rather than physical, performative, or optical facts; buildings relate us to the world, culture, and other humans. "The house is one of the greatest powers of integration for the thoughts, memories, and dreams of mankind,"[13] and "always in our daydreams, the house is a large cradle,"[14] Gaston Bachelard suggests.

Lived space

There are also fundamentally cinematic connections and experiences, as also cinematic events take place in specific places. Houses are built in the world of matter and geometry, but mentally they structure meaningless physical space for human purposes through inserting behavioral codes, aesthetic qualities, memories, desires, and existential meanings into it. Architecture turns our physical environment into an architecturally articulated reality; it presents a selective and deliberately structured and staged reality. The cities, houses and rooms of cinema serve similar mental purposes. Cinema creates, likewise, experiential settings for its narrative, dramatic, and psychological purposes. It also creates and mediates specific places and fuses them with its narratives and patterns of behavior. Even our ordinary lived spaces are experientially and essentially cinematic spaces, in their resemblance to dreams and the unconscious, collaged independently of the boundaries of physical and mental space, as well as of time and laws of nature. Our everyday lives are experientially compiled in a cinematic manner. We all know how little it takes to alter the order and balance of ordinary life and turn even a familiar place into a setting of depression, angst, or fear. In today's Consumerist and utilitarian culture, architects seem to have, regrettably, lost their interest in life. "Why is it that architecture and architects, unlike film and filmmakers, are so little interested in people during the design process? Why are they so theoretical, so distant to life in general," the Dutch film scholar Jan Vrijman laments.[15] Poet Jean Tardieu asks similarly: "Let us assume a wall: what takes place behind it?"[16] A curiosity for life ought to be also the architect's primary concern.

Lived space is a combination of external material space and inner mental space, perception and mood, memory and imagination, actuality and mental projection. Simply, we do not live in objectively given spaces; we exist in existential spaces and places of our own mental making. When experiencing lived space, memory and dream, fear and desire, value and meaning, fuse in the perceived situation and place. Lived space is inseparably integrated with the subject's consciousness and life situation. Italo Calvino gives a memorable formulation for the view that we do not live separately in material and mental worlds, as these dimensions are fully intertwined

> Who are we, who is each one of us, if not a combinatoria of experience, information, books we have read, things imagined? Each life is an encyclopedia, a library, an inventory of objects, a series of styles, and everything can be constantly shuffled and reordered in every way conceivable.[17]

We live in fused mental worlds, in which the experienced, remembered, and imagined, as well as the past, present, and future are intermixed. Henri Matisse gives a vivid description of this collaged and fused perception of the world:

> If I was able to unite in picture what was outside, the sea for example, and the interior, it is because the atmosphere of the landscape and that of my room are one and the same [...]. I don't have to bring together internal and external, both are united in my sensations. I can combine the armchair next to me in the studio and the cloud in the sky, the quivering of the palm tree by the waterside, without any effort in differentiating the places, without dissociating the different elements of my motif.[18]

This synthetic experience of a great painter is also the true architect's and filmmaker's manner of experiencing the world.

The modes of experiencing architecture and cinema become closely related in this experiential mental space, which meanders without fixed boundaries between the outer and inner worlds. Even in the art of building, a mental image is transferred from the imaginative and intuitive realm of the architect to the sensory, neural, and mental reality of the observer, and the material building is essentially a mediating object between the two realities: an image object and a messenger. The fact that images in architecture are eternalized in matter, whereas cinematic images are illusions projected momentarily on the screen, has no decisive significance in this respect. Both art forms define and articulate frames of life, situations of human interaction and realities of touching the world.

Existential experience and space

Cinema fuses the situational realities of place with sensory and imaginary realities of the cinematic narrative. In fact, the viewer themselves is in two realities at the same time: the reality of their situation of viewing and the imaginative reality of the cinematic narrative. This duality of experiential realities applies to all arts. Also, in a sensitive architectural space, we are simultaneously in the materially constructed reality and the imaginative realm of architecturally aestheticized and sensitized mental construction. The viewer's consciousness keeps shifting from one reality to the other, but the two are fused in the existential experience.

In the extremely reductively staged spaces of Lars von Trier's *Dogville* (2003),[19] various spaces or rooms are frequently indicated by mere white chalk lines and lettering on the black floor (e.g., "entry," "living room," "kitchen"), but that suffices to create the experience of the spaces of the story in the viewer's mind (see Figure 1.1). This film is close to theater, as the events take place in abstracted

FIGURE 1.1: Lars von Trier, *Dogville* (2003). The film takes place in vaguely suggested sets; various rooms are often indicated only by lines and the function of the space, written on the black floor by white chalk.

spaces without any intention to create a fully illusory experience. Both cinematic and architectural experiences create hallucinatory effects. "I can no longer think what I want to think. My thoughts have been replaced by moving images," as Georges Duhamel suggests.[20]

Distinct human acts and their architectural settings are strongly connected. This relativizes the meaning of events. One and the same event—a kiss or murder—is an entirely different story depending on whether it takes place in a bedroom, bathroom, library, elevator, or gazebo. An event obtains its particular meaning also through the time of the day, illumination, weather, and soundscape. In addition, every place has its history and symbolic connotations, which merge into the incident. Also, architecture conditions our existential experiences and guides us to encounter situations of specific meaning and emotional content.

In cinema, situations that are not shown at all on the screen are often emotionally more powerful than realistically presented events. Fritz Lang comments on the invisible content of his film *M* (1931):[21]

> There is no violence in my film *M*, or when there is, it occurs behind the scenes, as it were. Let's take an example. You will remember the sequence, where a little girl is murdered. All you see is a ball rolling and then stopping [see Figure 1.2]. The balloon flying off and getting caught in some telephone wires [...]. The violence is in your mind.[22]

FIGURE 1.2: Fritz Lang, *M* (1932). Two balloons of the young girl caught in the telephone wires suggesting that she has been murdered.

Similarly, in memorable architecture, singular ideas or details are not too explicit, as they are fused into the overall atmosphere and tuning of the experience. In great buildings, the experiential and mental meanings are not explicit or pronounced, either; they arise from the experience, and they are lived and encountered rather than given or intellectually understood. The stairway of Michelangelo's Biblioteca Laurentiana in Florence gives rise to associations with an underwater scene, but the imaginative sensation of water is conveyed by the unique architectural "melancholia," not any material suggestions. Gaston Bachelard uses the notion of "poetic chemistry," connecting the poetic metamorphoses with the sensory unexpectedness of chemical processes.[23] Who could imagine that combining two hydrogen atoms with one of oxygen creates the miraculous liquid substance of water, the condition of earthly life and the most poetic of all substances? Who could either expect the flowing forms of a stair, the columns partly sunk into the walls, suggesting an internal pressure, and the lines of the moldings, would make one sense the presence of water? Our perceptual reality, as well as the experiences of works of art are frequently a result of similar mental alchemy.

Cinematic architecture

The functional, perceptual, and emotive choreography projected by architecture is similar to cinematic structures. Jean Nouvel, an architect, who was initially a script writer, declares cinematic imagery and experience as a significant inspiration for his often radical architecture:

> Architecture exists, like cinema, in the dimension of time and movement. One conceives and reads a building in terms of sequences. To erect a building is to predict and seek effects of contrast and linkage through which one passes [...]. In the continuous shot/sequence that a building is, the architect works with cuts and edits, framings and openings.[24]

On the other hand, numerous film directors from Hitchcock (see Figures 1.3 and 1.4) and Bergman to Antonioni and Tarkovsky have used the architectural imagery of houses and rooms to structure and articulate their cinematic narratives and to evoke distinct expectations and feelings. A room can be a place of safety or of fear and torture.

Remarkably often, cinematic architecture has been deliberately invalidated in its structural and material reliability through intentionally neglected or destroyed functionality and material durability. Tarkovsky's *Nostalgia* (1983)[25] and *Stalker*

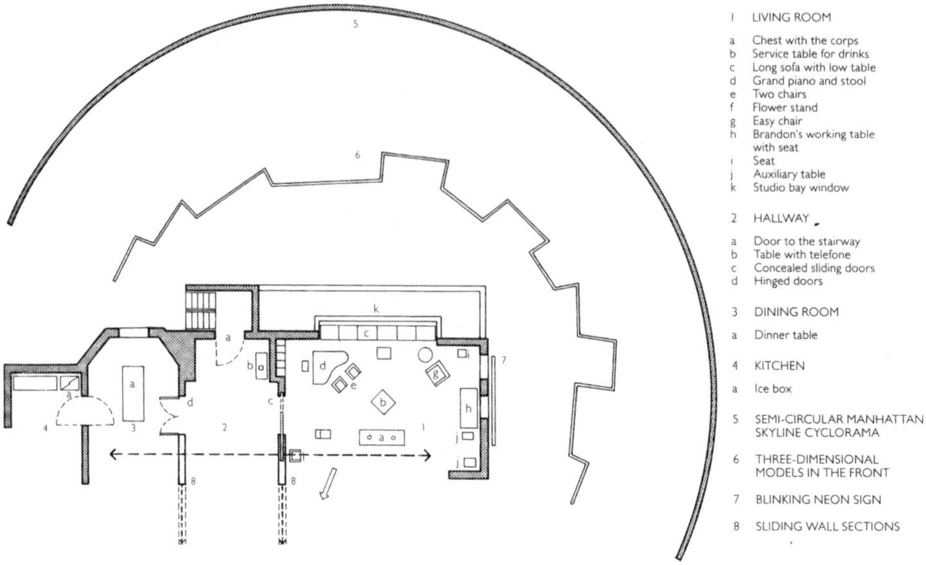

FIGURE 1.3: Alfred Hitchcock, *Rope* (1948). The entire film takes place in a single-staged Manhattan apartment built in a studio. The film was shot without cuts; as the film reel was changed, the camera turns to the back of an actor's coat and the new reel begins from this momentary black screen. Plan of the apartment, drawn based on numerous viewings of the film by the writer.

(1979)[26] portray the functional uselessness of leaking roofs, ruins, flooded floors, and broken windows to support an atmosphere of alienation, longing, and being lost. For many filmmakers, buildings seem to be cinematically more expressive in a dilapidated stage or even as ruins. Peter Brook, the radical theater director, explains that he intentionally destroyed the interior architecture of his *Bouffes-du-Nord* theater in Paris:

> A good space cannot be neutral, for an impersonal sterility gives no food to the imagination. The *Bouffes* has the magic and the poetry of a ruin, and anyone who has allowed themselves to be invaded by the atmosphere of a ruin knows strongly how the imagination is let loose.[27]

Sir John Soane memorably designed his magnificent house (1792–1824) at Lincoln's Inn Fields in London as a ruin.

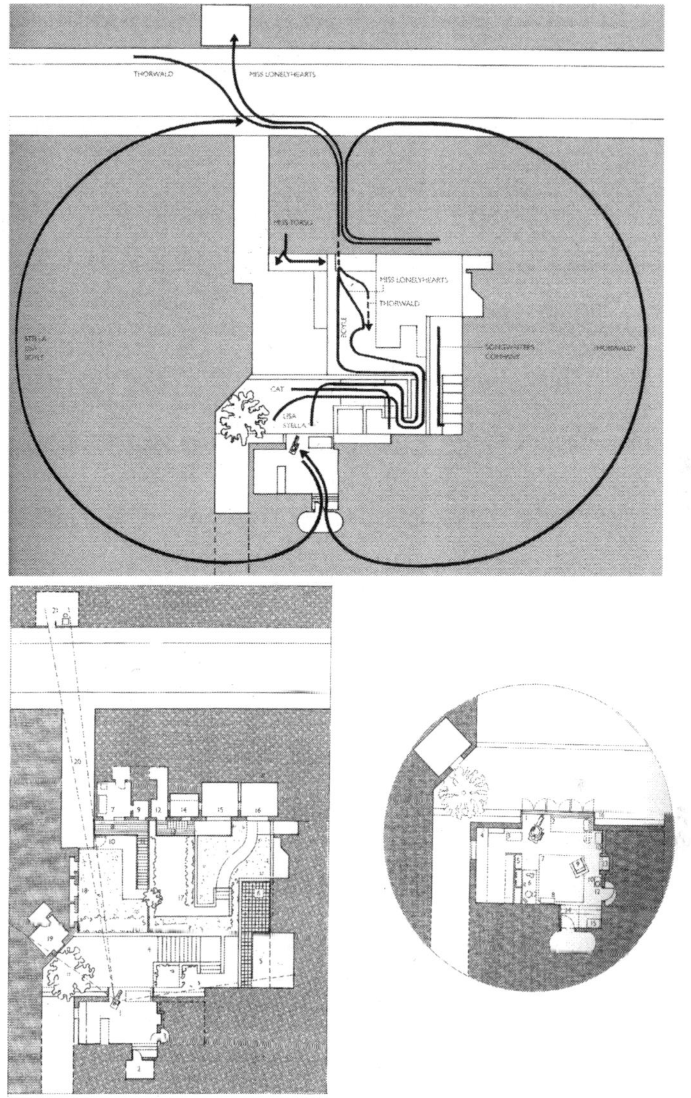

RECONSTRUCTION OF THE COURTYARD SETTING

1 Jeff's apartment
2 Stair/hallway
3 Bedroom (never shown in the film)
4 Lower courtyard
5 Part of the songwriter's studio apartment
6 Roof terrace attached to the studio apartment
7 Miss Torso's room / 1st floor
the sculptor woman's apartment / ground floor
8 Miss Torso's balcony
9 Miss Torso's bathroom
10 Sculptor woman's terrace / ground floor
11 Stair to Miss Torso's balcony
12 Corridor (on three floors)
13 Balcony with emergency stair
14 Thorwald's kitchen / 1st floor
Miss Lonelyheart's kitchen / ground floor
dog owner couple's kitchen / 2nd floor
15 Thorwald's living room / 1st floor
Miss Lonelyheart's living room / ground floor
dog owner couple's living room / 2nd floor
16 Thorwald's bedroom / 1st floor
Miss Lonelyheart's bedroom / ground floor
dog owner couple's bedroom / 2nd floor
17 Mr. Thorwald's flower bed
18 Lady with a bird cage
19 Room of the newly married couple
20 Passage to the street
21 Restaurant with Miss Lonelyheart's table

RECONSTRUCTION OF JEFF'S APARTMENT

1 Bay window / three bays that can be opened
2 High bed
3 Side table
4 Kitchen furniture
5 Open shelves in three parts with photographs, etc., below cupboards with doors / on the opposite side presumably kitchen cupboards
6 Table with broken camera, photographs, etc.
7 Carpet
8 Low drawer
9 Easy chair
10 Low table
11 Lamp suspended from ceiling
12 Table lamp
13 Fireplace
14 Three steps
15 Trunk
16 Possibly a balcony of the bedroom

FIGURE 1.4: Alfred Hitchcock, *Rear Window* (1954) takes place in a Manhattan apartment building. The film was shot in the largest studio set of its time. The top image, drawn by the author, shows the plan of the residential block and the movements of the characters. The bottom left plan shows the configuration of the apartments in the film. Bottom right is a plan of the photographer's flat.

The world of the senses and images

Walter Benjamin regarded architecture and cinema as "tactile arts," as in his view, they both engage haptic and bodily participation. However, embodied identification and unconscious participation engage our entire being in architectural and cinematic situations, not only one of our five senses. The sensation and self-consciousness in a real or an imaginary space are a single experience. The artistic internalization resembles "introjection," the psychoanalytic view of the infant's way of internalizing the world through the interior of the mouth. We fuse the situation with our own existential sense, the sense of being and self (the twelve senses of Steinerian philosophy include a "life sense" and an "ego sense," which, in my view, together constitute the "existential sense".)[28]

We do not record our being in the world primarily as a sequence of separate sensory perceptions, as we are part and parcel of the experiential reality, the world and our existence in it are a singular fused experience. Similarly, we do not experience a cinematic narrative and its physical location as separate entities. We are insiders and participants in our existential world. As we watch a movie, we are not really watching it, as we enter the events and are participants in its fictive reality. My perception and sense of self are fused. As I occupy the narrative, the world of the film also occupies my sense of self. "In the fusion of place and soul, the soul is as much a container of the place as the place is a container of soul; both are susceptible to the same forces of destruction," the American literary scholar Robert Pogue Harrison claims.[29]

Artistic images in general are generators of associations, emotions, and meanings. In his touching book, *Sculpting in Time*, Andrey Tarkovsky stresses the endlessness of artistic imagery. "In a word, the image is not a certain meaning, expressed by the director, but an entire world reflected as in a drop of water."[30] In the very end of his last film, *Beyond the Clouds* (1995), Michelangelo Antonioni, the architect of cinematic images (he actually studied architecture before becoming a filmmaker), expresses the complexity and enigma of artistic imagery through the concluding words of the protagonist, the photographer (played by John Malkovich):

> But we know that behind every image revealed, there is another image more faithful to reality, and in back of that image there is another, and yet another behind the last one, and so on, up to the true image of the absolute mysterious reality that no-one will ever see.[31]

In both cinema and architecture, the atmosphere, the shapeless and non-material feeling or tuning of the scene, situation or event, and its continuity and dynamic transformation through the artistic entity, has a central role in holding the experience together and creating its progression and internal dynamics. This mostly unconscious and embodied participation and existential identification engages our entire being. Both cinema and architecture take place in our existential consciousness, our sense of being, or in "the flesh of the world," to use a notion of Merleau-Ponty.[32] Situations and events in architecture and cinema interact with their contexts and fuse with their settings.

The existential space

The essential quality of lived space is that the observer is part of it. In the experience of both architectural and cinematic realities, we fuse the experienced space with our own sense of being. We are not outsider observers as we are part of the reality of the scene and event ourselves. The world is not outside us at a visual distance, we exist in the middle of the projected event and as part of the experienced reality. The existential experience is an exchange; I enter a space and the space enters me. This unifying experience of lived space firmly connects architecture and cinema.

I wish to suggest that the most important sense in architectural and cinematic experience is our existential sense, the sense of being in a place, space, or situation, not looking at it or recording it separately by any one of the five Aristotelian senses. The existential sense fuses the various separate sensations in the experience and consciousness of the self; self and the experienced situation constitute a singular sensation, consciousness of being and of lived reality. We do not experience artistic, architectural, or cinematic entities as outsiders; we share the same reality with the works and are existential participants in them. The intensity of individual association and identification naturally varies, and usually with works of high artistic quality the mental internalization is especially strong, whereas works of lesser quality leave us as unconcerned or critical observers. Through the capacity of empathic identification, we also share the fates and emotions of both real and enacted persons.

The intensity of belonging may weaken or be entirely lost due to both external and internal reasons. In his book, *Place and Placelessness*, Edward Relph introduces the alarming notion "existential outsideness" in reference to the growing loss of the sense of belonging, interiority, and domicile in contemporary cities. "Existential outsideness involves a self-conscious and reflective uninvolvement, an alienation from people and places, a homelessness, a sense of unreality of the world, and of not belonging."[33] The outsideness or alienation in relation to material places has the same sensory/mental ground as the experience of uninvolvement in relation to literary, theatrical, or cinematic encounters. From works of poetry and literature to painting, cinema, and architecture, the power of artistic experience arises from our sense of association and participation with the imaginative reality of the work.

Houses in books and films

Depictions and projections of houses, rooms, and specific spaces are also a central aspect of literature. Marilyn R. Chandler's book, *Dwelling in the Text: Houses in American Fiction*, studies the interactions of human character, place, and story.

> The book is an exploration of the ways in which a number of major [American] writers have appropriated houses as structural, psychological, metaphysical, and literary metaphors, constructing complex analogies between house and psyche, house and family, house and social environment, house and text. [...] The spaces we create and inhabit in our imagination are particularly fraught with significance, unlimited as they are by practical constraints of material and context but informed by the natural and architectural features of our actual environment.[34]

Henry James goes even further in comparing the writer building a "house of fiction" with "a thousand windows" to an actual craftsman builder.[35]

Houses in great films are similarly experientially "real"—they structure the fictitious human characters their behaviors and relations with the same power of suggestion. For me, many houses of cinema, such as the Bates House in Hitchcock's *Psycho* (1960),[36] or Andrey Gorchakov's hotel room and Domenico's ruined dwelling in Tarkovsky's *Nostalgia*, or the white family house in Tarkovsky's *The Sacrifice* (1986),[37] are as concrete and emotively charged in my memory as the memorable houses of books I have read, such as the tiny room of Raskonikov's double murder in Fyodor Dostoyevsky's *Crime and Punishment.* But also, the rooms of great paintings are experientially real, as Vincent van Gogh's simple bedroom in Arles (*Van Gogh's Bedroom,* 1888), and the amazing atmospheric space in J. M. W. Turner's painting *Interior at Betworth* (1837) demonstrate. Also convincing literary and painterly works mediate a continuum instead of presenting a singular and limited image. "If the painter presents us with a field or a vase of flowers, his paintings are windows, which are open on the whole world," Jean-Paul Sartre suggests.[38] The imposing spaces, rooms, and houses, which we have visited or experienced in lived reality, or through various art forms, are registered in our memory; and they are united in the mental reality of memories and dreams. The power of a memorized space is relative to its emotive impact and content. The rooms of great books and films are experientially as real for us as the material spaces we live in.

NOTES

1. Letter: *To George Keats*, March 19, 1819. Vol. II, p. 79, from Hyder E. Rollins's edition of *The Letters of John Keats*.
2. This formulation is usually remembered as an idea of Goethe, but he credits Novalis for the idea around the year 1800. The expression appears in Schelling's lecture *Philosophie der Kunst*, delivered in 1802–03 and published in 1856. In their comparisons of the two artforms, Schelling used the German adjective "*erstarrt*," while Goethe's adjective was "*verstummt*"—both are usually translated as "frozen."
3. Jeff Malpas in his lecture at the *Understanding and Designing Place Symposium* at Tampere University, April 2017 (the author's lecture note).
4. Maurice Merleau-Ponty. "Cezanne's Doubt," in *Sense and Non-Sense* (Evanston, IL: Northwestern University Press, 1964), 19.
5. John Dewey, *Art as Experience* (New York, NY: The Berkley Publishing Group, 1980), 123–24.
6. Walter Benjamin, "The Work of Art in the Age of Mechanical Reproduction," in *Illuminations*, ed. Hannah Arendt (New York, NY: Schocken Books, 1968), 217–51.
7. Maurice Merleau-Ponty, *The Primacy of Perception*, as quoted in Iain McGilchrist, *The Master and His Emissary: The Divided Brain and the Making of the Western World* (New Haven, CT: Yale University Press, 2009), 409.
8. Gaston Bachelard, *The Poetics of Space* (Boston, MA: Beacon Press, 1969), 4, 6.
9. Karsten Harries, "Building and the Terror of Time," in *Perspecta 19: The Yale University Journal* (Cambridge, MA: MIT Press, 1982), 59–69.
10. Sigfried Giedion, *Space, Time and Architecture: The Growth of a New Tradition* (Cambridge, MA: Harvard University Press, 1952), 376.
11. Andreĭ Tarkovsky, *Sculpting in Time: Reflections on the Cinema* (London: Bodley Head, 1986), 150.
12. Ibid., 21.
13. Gaston Bachelard, *The Poetics of Space* (Boston, MA: Beacon Press, 1969), 7.
14. Ibid., 4, 46.
15. Jan Vrijman, "Filmmakers Spacemakers," *The Berlage Papers 11*, January, 1994.
16. Jean Tardieu as quoted in Georges Perec, *Tiloja ja avaruuksia* (*Espéces d'espaces*) (Helsinki: Loki-kirjat, 1992), 72.
17. Italo Calvino, *Six Memos for the Next Millennium* (New York, NY: Vintage International, 1993), 124.
18. Henri Matisse in Georges Duthuit, *Le feu des signes* (Paris: Editions d'Art Albert Skira, 1962).
19. *Dogville* (2003), director Lars von Trier.
20. Georges Duhamel, *Scènes de la vie future* (Paris: Mercvre de France, 1930), 52.
21. *M* (1931), director Fritz Lang.
22. Fritz Lang, quoted in Peter von Bagh, "The Death of Emotion," in *Synnyt: Sources of Contemporay Art*, ed. Timo Valjakka (Helsinki: Museum of Contemporary Art, 1989), 202.

23. Gaston Bachelard, *Water and Dreams—An Essay on the Imagination of Matter* (Dallas, TX: Pegasus Foundation, 1983), 46.
24. Jean Nouvel, as quoted in Kester Rattenbury, "Echo and Narcissus," in *Architectural Design, Architecture & Film* (London: Academy Editions, 1994), 35.
25. *Nostalgia* (1983), director Andreï Tarkovsky.
26. *Stalker* (1979), director Andreï Tarkovsky.
27. Andrew Todd and Jean-Guy Lecat, *The Open Circle: Peter Brook's Theater Environments* (London: Palgrave MacMillan, 2003), 25.
28. Albert Soesman, *Our Twelve Senses: Wellsprings of the Soul* (Stroud: Hawthorne, 1998).
29. Robert Pogue Harrison, *Gardens: An Essay on the Human Condition* (Chicago, IL: The University of Chicago Press, 2008), 130.
30. Andreï Tarkovsky, *Sculpting in Time: Reflections on the Cinema* (London: The Bodley Head, 1986), 110.
31. *Par Delà des Nuages (Beyond the Clouds)* (1995), director Michelangelo Antonioni.
32. Merleau-Ponty describes "the flesh" in his essay "The Intertwining—The Chiasm," in *The Visible and the Invisible*, ed. Claude Lefort (Evanston: Northwestern University Press, 1969).
33. Edward Relph, *Place and Placelessness* (London: Pion Limited, 1986), 51.
34. Marilyn R. Chandler, *Dwelling in Text: House in American Fiction* (Berkeley-Los Angeles, Oxford: University of California Press, 1991), 10.
35. Henry James as quoted in Chandler, *Dwelling in Text*, "Introduction," 2.
36. *Psycho* (1960), director Alfred Hitchcock.
37. *The Sacrifice* (1986), director Andreï Tarkovsky.
38. Jean-Paul Sartre, "What is Literature?" *Jean-Paul Sartre: Basic Writings*, ed. Steven Priest (London, New York: Routledge, 2006), 272.

REFERENCES

Antonioni, Michelangelo, and Wim Wenders, directors. *Par-delà des nuages (Beyond the Clouds)*. Italy: Cecchi Gori Distribuzione, 1995.

Bachelard, Gaston. *The Poetics of Space*. Translated by Maria Jolas. Boston, MA: Beacon Press, 1969.

Bachelard, Gaston. *Water and Dreams: An Essay on the Imagination of Matter*. Dallas, TX: Pegasus Foundation, 1983.

Bagh, Peter von. "The Death of Emotion." In *Synnyt: Sources of Contemporary Art*, edited by Timo Valjakka. Helsinki: Museum of Contemporary Art, 1989.

Benjamin, Walter. *Illuminations: Essays and Reflections*. Edited by Hannah Arendt. New York, NY: Schocken Books, 1969.

Brook, Peter, Andrew Todd, and Jean-Guy Lecat. *The Open Circle: Peter Brook's Theatre Environment*. New York, NY: Palgrave MacMillan, 2003.

Calvino, Italo. *Six Memos for the Next Millennium*. New York, NY: Vintage International, 1993.

Chandler, Marilyn R. *Dwelling in Text: House in American Fiction*. Berkeley, Los Angeles, CA, Oxford: University of California Press, 1991.

Dewey, John. *Art as Experience*. New York, NY: Perigee Books, 1980.

Duhamel, Georges. *Scènes de la Vie future*. Paris: Mercure de France, 1930.

Duthuit, Georges. *Le feu des signes*. Paris: Editions d'Art Albert Skira, 1962.

Giedion, Sigfried. *Space, Time, and Architecture: The Growth of a New Tradition*. Cambridge, MA: Harvard University Press, 1952.

Harries, Karsten. "Building and the Terror of Time." *Perspecta 19: The Yale University Journal* 19 (1982): 59–69.

Harrison, Robert Pogue. *Gardens: An Essay on the Human Condition*. Chicago, IL: The University of Chicago Press, 2008.

Hitchcock, Alfred, director. *Psycho*. Los Angeles, CA: Paramount Pictures, 1960.

Lang, Fritz, director. *M*, Vereinigte Star-Film, 1931.

Malpas, Jeff. *Lecture at the Understanding and Designing Place Symposium*, Tampere University, Tampere, Finland, April 2017.

McGilchrist, Iain. *The Master and His Emissary: The Divided Brain and the Making of the Western World*. London: Yale University Press, 2009.

Merleau-Ponty, Maurice. *Sense and Non-sense*. London: Northwestern University Press, 1964.

Merleau-Ponty, Maurice. "The Intertwining: The Chiasm." In *The Visible and the Invisible*, edited by Claude Lefort. Evanston, IL: Northwestern University Press, 1969.

Perec, Georges. *Tiloja ja avaruuksia (Espéces d'espaces)*. Helsinki: Loki-kirjat, 1992.

Rattenbury, Kester. "Echo and Narcissus." In *Architecture & Film*, edited by Maggie Toy. London: Academy Editions, 1994.

Relph, Edward. *Place and Placelessness*. London: Pion Limited, 1986.

Rollins, Hyder E., ed. *The Letters of John Keats: Volume 2 1814–1821*. Cambridge, MA: Cambridge University Press, 2012.

Sartre, Jean-Paul. "What is Literature?" In *Jean-Paul Sartre: Basic Writings*, edited by Steven Priest. London, New York: Routledge, 2006.

Soesman, Albert. *Our Twelve Senses: Wellsprings of the Soul*. Stroud: Hawthorne, 1998.

Tarkovsky, Andreĭ, director. *Stalker*. Russia: Goskino, 1979.

Tarkovsky, Andreĭ, director. *Nostalghia (Nostalgia)*. Edinburgh: Grange Communications, Inc., 1983.

Tarkovskiĭ, Andreĭ, director. *The Sacrifice*. Russia: Sandrew, 1986.

Tarkovsky, Arseniĭ, and Andreĭ Arsen'evich Tarkovsky. *Sculpting in Time: Reflections on the Cinema*. London: Bodley Head, 1986.

Von Trier, Lars, director. *Dogville*, Columbia TriStar Film Distributors International, 2003.

Vrijman, Jan. "Filmmakers Spacemakers." *The Berglage Papers 11*, January, 1994.

2

Architecture After Affect

Jon Yoder

Affective architecture is now the norm. Practically every emergent design trajectory—from neo-pop to neo-primitivism, object-oriented ontology (OOO) to new materialism, and parametricism to the postdigital—grounds itself in some conception of affect. Like other cultural spheres including film, fashion, and food, architecture is now increasingly expected to elicit emotional and sensorial, *affective* responses. Unfortunately, architectural discourse on affect remains trapped between two ontological traditions: the essentializing phenomenology of Martin Heidegger and the post-humanist metaphysics of Gilles Deleuze. Heidegger's theories, with their essentializing emphases on the natural, fundamental, and original, have led to a notoriously conservative approach to the production and interpretation of architectural spaces and images.[1] Deleuze's theories, on the other hand, have prompted a reactionary turn to a vague vocabulary of mood, ambience, and cosmetics. As art historian Susanne von Falkenhausen explains, Deleuze's argument for affect has become so watered down that it often serves merely the ameliorative purpose of a "lifebelt against the helplessness felt in confronting the miseries of a postcommunist, post-colonial, post-human, post-digital, and neo-capitalist world."[2]

After phenomenology

In a sense, affect theory has become a successor to both phenomenology and post-structuralism in architectural discourse. Its construction of allusive or associative aesthetics seems to signal an appealing alternative to the self-righteous fundamentalism of phenomenological reduction and the cheap semiotic or syntactic didacticism of PoMo and Decon's initial incarnations. Indeed, affect-oriented architects are now fabricating a stunning range of post-human subjectivities: chunk models, synthetic landscapes, lively objects, tectonic swarms, pop confections, and bio-designed organisms, to name only a few.[3] Often these architects invoke the speculative aesthetics, realisms, fabulations, and materialisms of Jane Bennett, Donna Haraway, Graham Harman, Bruno Latour, or Jacques Rancière. Sometimes, however, they also make dubious claims about architectural origins and evolution. This is one similarity Peter Eisenman observes in phenomenology and parametricism: both ideological positions tend to make essentializing claims about the natural or inevitable tendencies of humans and architecture.[4] This fundamentalism is manifestly at odds with burgeoning conceptions of flat ontology, which assume an egalitarian universe of things, ideas, and possibilities. Ideological depth models no longer seem to apply.

As non-human subjectivities proliferate, phenomenology—whose lens focuses acutely on subjective perception—should be perfectly poised to lead the way. Unfortunately, its architectural incarnations have been surprisingly conservative regarding novel forms of cultural production. Even film phenomenology, which is traditionally more open to projective possibilities, has come to something of a standstill. *Post-phenomenology*, however, presents a fitting framework for exploring the territory between architecture and film—a liminal zone rife with visual images. Indeed, post-phenomenological approaches are ideal for analyzing imagery. Whereas phenomenology rejects images as superficial and ideologically deceptive, post-phenomenology embraces their projective potential. It celebrates visual and technological operations without resorting to the futile search for deep, humanistic essences. Unfortunately, post-phenomenological discourse has not really reached architecture.[5] Even when architects began invoking ontology again in the mid 2010s, it was without the concept's phenomenological baggage.[6] Object-oriented philosopher, Graham Harman, has been famously reframing architectural ontology in terms of "speculative realism," but the probative and projective approaches of post-phenomenology remain largely unknown to architects.[7]

So, what exactly is meant by post-phenomenology? The first sparks of post-phenomenological thinking appeared in the work of philosopher of science, Don Ihde. His ideas soon caught fire among a growing group of affect-oriented film and media studies scholars, some of whom were responsible for introducing phenomenology to cinema studies in the 1990s. Film scholars such as Vivian Sobchack, Steven Shaviro, and Laura U. Marks, for example, often emphasize the positive affective possibilities of cinematic vision.[8] Sobchack even celebrates an immersed "cinesthetic" subject whose cinematic spectatorship involves intense, multi-sensorial experience.[9] Not surprisingly, much of their film scholarship is heavily influenced by the visual theories of Maurice Merleau-Ponty. Unlike Heidegger's anti-visual phenomenology, Merleau-Ponty's "ocular-centric" phenomenology construes vision as a vital sensorial valence for cultural production. Post-phenomenologists therefore remain enthusiastic about vision whereas traditional phenomenologists tend to privilege the other senses, especially touch.

Post-phenomenological thinking also involves shifting from Heidegger's conception of technology to Merleau-Ponty's.[10] Although Heidegger's essay, "The Question Concerning Technology," has been enormously influential, his technological thinking was also surprisingly limited.[11] "To attend to the 'essence' of technology," Ihde argues, "blinds Heidegger to the differing contexts and multidimensionalities of technologies that a pragmatic-phenomenological account can better bring forth."[12] Merleau-Ponty's technological thinking, on the other hand, was about opening up possibilities instead of nostalgically retreating to essences. His conception of tools resembles Marshall McLuhan's later understanding of media as human "extensions."[13] Using the examples of a feather in a woman's hat, an automobile, and a blind man's cane, Merleau-Ponty elucidated the symbiotic relationships woven among humans, their tools, and the lifeworld. He wrote, "To get used to a hat, a car, or a stick is to be transplanted into them, or conversely, to incorporate them into the bulk of our own body."[14] As Ihde explains, "In [Heidegger's] hammer example, the tool 'withdraws'; but in the Merleau-Pontean feather or cane, it is a part of the world which is reached through this withdrawal."[15] Bodies, images, and technologies thus become sites of affective potentials instead of mythical origins.

Finally, post-phenomenological thinking also requires abandoning the fundamentalist pursuit of essences in favor of open-minded speculation and projection. As early as 1984, Ihde called for a "nonfoundational phenomenology," which he described as "just another way of characterizing it as different from, but owing to its ancestry."[16] His use of phenomenological methods for experimental post-phenomenological purposes predicted how some architects today use digital techniques for post-digital projects. Designers increasingly use the term postdigital to indicate a new type of digitally savvy work that is no longer naively enamored with the utopian frenzy surrounding early digital form-making.[17] Neither post-digital nor post-phenomenological approaches involve an ideological search for essences. Instead, post-phenomenology uses phenomenological reduction as a key to unlock projective opportunities. It emerges in the wake of the critical and digital projects of the last century to offer a new mode of image analysis and production—one that is incisively optimistic about vision and technology, but decidedly wary of essentialism.

After cinema

It makes sense that film and media scholars would be early adopters of post-phenomenological points of view. Because it is literally impossible to escape the screen in cinema, filmmakers have invented an impressive array of techniques to intensify the cinematic experience. They are always on the lookout for new ways to viscerally engage audiences. Film theorists therefore rhapsodize erotically about effects of color, texture, reflection, duration, luminosity, rhythm, and resolution in ways that might mortify architectural phenomenologists. In short, post-phenomenological film theorists write precisely about the kind of affective abundance to which architectural theorists often merely allude. Nonetheless, architects remain famously fascinated with film. From Le Corbusier's *promenade architecturale* to Bernard Tschumi's cinematographic promenade, from Juhani Pallasmaa's cinematic tactility to Jean Nouvel's cinematic scenography—phenomenologists and post-structuralists alike have fetishized filmic techniques as (literally) sensational, image-oriented models for making architecture.

The buildings of Los Angeles architect John Lautner (1911–94) have appeared in feature films more frequently than those of practically any other architect.[18] This is partly because Lautner's broad expanses of glass often frame *widescreen* views of landscape. In fact, the panoramic parameters of these vistas sometimes simulate the stretched aspect ratios of contemporaneous widescreen film formats of the 1950s and 1960s.[19] This hedonistic ocular revelry produced a persistent "scopic pulsion" (an irresistible urge to look) that tends to make anti-visual phenomenologists blush. It leads Kenneth Frampton to question the "latent erotic content" of Lautner's lush, image-oriented designs.[20]

This image orientation concerns Karsten Harries, who considers the implications of Lautner's ocular-centrism "very dangerous" for architecture.[21] Lautner, however, made no apologies for taking vision as a primary concern. He explained the exotic curvilinear shapes of his buildings as part of the simple desire to frame panoramic vistas. "Usually in the hills you have a panoramic view that people are interested in right away," he noted. "And so most of my things are curved."[22] Architectural photographer Julius Shulman, who photographed many Lautner houses including the iconic Malin House *Chemosphere* (1960), understood this about Lautner's enveloping ocular-centric form-making. "The view [from Lautner buildings] was peripheral," he explained. "It requires a circular form" (see Figure 2.1).[23]

Still, although Lautner's work seems synchronized with widescreen cinema, it is not necessarily cinematic in the traditional sense. Cinematic architecture requires movement through space. This is why the vocabulary of architectural cinema is rife with kinesthetic terms such as space–time, parallax, distraction, montage and

FIGURE 2.1: Photo by Julius Shulman (1961). John Lautner, Malin House *Chemosphere*, Los Angeles, 1960. Getty Research Institute.

promenade. Witness Steven Holl's emphasis on the "mobile" body in architectural experience:

> Our faculty of judgment is incomplete without this experience of crossing through spaces. The turn and twist of the body engaging a long and then short perspective, an up-and-down movement, an open-and-closed or dark-and-light rhythm of geometries—these are the core of the spatial score of architecture.[24]

Instead of presenting this kind of gradually unfolding picturesque pathway to mobile viewers, Lautner's houses tend to envelope viewers at rest. This different type of immersive viewing led film theorist Anne Friedberg, herself a Lautner client, to suggest that his architecture might qualify as "post-cinematic."[25] His architecture assumes neither the static viewer of photography nor the mobile viewer of cinema. Instead, Lautner's architecture posits a third type of viewer: the "cineramic" subject. In this model, the body is mainly at rest, but the eyes continue to navigate in a sea of widescreen imagery. Although this type of immersive spectatorship might smack of guilty architectural pleasure (or even panoptic oppression), there is nothing to suggest that cineramic subjectivity is inherently passive or oppressed simply because it does not involve wandering cinematically through space. Like the cinesthetic subject, the cineramic subject opens exhilarating new opportunities for cultural production by celebrating the seductive, post-cinematic territory between architecture and film.

If Lautner's buildings are indeed post-cinematic, they also constitute a remarkably affective body of post-phenomenological architecture. After all, vision and technology were central concerns in his design process. Stretched to widescreen extremes, Lautner's windows sometimes create projection screens for superimposing images of architecture and film. Here, Ihde's rumination on the mediating role of windows is instructive. He understands the window as simultaneously a divider and facilitator for the symbiotic relationship between building and occupant. Ihde notes, "the window occupies a position *between* the observer and what is observed. The I-world relation is changed to I-window-world. This is more than a formal change; the way world is experienced is changed *ontologically*."[26] Any time ontology is invoked in architectural discourse, the work of Heidegger (and more recently, Harman) immediately comes to mind. In fact, the current dubious status of phenomenology in architectural discourse stems largely from the longstanding dominance of Heidegger's essentialist emphases on being, truth and origins. An allegiance to Heideggerian clichés is one reason some architects have not explored the generative possibilities of image-making more liberally. In fact, Heidegger's championing of art and orality over technology and visuality makes him a primary antagonist of Lautner's ocular-centric architecture.

The work of Merleau-Ponty, however, provides an inviting visual alternative. Although Martin Jay concludes that Merleau-Ponty's valiant attempt to reconstruct our understanding of vision did little to turn the anti-visual tide of the twentieth-century French discourse, his work still has enormous potential for architecture.[27] Because Merleau-Ponty wrote very little about buildings, however, architects often understand his work, when we read it at all, as a lesser addendum to Heidegger's. In the arena of vision and visuality, however, their bodies of work could hardly be more different. Merleau-Ponty, like Lautner, emphasized the central position of the subject in visual experience. As he put it, "because [my body] moves itself and sees, it holds things in a circle around itself."[28] This focus on the centrality and implicit agency of the individual viewer marks an important shift. If philosopher Edmund Husserl developed his early phenomenology largely in response to the dominance of Cartesian assumptions, then Lautner did a similar thing for architecture.[29] Many of Lautner's contemporaries pushed the possibilities of linear perspective in their designs. The buildings of Richard Neutra, Pierre Koenig, and other Case Study architects, for example, were popularized through the lenses of Shulman's cameras and the pages of *Arts & Architecture* magazine (see Figure 2.2).

Indeed, mid-century Rationalist architecture in Los Angeles often exuded the strong photographic qualities of one-point perspective. Lautner, on the other hand,

FIGURE 2.2: Photo by Julius Shulman (1960). Pierre Koenig, Stahl House (CSH #22), Los Angeles, 1960. Getty Research Institute.

rejected Cartesian perspectivalism. Like a widescreen filmmaker, he celebrated peripheral vision and its catalytic promise of infinite vanishing points.

After apparatus

Whereas many architects owe debts to Heidegger, Holl is one of the few to mobilize Merleau-Ponty's writings. He bases a concept he calls "enmeshed experience" on Merleau-Ponty's model of immersion, but there is an important difference between the two.[30] While Holl suggests a blurring of figure/ground, Merleau-Ponty suggested a reversal. He wrote,

> The idea we have of the world would be overturned if we could succeed in seeing the intervals between things (for example, the space between the trees on the boulevard) as *objects* and, inversely, if we saw things themselves—the trees—as the ground.[31]

This model of tangible, plastic space echoes Lautner's mentor Frank Lloyd Wright's central tenet of organic architecture: that space itself is the object of design and the walls and roof are merely incidental.[32] His parallel emphasis on space and environment over things and materials is arguably where Merleau-Ponty became most architectural. While Heidegger and Harman remind us that even concepts are things (or objects), Merleau-Ponty identified important perceptual and environmental relations in art. In fact, the relationship between viewer and viewed in Lautner's architecture is strikingly similar to Merleau-Ponty's description of the experience of Paleolithic cave paintings in France:

> The animals painted on the walls of Lascaux are not there in the same way as the fissures and limestone formations. But they are not *elsewhere*. Pushed forward here, held back there, held up by the wall's mass they use so adroitly, they spread around the wall without ever breaking from their elusive moorings in it. I would be at great pains to say *where* is the painting I am looking at. For I do not look at it as I do at a thing; I do not fix it in its place. My gaze wanders in it as in the halos of Being. It is more accurate to say that I see according to it, or with it, than that I *see it*.[33]

It makes sense that Merleau-Ponty would locate his cavernous consideration of intersubjective viewing underground. Caves have long played important roles in discussions of visual production. Not surprisingly, cave metaphors also abound in descriptions of Lautner's architecture. Lionel March called him "the great architect of the cave."[34] And Lautner himself often described the Segel House (1980) in Malibu as a "cave on the beach."[35] Lautner incorporated boulders and existing rock outcroppings into the walls and floors of the Arango House (1973) in Acapulco and the Elrod House (1968) in Palm Springs (see Figure 2.3).[36] The Arango House and unbuilt Aita Private Discotheque (1978) both employ cave-like forms with water encircling their outer edges. Jim Charlton's exquisite pencil renderings for Lautner emphasize the cavernous interiors of his seemingly primordial projects (see Figure 2.4).

These projects implicitly, if unintentionally, relate Lautner's architecture to cinema. After all, film theorists frequently invoke Plato's "Allegory of the Cave" to describe viewers' relationship with the cinematic apparatus. Most people are like prisoners who are forced to watch shadows against the wall of a cave, Plato argued. We have our backs to the light that casts the shadows, so we are not prepared to recognize the source of the shadows even if it were shown to us.[37] Apparatus

FIGURE 2.3: Photo by Jon Yoder. John Lautner, Elrod House, Palm Springs, 1968.

FIGURE 2.4: Drawing by Jim Charlton. John Lautner, Arango House, Acapulco, 1973. John Lautner Papers. Getty Research Institute.

theorists frequently use this allegory to describe the mind control that cinema ostensibly wields over its viewing subjects. Moviegoers are like Plato's prisoners in a specular cave, the theory goes, willingly entranced by the cinematic apparatus. Film theorist Jean-Louis Baudry, for example, described the constellation of elements that conspire to produce the effect of obedience through the internalized illusion of cinema's comprehensiveness:

> No doubt the darkened room and the screen bordered with black like a letter of condolences already present privileged conditions of effectiveness—no exchange, no circulation, no communication with any outside. Projection and reflection take place in a closed space and those who remain there, whether they know it or not (but they do not), find themselves chained, captured, or captivated.[38]

Apparatus theory, which dominated cinema studies in the 1970s, maintained that films are inherently deceptive and ideologically coercive because the image-oriented medium of film hides the "reality" of its production and projection. Still frames of celluloid pass before the eyes so fast that the actual mechanics of cinema always remain veiled from the audience.

Like caves, mirrors also figure prominently in apparatus theory. They are often employed to explain similar illusory or deceptive effects. Apparatus theorists such as Baudry and Jean-Louis Comolli invoke psychoanalyst Jacques Lacan's "mirror stage" concept to describe the formative role of cinema in the construction of subjective identity.[39] According to their models, we see ourselves on screen whether we want to or not and are thus subject to the ideological conditioning of the cinema.[40] Baudry even portrays the cinematic apparatus as nothing less than a synthesis of Plato's cave and Lacan's mirror stage.[41]

Lautner used mirrors prolifically, but he almost never used them to construct one-to-one reflections for viewers. He avoided simple frontal reflections whenever possible. This is one reason Lautner often tilted, accordioned, or curved the fenestration of his buildings. He worked to dissipate his viewers' awareness of self whenever they inhabit the widescreen images he constructed. Lautner intentionally fragmented and facetted the surfaces of transparent glass in order to disperse reflections and enhance visual immersion. He also used mirrors in an explicitly Loosian way to expand the impression of space. For example, he surfaced the Elrod House kitchen walls with mirrors above eye level in order to reflect its massive concrete ceiling and create the impression that space continues above the cabinets. At the Goldstein Properties Offices (1989) in Century City, and the Shearing House (1992) in Coronado, Lautner used mirrors to construct widescreen vistas that did not otherwise exist. The expansive mirrored surfaces in his 1980s renovation of the Sheats/Goldstein House go even farther in producing a funhouse effect that transforms a single image into a multiplied field.

Both architecture critics and apparatus theorists have often dismissed these specular effects as unnecessary gimmicks or tricks. Post-phenomenological film theorists, however, tend to emphasize the positive intersubjective relations construed by the cinematic apparatus. It is not so much that we learn who we are in cinema's mirror, they suggest, but rather that we relate to the screen itself as a subject. For these theorists, the cinematic apparatus becomes a locus of projective potentials instead of ideological discipline. This projective model hints at some crucial differences between Lautner's architecture and the cave and mirror allegories of apparatus theorists. It would be a mistake to literally compare Lautner's viewing subjects to infants sitting before Lacan's mirror or prisoners chained in Plato's cave. Through their immersion in widescreen images, Lautner's cineramic subjects are confronted—or better, wrapped—by the technologically constructed nature of vision. Partly because they often cannot see themselves as singular reflections, Lautner's cineramic subjects tend to intimately identify with the buildings that frame their vision. Like the viewers of Paleolithic cave paintings described by Merleau-Ponty, Lautner's clients see *with* the buildings he designed for them, and *according* to the enveloping images he framed.

After automation

This close relationship between vision and technology signals an affective immersion of which some art critics remain wary. Rosalind Krauss, for example, dismisses the immersive environments of new media art as "kitsch."[42] And Hal Foster claims that those same environments are not authentically phenomenological because they are so highly mediated.[43] Although these critics are focused on the work of installation artists such as James Turrell (see Figure 2.5) and Bill Viola—not buildings designed by architects—Foster's opposition of phenomenology and mediation deserves scrutiny. It reflects a distinctly Heideggerian thinking that applauds "thingness" while seeking essential truth. Whereas Heidegger conceptualized equipment as occupying a middle position between mere things and works of art, Merleau-Ponty placed equipment in a position of mediation between viewer and environment, a location closer to Ihde's "I-window-world" model.[44] For Merleau-Ponty and Ihde, the mediating role of technology is inevitable. As Ihde points out, "Virtually every area of praxis implicates a technology [...] *human activity from immemorial time and across the diversity of cultures has always been technologically embedded.*"[45] While Krauss and Foster fear the loss of individual agency implied by immersion, Ihde insists that immersion is ultimately flexible and dynamic.

Similarly, Merleau-Ponty did not envision immersion as a trap, but rather as an infinite storehouse of possibilities. For him, technology is something that sharpens our vision, not something that obscures it, hence his famous example of the blind man's cane. Through technological immersion, our horizon of experience expands.

FIGURE 2.5: Photo by Jon Yoder. James Turrell, Skyspace *Above Horizon*, Beverly Hills, 2004.

As Merleau-Ponty wrote, "Immersed in the visible by his body, itself visible, the see-er does not appropriate what he sees; he merely approaches it by looking, he opens himself to the world."[46] In this spirit of opening oneself to a world of visual possibilities, Lautner deployed automation technologies to dramatic effect. For him, immersion involved more than spatial envelopment; it also relied on push-button automation for its special effects. At the Sheats/Goldstein House, for example, Lautner's automated effects include a large-screen TV that rises miraculously from a built-in concrete table, skylight and hot tub covers that retract at the touch of a button, retractable glass walls that expose an unprotected cantilevered corner, and a functioning all-glass sink in a glass wall.

In an early article from 1905, Lautner's professor father described the desire to achieve maximum effect with minimum effort as a quintessentially American pragmatic mentality. He wrote,

> The first and chief aim of inventions is to secure the necessaries of life at a less expenditure of human energy. A second aim is to free man from the narrow bonds of his physical environment and to secure for him a larger sphere of action.[47]

In his ocular-centric houses that substitute electric energy for human energy wherever possible, Lautner took the goal of designing a "larger sphere of action" literally.

Perhaps the pinnacle of Lautner's automated explorations is the Reiner House *Silvertop* (1963). Together with his inventor client Kenneth Reiner, Lautner questioned every scale of domestic living and designed numerous details and pieces of hardware in the process.[48] The house became a kind of research and development laboratory for testing new products and construction systems. Esther McCoy credited *Silvertop* as "the first time gadgetry on a large scale has come under the hegemony of architecture."[49] Miles of wiring run in extensive utility tunnels beneath the house, whose automated features include a skylight with motorized vanes for light control, pivoting wall segments on the West facade that expose views of Hollywood, basins that automatically fill with water from hidden sources at their rims, a retractable glazed partition in the bathroom that promotes interior sunbathing, and a retractable curving glass wall in the main living space (see Figure 2.6). According to Alan Hess, "It was a building of its age, a building capturing and defining the age's confidence that technology could improve human lives."[50]

This optimism is a far cry from Heidegger's concept of "standing-reserve" that describes the devastating transformation of nature and humanity at the hands of modern technology.[51] Indeed, it is difficult to imagine two more opposed views of technology. Instead of interrogating technology's insidious essence with Heidegger, Lautner questioned technology's unexpected potentials with Merleau-Ponty. Seemingly with Professor Heidegger in mind, Merleau-Ponty wrote,

FIGURE 2.6: Photo by Jon Yoder. Reiner House *Silvertop*, Los Angeles, 1963.

> And so it is not a question asked of someone who doesn't know by someone who does—the schoolmaster's question. The question comes from one who does not know, and it is addressed to a vision, a seeing, which knows everything and which we do not make, for it makes itself in us.[52]

By blending Ihde's vision of technology with Merleau-Ponty's emphasis on projective vision, Lautner's designs opened post-phenomenological possibilities for architecture. Seemingly equal parts technological and psycho-physiological, his radically ocular-centric "machines for viewing" supersede Le Corbusier's comparatively benign "machines for living."

Some architects still see technological mediation as an unwelcome interloper, however. Holl, for example, poses a common question loaded with architectural anxiety:

> As our technological means multiply, are we growing—or becoming stunted—perceptually? We live our lives in constructed spaces, surrounded by physical objects. But, born into this world of things, are we able to experience fully the phenomena of their interrelation, to derive joy from our perceptions?[53]

Even in the age of Instagram, some architects are still staging the age-old battle of reality versus its representation. This fear that our perceptive abilities will flatten with the reduction of the real world to two-dimensional images haunts phenomenological discourse in architecture. As Holl insists, "If we allow magazine photos or screen images to replace experience, our ability to perceive architecture will diminish so greatly that it will become impossible to comprehend it."[54] Pallasmaa agrees, arguing,

> Architecture at large has become an art of the printed image fixed by the hurried eye of the camera. The gaze itself tends to flatten into a picture and lose its plasticity; instead of experiencing our being in the world, we behold it from outside as spectators of images projected on the surface of the retina.[55]

Once again, Merleau-Ponty's own interpretations are at odds with his interpreters. Shortly before his death, he testified convincingly, and provocatively, in defense of visual images:

> The word "image" is in bad repute because we have thoughtlessly believed that a design was a tracing, a copy, a second thing, and that the mental image was such a design, belonging among our private bric-a-brac. But if in fact it is nothing of the kind, then neither the design nor the painting belongs to the in-itself any more than the image does.[56]

After human

In a sense, phenomenological fears that the human sensorium will flatten are well-founded. As Walter Benjamin famously observed, human perception is malleable and changes tangibly from generation to generation.[57] An important difference today is that post-phenomenologists welcome these transformations. Even Michael Benedikt, whose influential book *For an Architecture of Reality* became something of a post-modern phenomenological manifesto, is now working more in terms of projection than traditional phenomenological reduction. His new book *Architecture Beyond Experience* casts buildings as sentient beings and rooms as relational subjects that crackle with social electricity.[58] Indeed, philosopher of science Donna Haraway's cyborg dreams seem to be coming true as post-human subjectivities proliferate. Media scholar Christian Stiegler describes a hybrid organicism that embraces new technology the way Lautner's earlier organicism embraced automation. "Posthuman hybridity is the *merging of organic data and mediated features* such as technology," he explains. "The result is an artificial, mutated *posthuman organism.*"[59]

Lautner's unconventional embrace of automation technologies imbued his organic architecture with an extraordinarily affective ergonomics. His push-button special effects produce hybrid relationships between house, human, and horizon. In this respect, Lautner's houses sometimes seem to visually propel their occupants into the distant landscape—freeing viewers, in a sense, from the confines of their immediate surroundings through the collaboration of visual envelopment and technological interactivity. The scale of these effects sometimes borders on the sublime. Indeed, Lautner's enormous widescreen frames challenge traditional notions of domestic propriety, banishing quaint tropes like the picture window, sash, and shutter. Sometimes their visual expansiveness even seems to transcend human subjectivity. As Eric Lloyd Wright insists, "John Lautner went very much beyond the human scale."[60]

Three decades ago, art historian Jonathan Crary insightfully predicted that the (first) digital revolution would have enormous consequences for culturally constructed post-human vision:

> Computer-aided design, synthetic holography, flight simulators, computer animation, robotic image recognition, ray tracing, texture mapping, motion control, virtual environment helmets, magnetic resonance imaging, and multispectral sensors are only a few of the techniques that are relocating vision to a plane severed from a human observer.[61]

Indeed, the recent wave of design practices dedicated to exploring the architectural implications of artificial intelligence and object-oriented ontology seems to reinforce Crary's suggestion that technological vision is leaving the human body behind.[62] To Crary's 30-year-old list of visualization techniques, architects can now add newer imaging technologies such as virtual and augmented reality systems, aerial drone photography, robotic videography, 3D laser scanning, and parametric projection mapping. Stiegler reminds us that this current fascination with immersion is nothing new:

> In fact, the current hype around human-machine interactions, artificial intelligence (AI), and extended reality (XR) like virtual reality (VR), augmented reality (AR), and mixed reality (MR) needs to be seen as a culmination of a long history of immersive experiences in media, ranging across literature, theater, film, and games.[63]

Even the ubiquitous array of digital fabrication systems in architecture studios produces different types of visual immersion, inviting users to expand their human sensoria by seeing according to non-human systems. It is important to note, however, that in alienating users from normative modes of vision, these systems also expand users' perceptive apparata. New modes of immersive viewing might construct post-human subjects, but they are also—as in Lautner's architecture—radically and projectively embodied.

In "The Question Concerning Technology," Heidegger famously argued,

> Everywhere we remain unfree and chained to technology, whether we passionately affirm or deny it. But we are delivered over to it in the worst possible way when we regard it as something neutral; for this conception of it, to which today we particularly like to do homage, makes us utterly blind to the essence of technology.[64]

Today, architecture remains unfree and chained between the dichotomous ideological legacies of phenomenology and post-structuralist metaphysics. Merleau-Ponty would hardly be concerned. For him, these distinctions do not apply to artists anyway. He wrote,

> Rather than apply to [Cézanne's] work dichotomies more appropriate to those who sustain traditions than to those men [sic], philosophers or painters [and here we should add architects], who initiate these traditions, he preferred to search for the true meaning of painting, which is continually to question tradition.[65]

So, of course, Heidegger was right to question. But in looking inward for essences, he inadvertently stifled creative design exploration. What might be produced through a new focus on the projective possibilities—or scopic pulsions—opened up by immersive image-making? New modes of post-cinematic and post-human vision are already proliferating, and the ocular-centric designs of Lautner and writings of Merleau-Ponty suggest some exciting trajectories for architecture. In fact, Lautner's cineramic apparata instantiate one form of the experiential horizon about which Merleau-Ponty wrote: "The openness upon the world implies that the world be and remain a horizon, not because my vision would push the world back beyond itself, but because somehow he who sees is of it and is in it."[66] In our highly mediated cultures, where multiple screens increasingly form environments in multiple ways, it is important for designers to acknowledge and continue to explore the immersive, image-oriented territory between architecture and film. This goes beyond the clichéd call for slow architecture to catch up with fast media. Instead, it invites affect-oriented architects to experiment promiscuously across disciplines with the exhilarating, post-phenomenological possibilities of cinesthetic and cineramic subjectivity.

NOTES

1. Heidegger's influential body of work includes not only the massive book *Being and Time* (1927), but individual essays such as "The Origin of the Work of Art" (1935), "The Age of the World Picture" (1938), "Building Dwelling Thinking" (1952), and "The Question Concerning Technology" (1954).
2. Susanne von Falkenhausen, "The Trouble with 'Affect Theory' in our Age of Outrage," *Frieze*, no. 204, June 6, 2019. https://www.frieze.com/article/trouble-affect-theory-our-age-outrage.
3. Jon Yoder, "Design vs. History: Materializing Theory After the Post-Linguistic Turn," Paper presented in *Architectural Theory Now?* Conference, University of Pennsylvania Weitzman School of Design, April 4–6, 2019.
4. "Peter Eisenman in Conversation with Greg Lynn": https://www.youtube.com/watch?v=-DUrA1Lod--g.
5. I first engaged post-phenomenological ideas in a paper titled "An Answer Concerning Technology: Or, Some Questions Concerning Phenomenology" at the Second International Architecture + Phenomenology Conference at Kyoto Seika University in Japan (June 2009).
6. Kivi Sotamaa, for example, invoked ontology in a non-phenomenological context in Neil Denari's "Of a Controlling Nature" graduate design studio review at UCLA on June 10, 2014.
7. Graham Harman, *Is There an Object Oriented Architecture?*, ed. Joseph Bedford (London, New York, NY: Bloomsbury Academic, 2020); and *Object-Oriented Ontology: A New Theory of Everything* (London: Penguin, 2018).
8. Vivian Sobchack: *Address of the Eye: A Phenomenology of Film Experience* (Princeton, NJ: Princeton University Press, 1992); and *Carnal Thoughts: Embodiment and Moving Image Culture* (Berkeley, Los Angeles, CA: University of California Press, 2004); Steven Shaviro, *Post-Cinematic Affect* (Ropley, Hants: Zero Books, 2010);

and Laura U. Marks: *The Skin of the Film: Intercultural Cinema, Embodiment, and the Senses* (Durham, NC: Duke University Press, 2000); and *Touch: Sensuous Theory and Multisensory Media* (Minneapolis, MN: University of Minnesota Press, 2002).

9. Vivian Sobchack, "What My Fingers Knew: The Cinesthetic Subject, or Vision in the Flesh," in *Carnal Thoughts: Embodiment and Moving Image Culture* (Berkeley, Los Angeles, CA: University of California Press, 2004), 53–84.
10. According to Bryan E. Norwood,

> the architectural appropriations of phenomenology have hinged their account of the primacy of embodiment on the opposition of wholeness and place to scientific and technological displacement to such a degree that they have reified an alternative set of unbracketed, abstract clichés.

Norwood, "Disorienting Phenomenology," in *Log* 42 (Winter/Spring 2018), 15.

11. Martin Heidegger, "The Question Concerning Technology" (1953), in *The Question Concerning Technology and Other Essays*, trans. William Lovitt (New York, NY: Harper & Row, Publishers, Inc., 1977), 3–35.
12. Don Ihde, Heidegger's *Technologies: Postphenomenological Perspectives* (New York, NY: Fordham University Press, 2010), 115.
13. Marshall McLuhan, *Understanding Media: The Extensions of Man* (Cambridge, MA: MIT Press, 1994).
14. Merleau-Ponty, *Phenomenology of Perception* (1945), trans. Colin Smith (London: Routledge & K. Paul; New York, NY: Humanities Press, 1962), 165–66.
15. Don Ihde, *Technology and the Lifeworld: From Garden to Earth* (Bloomington, IN: Indiana University Press, 1990), 40.
16. Don Ihde, *Postphenomenology: Essays in the Postmodern Context* (Evanston, IL: Northwestern University Press, 1993), 1.
17. Ellie Abrons and Adam Fure, "Postdigital Materiality," in *Lineament: Material, Representation and the Physical Figure in Architectural Production*, eds. Gail Peter Borden and Michael Meredith (New York, NY: Routledge, 2018), 194.
18. Jon Yoder, "Vision and Crime: The *Cineramic* Architecture of John Lautner," in *Archi.Pop: Mediating Architecture in Popular Culture*, ed. D. Medina Lasansky (London, New York, NY: Bloomsbury Academic, 2014), 45–58.
19. John Belton, *Widescreen Cinema* (Cambridge, MA: Harvard University Press, 1992).
20. Kenneth Frampton, interview with author, New York, NY, February 13, 2005.
21. Karsten Harries, conversation with author, Second International Architecture + Phenomenology Conference, Kyoto Seika University, Japan, June 2009.
22. Lautner, interview with Marlene L. Laskey, *Responsibility, Infinity, Nature Oral History Transcript* (1982). (Los Angeles, CA: Oral History Program, UCLA, 1988), 15–19.

23. Julius Shulman, interview with author, Los Angeles, CA, September 20, 2005.
24. Steven Holl, *Parallax* (New York, NY: Princeton Architectural Press, 2000), 26.
25. Anne Friedberg, e-mail correspondence with author, March 2003.
26. Ihde, *Technology and the Lifeworld*, 47.
27. Martin Jay, *Downcast Eyes: The Denigration of Vision in Twentieth-Century French Thought* (Berkeley, Los Angeles, CA: University of California Press, 1993).
28. Maurice Merleau-Ponty, "Eye and Mind," trans. Carleton Dallery, *The Primacy of Perception*, ed. James M. Edie (Evanston, IL: Northwestern University Press, 1964), 159–90.
29. Edmund Husserl, *Logical Investigations* (1900), trans. J. N. Findlay (London: Routledge and K. Paul; New York, NY: Humanities Press, 1970).
30. Holl, *Parallax*, 56–67.
31. Merleau-Ponty, "The Film and the New Psychology," in *Sense and Non-Sense*, trans. Hubert L. Dreyfus and Patricia Allen Dreyfus (Evanston, IL: Northwestern University Press, 1964), 48–59.
32. Peter Blake, *Frank Lloyd Wright: Architecture and Space* (1960) (New York, NY: Pelican Books Inc., 1965).
33. Merleau-Ponty, "Eye and Mind," 164.
34. Lionel March, interview with Bette Jane Cohen, Los Angeles, CA, 1988 (transcription by author).
35. John Lautner, "Lyrical Technology," presented in "Structures: Style and Substance," lecture series at Westweek, Pacific Design Center, Los Angeles, CA, March 25, 1987.
36. Lautner's work prefigured the fetishization of rocky surfaces found in the work of today's neo-primitivist/paleo architecture practices such as Ensamble Studio, Matter Design and T+E+A+M.
37. Plato, *The Republic* ("Allegory of the Cave," circa 380 B.C.E.), ed. G. R. F. Ferrari, trans. Tom Griffith (Cambridge: Cambridge University Press, 2000), 220–25.
38. Jean-Louis Baudry, "Ideological Effects of the Basic Cinematographic Apparatus" (1970), trans. Alan Williams, *Film Quarterly* 28, no. 2 (Winter 1974–75), 44.
39. Jacques Lacan, "The Mirror Stage as Formative of the I Function as Revealed in Psychoanalytic Experience" (1949), *Écrits: A Selection*, trans. Bruce Fink (New York, NY: W.W. Norton & Company, Inc., 2002).
40. Jean-Louis Comolli, "Machines of the Visible" (1971), in *The Cinematic Apparatus*, eds. Teresa de Lauretis and Stephen Heath (New York, NY: St. Martin's Press, 1980), 121–42.
41. Baudry, "Ideological Effects of the Basic Cinematographic Apparatus," 45.
42. Rosalind Krauss, lecture in the UCLA Dept. of Architecture + Urban Design, Los Angeles, CA, November 24, 2004.
43. Hal Foster (in conversation with Marquard Smith), "Polemics, Postmodernism, Immersion, Militarized Space," *Journal of Visual Culture* 3, no. 3 (December 2004), 327–28.

44. Heidegger elaborated his tripartite model of *mere things*, *equipment*, and *works of art* in "The Origin of the Work of Art" (1935), in *Poetry, Language, Thought*, trans. Albert Hofstadter (New York, NY: Harper & Row, 1971), 17–87.
45. Ihde, *Technology and the Lifeworld*, 20.
46. Merleau-Ponty, "Eye and Mind," 162.
47. John E. Lautner [Sr.], "American Materialism," in *Normal College News* 3, no. 9 (November 24, 1905).
48. John Reese, "Dream House or Nightmare?" *The Saturday Evening Post* (August 20, 1960), 64.
49. Esther McCoy, "West Coast Architects V/John Lautner," in *Arts & Architecture* 82 (August 1965), 27.
50. Alan Hess, *The Architecture of John Lautner* (New York, NY: Rizzoli International Publications, 1999), 104.
51. Heidegger, "The Question Concerning Technology," 17.
52. Merleau-Ponty, "Eye and Mind," 167.
53. Steven Holl, Juhani Pallasmaa, and Alberto Pérez-Gómez, *Questions of Perception: Phenomenology of Architecture* (Tokyo: A+U Publishing Co., Ltd., 1994), 40.
54. Holl, *Parallax*, 26.
55. Pallasmaa, "An Architecture of the Seven Senses," in *Questions of Perception*, 29.
56. Merleau-Ponty, "Eye and Mind," 164.
57. Benjamin wrote,

    > During long periods of history, the mode of human sense perception changes with humanity's entire mode of existence. The manner in which human sense perception is organized, the medium in which it is accomplished, is determined not only by nature but by historical circumstances as well.

    See Benjamin, "The Work of Art in the Age of Mechanical Reproduction" (1936), in *Illuminations*, ed. Hannah Arendt, trans. Harry Zohn (New York, NY: Schocken Books, 1969), 222.
58. Michael Benedikt, *Architecture Beyond Experience* (San Francisco, Los Angeles, CA, New York, NY, Hong Kong: Applied Research + Design Publishing, 2020).
59. Christian Stiegler, *360° Gaze: Immersions in Media, Society, and Culture* (Cambridge, MA: MIT Press, 2021), 205.
60. Eric Lloyd Wright interview with the author, Malibu, CA, 9 February 2006. Stephen Burum, director of photography for Brian De Palma's 1984 film *Body Double*, which used Lautner's *Chemosphere* as a location, notes that widescreen cinema also goes beyond the human scale. Architecture and cinema are two *different* disciplines, he emphasizes. Whereas architecture deals with relationships and proportions for the human scale, Burum claimed, designing for movies requires proportioning things for the camera lens. Burum, telephone interview with author, July 3, 2006.

61. Jonathan Crary, *Techniques of the Observer: On Vision and Modernity in the Nineteenth Century* (Cambridge, MA: MIT Press, 1990), 1.
62. See, for example, the pioneering practices of SPAN (Matias del Campo and Sandra Manninger: https://span-arch.org) and Ruy Klein (David Ruy and Karel Klein: http://ruyklein.com/about_rk.html).
63. Stiegler, *360° Gaze*, 4–5.
64. Heidegger, "The Question Concerning Technology," 4.
65. Merleau-Ponty, "Cézanne's Doubt" (1945), in *Sense and Non-Sense*, trans. Hubert L. Dreyfus and Patricia Allen Dreyfus (Evanston, IL: Northwestern University Press, 1964), 13.
66. Merleau-Ponty, *The Visible and the Invisible* (1964), ed. Claude Lefort, trans. Alphonso Lingis (Evanston, IL: Northwestern University Press, 1968), 100.

REFERENCES

Abrons, Ellie, and Adam Fure. "Postdigital Materiality." In *Lineament: Material, Representation and the Physical Figure in Architectural Production*, edited by Gail Peter Borden and Michael Meredith, 185–95. New York, NY: Routledge, 2018.

Baudry, Jean-Louis. "Ideological Effects of the Basic Cinematographic Apparatus." Translated by Alan Williams. *Film Quarterly* 28, no. 2 (Winter 1974–75) (1970): 39–47.

Belton, John. *Widescreen Cinema*. Cambridge, MA: Harvard University Press, 1992.

Benedikt, Michael. *Architecture Beyond Experience*. San Francisco, Los Angeles, CA, New York, NY, Hong Kong: Applied Research + Design Publishing, 2020.

Benjamin, Walter. "The Work of Art in the Age of Mechanical Reproduction" (1936). In *Illuminations*, edited by Hannah Arendt. Translated by Harry Zohn. New York: Schocken Books, 1969.

Bennett, Jill. "Atmospheric Affects." In *Carnal Aesthetics: Transgressive Imagery and Feminist Politics*, edited by Bettina Papenburg and Marta Zarzycka, 102–18. London, New York, NY: I.B. Tauris, 2013.

Blake, Peter. *Frank Lloyd Wright: Architecture and Space* (1960). New York, NY: Pelican Books Inc., 1965.

Comolli, Jean-Louis. "Machines of the Visible" (1971). In *The Cinematic Apparatus*, edited by Teresa de Lauretis and Stephen Heath, 121–42. New York, NY: St. Martin's Press, 1980.

Crary, Jonathan. *Techniques of the Observer: On Vision and Modernity in the Nineteenth Century*. Cambridge, MA: MIT Press, 1990.

Foster, Hal (in conversation with Marquard Smith). "Polemics, Postmodernism, Immersion, Militarized Space," *Journal of Visual Culture* 3, no. 3 (December 2004): 327–28.

Harman, Graham. *Is There an Object Oriented Architecture?*, edited by Joseph Bedford. London, New York, NY: Bloomsbury Academic, 2020.

Harman, Graham. *Object-Oriented Ontology: A New Theory of Everything*. London: Penguin, 2018.

Heidegger, Martin. "Building Dwelling Thinking" (1954). In *Basic Writings from Being and Time to The Task of Thinking*, edited by David Farrell Krell, 323–39. New York, NY: Harper and Row, 1977.

Heidegger, Martin. "The Origin of the Work of Art" (1935). In *Poetry, Language, Thought*, translated by Albert Hofstadter, 17–87. New York, NY: Harper & Row, 1971.

Heidegger, Martin. "The Question Concerning Technology" (1954). In *The Question Concerning Technology, and Other Essays*, translated by William Lovitt, 3–35. New York, NY: Garland Publishing, 1977.

Hess, Alan. *The Architecture of John Lautner*. New York, NY: Rizzoli International Publications, 1999.

Holl, Steven. *Parallax*. New York, NY: Princeton Architectural Press, 2000.

Holl, Steven, Juhani Pallasmaa, and Alberto Pérez-Gómez. *Questions of Perception: Phenomenology of Architecture*. Tokyo: A+U Publishing Co., Ltd., 1994.

Husserl, Edmund. *Logical Investigations* (1900). Translated by J. N. Findlay. London: Routledge and K. Paul; New York, NY: Humanities Press, 1970.

Ihde, Don. *Bodies in Technology*. Minneapolis, MN: University of Minnesota Press, 2002.

Ihde, Don. *Expanding Hermeneutics: Visualism in Science*. Evanston, IL: Northwestern University Press, 1998.

Ihde, Don. *Heidegger's Technologies: Postphenomenological Perspectives*. New York, NY: Fordham University Press, 2010.

Ihde, Don. *Postphenomenology: Essays in the Postmodern Context*. Evanston, IL: Northwestern University Press, 1993.

Ihde, Don. *Technology and the Lifeworld: From Garden to Earth*. Bloomington, IN: Indiana University Press, 1990.

Jay, Martin. *Downcast Eyes: The Denigration of Vision in Twentieth-Century French Thought*. Berkeley, Los Angeles, CA: University of California Press, 1993.

Lacan, Jacques. "The Mirror Stage as Formative of the I Function as Revealed in Psychoanalytic Experience" (1949). In *Écrits: A Selection*. Translated by Bruce Fink. New York, NY: W.W. Norton & Company, Inc., 2002.

Lautner, John. *Responsibility, Infinity, Nature Oral History Transcript* (1982). Interview with Marlene L. Laskey. Los Angeles, CA: Oral History Program, UCLA, 1988.

Lautner [Sr.], John E. "American Materialism." In *Normal College News* 3, no. 9 (November 24, 1905).

Marks, Laura U. *Touch: Sensuous Theory and Multisensory Media*. Minneapolis, MN: University of Minnesota Press, 2002.

McCoy, Esther. "West Coast Architects V/John Lautner." In *Arts & Architecture* 82 (August 1965): 22–27.

McLuhan, Marshall. *Understanding Media: The Extensions of Man* (1964). Cambridge, MA: MIT Press, 1994.

Merleau-Ponty, Maurice. "Eye and Mind." In *The Primacy of Perception*. Edited by James M. Edie. Translated by Carleton Dallery, 159–90. Evanston, IL: Northwestern University Press, 1964.

Merleau-Ponty, Maurice. *Phenomenology of Perception* (1945). Translated by Colin Smith. London: Routledge & K. Paul; New York, NY: Humanities Press, 1962.

Merleau-Ponty, Maurice. *Sense and Non-Sense*. Translated by Hubert L. Dreyfus and Patricia Allen Dreyfus. Evanston, IL: Northwestern University Press, 1964.

Merleau-Ponty, Maurice. *The Visible and the Invisible* (1964). Edited by Claude Lefort. Translated by Alphonso Lingis. Evanston, IL: Northwestern University Press, 1968.

Michalka, Matthias, ed. *Dorit Margreiter: 10104 Angelo View Drive*. Köln: Verlag der Buchhandlung Walther König; Vienna: Museum Moderner Kunst Stiftung Ludwig Wien, 2004.

Norwood, Bryan E. "Disorienting Phenomenology." In *Log* 42 (Winter/Spring 2018): 10–22.

Pallasmaa, Juhani. *The Eyes of the Skin: Architecture and the Senses*. Chichester: Wiley-Academy, 2005.

Papenburg, Bettina and Marta Zarzycka, eds. *Carnal Aesthetics: Transgressive Imagery and Feminist Politics*. London, New York, NY: I.B. Tauris, 2013.

Plato. *The Republic* (Allegory of the Cave, circa 380 B.C.E.). Edited by G. R. F. Ferrari. Translated by Tom Griffith. Cambridge, MA: Cambridge University Press, 2000.

Rancière, Jacques. *The Emancipated Spectator*. Translated by Gregory Elliott. London, New York, NY: Verso, 2009.

Reese, John. "Dream House or Nightmare?" *The Saturday Evening Post* 30 (August 20, 1960): 62–64.

Shaviro, Steven. *Post-Cinematic Affect*. Ropley: Zero Books, 2010.

Shaviro, Steven. *The Universe of Things: On Speculative Realism*. Minneapolis, MN: University of Minnesota Press, 2014.

Sobchack, Vivian. "The Scene of the Screen: Envisioning Cinematic and Electronic Presence." In *Materialities of Communication*, edited by H. U. Gumbrecht and K. L. Pfeiffer, 83–106. Stanford, CA: Stanford University Press, 1994.

Sobchack, Vivian. "What My Fingers Knew: The Cinesthetic Subject, or Vision in the Flesh." In *Carnal Thoughts: Embodiment and Moving Image Culture*, 53–84. Berkeley, Los Angeles, CA: University of California Press, 2004.

Stiegler, Christian. *360° Gaze: Immersions in Media, Society, and Culture*. Cambridge, MA: MIT Press, 2021.

Van Den Eede, Yoni, Stacey O'Neal Irwin and Galit Wellner, eds. *Phenomenology and Media: Essays on Human-Media-World Relations*. Forward by Don Ihde. London: Lexington Books, 2017.

Von Falkenhausen, Susanne. "The Trouble with 'Affect Theory' in our Age of Outrage." *Frieze*, no. 204, June 6, 2019. https://www.frieze.com/article/trouble-affect-theory-our-age-outrage.

Yoder, Jon. “Design vs. History: Materializing Theory After the Post-Linguistic Turn.” Paper presented in *Architectural Theory Now?* Conference, University of Pennsylvania Weitzman School of Design, April 4–6, 2019.

Yoder, Jon. “Vision and Crime: The *Cineramic* Architecture of John Lautner.” In *Archi.Pop: Mediating Architecture in Popular Culture*, edited by D. Medina Lasansky, 45–58. London, New York, NY: Bloomsbury Academic, 2014.

3

Walled Fantasies

Vahid Vahdat

Who framed Hugo Cabret?

Writings on architecture and film appear to take pleasure in re-counting the similarities between the two disciplines. And among the parallels, the act of framing the view seems an obvious item of discussion. Architectural aperture, such as doors and windows frame visible content much like the view of a camera. Openings hence curiously gain ontological autonomy—they no longer exist as a void or an absence of material. It is rather the wall that despite its heavy material presence, becomes invisible—a mere container of the openings that gains importance only with its moments of absence.

The continuity of the view gets disrupted with the wall. And from one view to another, the wall occupies a position of nothingness between the framed content. By interrupting the act of viewing, the wall without an opening functions like montage. Montage juxtaposes multiple views, when continuous viewing (with camera movements such as pan and zoom) is not possible or desired. But the moment between two montaged scenes is never a subject of discussion, because it has no autonomous existence—it has no content, not even as much as the milliseconds of blackness in a fade-in. Wall is similarly transformed to a depthless surface of nothingness, when "viewing" is the privileged architectural desire.

But aside from the more direct (or literal, as Graham Harman might suggest) act of viewing, architecture can enable imagination. And when "imagining" is the privileged architectural desire, the hidden, the withdrawn, and the invisible become triggers of imaginative inspiration. The concealing nature of walls has thus bestowed them a mystical (and mythical) significance not simply because of what lies behind them, but also within them.

While the spectatorial flatness of the view renders a wall as a (blank) surface, imaginative speculation adds another dimension to it. A dimension that can be expanded and unfolded through cinematic imagination. This alliance of film and architecture in reconceptualizing the concealed thickness of a wall allows it to function as a perfect house for imagination, either the horrific or the fantastic. James Kerestes shall discuss the horrors that the cinematic lens reveals within the otherwise inaccessible interiority of a wall. Here, I will focus on the fantasies that live and grow within its belly.

The belly of a wall

I cannot quite recall when I first laid eyes on the interior of Jerry's house. But the tiny archway on the wall where he sought refuge after an entire episode of mischievously harassing a helpless blue cat was a gateway to my infantile imagination. Through similar gateways of wardrobes, rabbit holes, and bricked-up walls, many like me have visited fantastical hidden spaces occupied by deep-voiced lions, hookah-smoking caterpillars, and button-eyed doppelgangers.

Fantasies about the hidden space behind a wall, beneath a floor, and beyond the ceiling have for centuries inspired imaginative spaces where fantasies unfold. Disfigured protagonists roaming above the dark stone walls of a daunting cathedral and beneath the richly decorated walls of a majestic opera house are only examples of a genre of habitable pochés.[1] Notre Dame and Opéra Garnier are no less central to the story than the hunchback and the phantom. Their hidden corners correspond to hidden dimensions of the characters. This historical lineage of Parisian grand architecture from the cavernous gothic to the extravagant Beaux-Arts, before arriving at the inside-out architecture of Centre Pompidou, has a major stop at an industrial typology, where a modern myth can continue the genre of occupiable poché—the nineteenth-century train station.

Layered interiorities

Martin Scorsese's 2011 *Hugo*[2] adopts the interiority of the nineteenth-century Parisian train station as an urban laboratory that situates the narrative within the manageable limits of a controlled metropolitan ecosystem.[3] The train station thus becomes a microcosm of metropolitan life—a small world that much like the world of movies is compact yet complicated, fragmented yet generalizable, and autonomous yet highly dependent upon the realities of the outside world. Through *Hugo*, the interiority of the movie intersects with the interior urbanism of the metropolitan world of the station. The train station is a model within a model—a simulation of the real, erected in the virtual world of filmic imagination.

This layering of worlds within worlds however does not stop at the station level. In fact, the main narrative that the camera chases throughout the movie does not take place in the locations that people habitually occupy, mingle, and interact. The movie peels the central architectural space to give the viewer a peek through its poché. Poché is an architectural drawing convention by which the spatial elements that intersect with the section plane are filled in—either blackened or cross-hatched. The inside components of spatial elements such as walls, floors, ceilings, and columns in architectural plans and section are retracted; their structural, material, mechanical, and electrical details are unworthy of the drawing's intention.

This blackened homogenously solid mass of nothingness is however penetrated by the filmic imagination. It is hollowed, expanded, and furnished to create a betwixt space, where one space ends, but before the other starts—a liminal condition appears within the wall, independent of its adjacent spaces. The concept of "betwixt," as developed in the late 1960s by British cultural anthropologist Victor Turner, is fluid, migratory, mediatory, and elusive.[4] It possesses a transitive quality that occupies a space between the assumed dichotomies of here/there, interior/exterior, figure/ground, real/virtual, built/natural, and present/absent. This possibly explains why the betwixt condition has for long been privileged in architectural theory. Architects have long studied betwixtscapes through the lens of the interstitial, blurred zone, zones of undecidability, unstructured spaces, and gradient architecture, to name a few.[5]

The cinematically habitable pochés of the train station in *Hugo* are liminal not only because they lie between conventionally occupiable spaces, or because they give the neglected ground of the crosshatched a figural prominence, or because they buffer the reductionist dualism of interior and exterior, but more importantly because they are produced somewhere between the virtual and the real—the architectural space and the cinematic.

Following its generic predecessors, and via the X-ray vision of the camera, *Hugo* circulates its audience through the liminal space within the walls of the train station that are otherwise visually inaccessible to both the audience and the inhabitants of this interior city. Deep within the assumed pochés of the station, a maze of mechanical infrastructure houses the central narrative of the movie (see Figure 3.1). The narrative of Hugo Cabret, a teenage orphan, whose attempts to refurbish an automaton eventually leads him to Georges Méliès (1861–1938), a French film director who pioneered fictional narratives in cinema.

The liminal space of Hugo Cabret's residence, continuously wrapping all sides of the station, below its floors, above its ceilings, between levels, within walls, columns, and objects, is however temporary and transitionary. It operates only

FIGURE 3.1: A film still from *Hugo* juxtaposed next to an image from the book, *The Invention of Hugo Cabret*. Gare Montparnasse was imagined and recreated by Brian Selznick as a collage of "pieces from many other stations."

as a mediatory phase starting with the traumatic death of his father and ending with his arrival at a new family. And in this process of filling his inner void and finding meaning for his life, the liminal space that he occupies acts with agency. This transitionary nature of the betwixt is emphasized by Turner. Discussing the rites of passage, Turner observed a liminal stage in the initiand's transition from one social status to another. "Transitional beings," according to Turner,

> are particularly polluting, since they are neither one thing nor another; or may be both; or neither here nor there; or may even be nowhere (in terms of any recognized cultural topography), and are at the very least "betwixt and between" all the recognized fixed points in space time of structural classification.[6]

The extension of the anthropological concept of betwixt and between to the architectural can find reflection in how the liminal condition of Hugo Cabret intersects with the in-between space of the occupiable poché. "Spaces within walls," as Unwin points out, "are never quite 'of' the interior nor the exterior."[7] By relocating the center of the narrative to this in-between space, the station is pushed to a peripheral position—a left-over space. And in this dialectic of interior/exterior, the station for Hugo Cabret becomes an outside world to his home—one that provides amusing but distant urban views, similar to how Paris becomes peripheral to the station.[8] Paris is an outside world that glimpses of its reality is reflected in the public life of the station, in the same way that the virtual world of movies capture glimpses of reality within their frame.

Mechanization of space

It is within this continuous Deleuzian folding and unfolding of space that the story takes place.[9] The movie subverts the interior/exterior dualities as part of a larger attempt to reposition the center and periphery, in artistic productions, including cinema and architecture. While some critics have tried to locate the movie within auteurist discourses, *Hugo* is more so a celebration of artistic processes over products. Scorsese's in-depth knowledge of and interest in the history of cinema explains why he took on *Hugo*.[10] Scorsese, as Legato confirms, "adores the history of movie making, and this film is about the history of moviemaking."[11] But where does the history of movie making originate from? "Scorsese's film," as Davidson suggests, "situates the origins of movies in *fin-de-siècle* Paris as *the* modern industrial city."[12]

Hugo is thus not a teleological glorification of Méliès's oeuvre, but it is more so about the cinematic processes he introduced and used to create his work: his early career as a magician and an entertainer, his collaboration with the Lumière brothers, his not-so-conventional team, and above all, his palace-like glass studios, where "dreams [are] cultivated in a green-house of industrial activity."[13] And *Hugo* is not a mere celebration of the creative authorship of an individual inspiring mind, but it is more so about Méliès's role in the greater history of cinema—a "part," if you will, of a larger cinematic machine.[14]

Much like Hugo Cabret, Scorsese sees the objects of his inquiry as machines that cannot function unless their mechanical processes are fully understood. "The whole world," according to Hugo Cabret, "is one big machine." Even living forms are treated as such—and the signs are endless: the automaton and its consumption of Hugo Cabret's body in his dream, the mechanical mouse that he fixes and brings to life, and the prosthetics enabling the station inspector to bring some excitement and humor into the film. The film is thus an attempt to reverse engineer all objects, from cinema to life itself. And if objects such as the anthropomorphic moon of Méliès's 1902 short *Le Voyage dans la Lune (A Trip to the Moon)*[15] are seen to have life and their behind-the-scenes mechanics can be brought to the forefront, so can architecture.

The architecture of *Hugo*'s liminal spaces diverts the focus of attention to the assumed mechanical infrastructure of space (see Figure 3.2). It is within this maze of pipes, gears, studs, ductwork, beams, chains, and stairs that the main story resides. What is conventionally appreciated as the figural space in architecture is

FIGURE 3.2: A collage of two images from *The Invention of Hugo Cabret* showing the narrative as it moves through the walls of the train station. Through the free movement of the camera beyond the otherwise impenetrable pochés of the station, the film exposes another layer of interiority within the interior urbanism of the station.

secondary to this processual infrastructure and also to Hugo Cabret, who treats it as an exteriority whose views can be enjoyed through ducts and vents and screens that in his world replace doors and windows.

To emphasize the infrastructural significance of architecture, what typology better than a nineteenth-century train station;[16] and to celebrate the mechanical processes that bring life to architectural space, what style better that that of contemporaneous Paris, through structures like Gare Montparnasse, Gare du Nord, and Henri Labrouste's Sainte-Geneviève Library, all of which were built around the same time in the 1840s? The significance of these buildings, as architectural historians explain, is not merely for their innovative use of cast iron for building structure, but more so for their attempt to bring architectural (infra)structure to the forefront of space.[17] The intricate metal framework and gas lighting that cover and illuminate their vast interiors are no longer hidden (see Figure 3.3). They are privileged and exposed the same way *Hugo* brings them to the forefront of attention.[18] Quite like the urban interiority of the station, which owes its vitality to its infrastructure, the metropolis in *Hugo* gains life from mechanical processes. Isn't that what the opening scene of the movie where the aerial shot of Paris centering the Arc de Triomphe de l'Étoile fades into a series of mechanical gears is all about?[19]

FIGURE 3.3: A collage of two stills from *Hugo* showing how the otherwise-neglected mechanical infrastructure of the station assumes agency through filmic imagination.

Kitbashing an interior Collage City

Earlier, I argued how in the act of framing, walls function through the logic of montage. They cut the continuity of spatial experience while simultaneously stitching different spatial events together. Through the power of cinematic montage, architectural poché becomes habitable and thus gains its liminal condition. The spatio-cinematic inhabitation of the liminal architecture of the train station in *Hugo* is however part of a larger theme of montage/collage.

In their discussion of the "Collage City," Colin Rowe and Fred Koetter advocate for a radical heterogeneity of architectural and urban form, by referencing another anthropologist, Claude Lévi-Strauss, when he calls for a balance "between structure and event, necessity and contingency, the internal and the external."[20]

Hugo can be considered a cinematic depiction of collage city through the interior confines of a Parisian train station. And within the forgotten spaces of this cinematically manageable collage city, Hugo Cabret manages to revive a broken automaton, through a similar act of collaging, i.e., by taking parts from items he steals, including from the station's old toy shop, operated by Méliès. The movie itself is similarly a collage of historic film sequences as I have previously discussed.[21] The background presence of figures such as jazz guitarist Django Reinhardt (1910–63) who is seen briefly as he plays at the station's café to an audience that includes painter Salvador Dalí (1904–89) and the novelist James Joyce (1882–1941)[22] shows that the same superimposed assemblage of parts is at work in the entourage that occupies the station, unbothered by historic accuracy.

Unbothered by spatial consistency, the architecture of the station enjoys a similar fragmentation that allows the pocket-spaces within it to function as part of the dynamic and ever-changing spatial relationships of the station as a whole. The movie was based on the award-winning children's book by Brian Selznick.[23] The author discusses his rendition of Gare Montparnasse, which housed the actual location to Méliès's shop but was eventually torn down in 1969, through a similar collage-like assemblage process. Gare Montparnasse, Selznick describes (see Figure 3.4),

> is the only one that has been torn down, so to create the station in my book, I used vintage photographs of the original station, as well as bits and pieces from many other stations in Paris, especially the Gare du Nord. I also used details from Grand Central Terminal in New York City.[24]

How is this process any different from Hugo Cabret's kitbashed automaton that only finds life through an assemblage of external pieces?

This playful juxtaposition of spatial elements is intensified in the filmic representation of the station. While the film crew had taken extreme measures to rebuild Méliès's original studio, "constructing it to the exact plans," as Rob Legato, second unit director and visual effect supervisor to the movie, puts it, they "didn't build much of the train station."[25] In fact, unlike the obsessive realism required for recreating Méliès's studio, the train station enjoyed an unreal, if not

FIGURE 3.4: A film still from *Hugo* juxtaposed next to an image from the book, *The Invention of Hugo Cabret*. The mid-nineteenth-century train stations with their exposed structure become a site to Hugo's playful celebration of mechanical processes.

surreal, configuration, allowing it to accommodate contradictory/impossible shots. "The big problem for our asset team was that in visual effects, we're obsessed with taking things realistic," Ben Grossmann, the film's visual effect director, says. "The Eiffel Tower moved where it needed to be. Some routes made no sense at all, the train station would look different in some shots—but there was consistency in that everything looked good."[26]

Spatial consistency here is not sought through a rational functioning of architectural elements and their relationships. What Scorsese seeks is not the recovery of Paris' historical reality, or the station for that matter, but as Annett puts it, "a creative engagement with the cinematic construction of memory."[27] It is only through the kitbashing of spaces and architectural elements that an opportunity opens to create a fluid space that can adjust its properties to accommodate the best views of Paris, the movement of cameras and characters, and the suspense/action of the movie. In fact, the metropolitan spirit of the train station allows and welcomes this fragmentation. As an interior urban space, the station becomes a Collage City with fragments from the past, present, and future that defies the centralized, controlling, and dominating nature of total-design, in favor of a juxtaposition strategy that allows autonomous spatial microcosms to perpetually create themselves within the station.

"These walls are solidly put together"[28]

Back in the early 1990s, the artist Monica Wyatt conducted an experiment that started with a simple question: "can I be (in) a wall?" Responding to this desire to "get into the wall," she symbolically constructed the interior of a brick wall by wrapping a brick in lead sheet, re-flattening the wrapping through a printing press (which keeps the traces of its former volume), impressing on paper, cutting out the pattern on the wall's wallpaper, peeling it off, and using the wallpaper to create a body-dress.[29]

Architectural practices of "equipped wall," "habitable interstice," "inhabited wall," "thickened wall," "occupiable poché," which might possibly date back to cave excavations, allowed their occupants to live this fantasy. From Renaissance cabinets to Baroque churches, from Swabian fortresses to Scottish castles, from Egyptian temples to Japanese engawa, from Louis Kahn's "hollow column" to Manuel Aires Mateus's "living in the boundary," the fantasy of evading the center and experiencing nonexistence in the invisible space of the in-between has been manifested in a variety of architectural traditions.[30]

But with the spatio-cinematic opportunities that the intersection of film and architecture provides, a new form of embodied experience of Wyatt's desire to occupy the unstructured cavity becomes possible. The power of filmic frame expands the architectural frame, hollows the poché, and replaces the eliminated material evidence of construction with visual narratives of fantasies.

And while the fantasies of inhabiting the wall have a rich literary history, so too have its horrors. All one must do is to follow the screeching of Edgar Allan Poe's one-eyed "Black Cat" to find the terrors buried in the walls.[31] This is where James Kerestes will take you in his chapter.

NOTES

1. A delayed definition of poché will be offered in the next section.
2. *Hugo* (2011), director Martin Scorsese.
3. The title of the movie is taken from its main character, Hugo Cabret. To distinguish the two throughout the chapter, I have used "*Hugo*" to refer to the film and "Hugo Cabret" to signify the protagonist.
4. Victor Witter Turner, *The Forest of Symbols: Aspects of Ndembu Ritual* (Ithaca, NY: Cornell University Press, 1967), 97.
5. Andrew E. Benjamin, *Blurred Zones: Investigations of the Interstitial: Eisenman Architects, 1988–1998* (New York, NY: Monacelli Press, 2003). Roger Trancik, *Finding Lost Space: Theories of Urban Design* (New York, NY: Van Nostrand Reinhold, 1986). Peter Eisenman, "Zones of Undecidability: The Interstitial Figure." Paper presented at the Anybody, Buenos Aires, Argentina, 1996; "Zones of Undecidability: The Processes of the Interstitial." Paper presented at the Anyhow, Rotterdam, Holland, 1997.
6. Victor Witter Turner, *The Forest of Symbols: Aspects of Ndembu Ritual* (Ithaca, NY: Cornell University Press, 1967), 97.
7. Simon Unwin, *Analysing Architecture* (London: Routledge, 2014), 229.
8. The exteriority of Paris to Hugo Cabret's world is emphasized in a scene in which he is chasing Méliès to get his notebook back. As Méliès steps out of the station, the camera shows Hugo Cabret's hesitance to set foot in the unchartered territory of Paris.
9. In Deleuze's materialist metaphysics, the universe (including consciousness) is the result of folded matter. Influenced by Leibniz's theory of the monad that suggests the whole universe is contained within each being, it is this process of folding that, according to Deleuze, constitutes the basic unit of existence. This infinite process of folding and unfolding the outside generates interiorities that are not separated from an autonomous exterior world but rather result from doubling/multiplying of the outside. The fold is thus best understood as an ontology of becoming (and of differentiation) while maintaining continuity. The conceptualization of interiority as folded exterior has allowed architects to rethink the figure-ground relationship as a reversible extension of one another and thereby blur the boundaries between inside/outside, solid/void, and mass/space. The same uncertain, open-ended, inexhaustive, and non-exclusive relationship between exterior and interior in

the film (and outside of it for that matter) is what makes the concept of folding evermore significant in understanding/unfolding the movie. For more information see Gilles Deleuze, *Foucault*, Collection "Critique" (Paris: Editions de Minuit, 1986); *The Fold: Leibniz and the Baroque* (Minneapolis, MN: University of Minnesota Press, 1993).

10. Obviously, *Hugo* is not Scorsese's only attempt to pay tribute to film history and Méliès is not the only film-maker that he showcases in his movies. For example, in his 2004 *Aviator*, Scorsese reflects on the life and works of Howard Hughes. See Martin Scorsese, *The Aviator* (Sydney, N.S.W.: Gem, 2013). For Scorsese's take on the history of cinema, see Martin Scorsese and Michael Henry Wilson, *The Century of Cinema: A Personal Journey with Martin Scorsese through American Movies* (London: British Film Institute, 2000).
11. Barbara Robertson, "Visual Effects Artists Push Deep into Cinema History to Help Martin Scorsese Create *Hugo* Magic Man," *Computer Graphics Magazine*, 2011, 22.
12. John E. Davidson, "Industry in Idealized Form: The Work of Movies in Film's First One Hundred Years," *PMLA* 127, no. 4 (2012): 11.
13. Ibid.
14. In fact, through *Hugo*, Scorsese pays homage to many films and film-makers. Some scenes, for example from Edwin S. Porter's *The Great Train Robbery* (United States: Edison Manufacturing Co., 1903) and Lumière brothers' *L'arrivée D'un Train À La Ciotat* (New York, NY; Chatsworth, CA: Kino on Video; Image Entertainment [distributor], 1896) are directly shown in their original format and others such as Harold Lloyd's 1923 *Safety Last!* (1923) and Hitchcock's (1958) famous staircase scene in *Vertigo* (1958) are recreated and indirectly alluded to within the movie. Visually, it also pays homages to René Clair's 1930 *Sous Les Toits De Paris (Under the Roofs of Paris)* (1930) and Jean Renoir's (1938) *La Bête Humaine* (1938). For more, see Scott Higgins, "3d in Depth: *Coraline*, *Hugo*, and a Sustainable Aesthetic," *Film History: An International Journal* 24, no. 2 (2012).
15. *Le Voyage dans la Lune (A Trip to the Moon)* (1902), director Georges Méliès.
16. Romanticization of steam locomotives and train stations has been a reoccurring theme in art and literature. As the subject or backdrop of artistic imagination, train stations have glorified the industrial power of human will over nature, represented nostalgia for the machine age, or celebrated the role of infrastructure as a catalyst for social justice. Numerous masterpieces by nineteenth- and twentieth-century artists, e.g. William Turner, Claude Monet, Charles Sheeler, Camille Pissarro, and Edward Hopper capture the aesthetics of the machine through railroads, train stations, and steam locomotives. For more, see Susan Danly Walther, *The Railroad in the American Landscape, 1850–1950* (Wellesley, MA: Wellesley College Museum, 1981); Ted Rose, *In the Traces: Railroad Paintings of Ted Rose*, Railroads Past and Present (Bloomington, IN: Indiana University Press, 2000); Ian Kennedy and Julian Treuherz, *The Railway: Art in the Age of Steam*, Hardcover ed. (New Haven, CT: Yale University Press, 2008).

17. Interestingly, Bibliotheque Sainte Geneviève is dubbed by the Encyclopedia of Art Education as the "first non-utilitarian building to show exposed metalwork." Neil Collins, "19th Century Architecture," visual-arts-cork, www.visual-arts-cork.com/history-of-art/nineteenth-century-architecture.htm.
18. The filmic imagination of metropolis as an outcome of infrastructural processes has probably first been depicted in Walter Ruttmann's (1927) "Berlin: Die Symphonie Der Grossstadt (Symphony of a Metropolis)" (1927). Ruttmann's camera provides the audience with visuals that would be otherwise hidden to the wondering eyes of the urban *flâneurs*. Objects such as light bulbs, bottles, bread loafs, newspapers, and even the food served at a restaurant are demystified as products of often-mechanical processes of manufacture and labor. Ruttmann's metropolis should also be read in this context as an outcome of mechanical infrastructure—scenes of which are montaged throughout the movie. The film's emphasis on roads, railways, subways, water pipes, sewage, and other forms of urban services becomes a predecessor to Hugo's mechanical metropolitan lab.
19. Legato articulates the "philosophy" behind this scene as creating a subconscious visual of "Paris as a mechanism." Robertson, "Visual Effects Artists," 11.
20. Collage City is also the title of their book published in 1979, which was an extension of Colin Rowe and Fred Koetter's earlier essay with the same title. Collage becomes a central concept through which the authors articulate their theory of architecture—one that negates the holistic and decontextualized hegemony of "total design" in modern utopianism and offers an alternative proposal by embracing the contingent and the chaotic through radical heterogeneity of architectural and urban form. The quote from Lévi-Strauss is cited in Colin Rowe and Fred Koetter, *Collage City* (Basel: Birkhäuser, 2009), 136.
21. "In *Hugo*," as Sandra Annett argues "we see that digital cinema is a machine made from the parts of many other machines." Sandra Annett, "The Nostalgic Remediation of Cinema in *Hugo* and *Paprika*," *Journal of Adaptation in Film and Performance* 7, no. 2 (2014): 175.
22. Crystal Downing, *Salvation from Cinema: The Medium Is the Message* (2016), 170.
23. Brian Selznick, *The Invention of Hugo Cabret: A Novel in Words and Pictures* (London: Scholastic, 2008).
24. Brian Selznick, Martin Scorsese, David Serlin, and Jaap Buitendijk, *The* Hugo *Movie Companion: A Behind the Scenes Look at How a Beloved Book Became a Major Motion Picture* (New York, NY: Scholastic Press, 2011), 21.
25. Robertson, "Visual Effects Artists," 22.
26. Ibid. He also explains how the asset team who built the train station got frustrated by constant changes in their model to accommodate demands about relocating walls, removing roofs, and even shifting the Eiffel Tower or Arc de Triomphe to provide more compelling imagery.
27. Annett, "The Nostalgic Remediation," 174.
28. From Edgar Allan Poe, *The Black Cat* (Carlisle, MA: Applewood Books, 2016).
29. Lois Weinthal, "Toward a New Interior: An Anthology of Interior Design Theory," (2011): 342.

30. Steven Kent Peterson, "Space and Anti-Space," *Harvard Architecture Review* 1 (1980): 89–113. Lukas Pauer, "Spatial Efficiency on the Edge: On Formal Excess and Surface Strategies in Boundary Conditions," *Very Vary Veri*, no. 1 (2014). Simon Unwin, *An Architecture Notebook: Wall* (London: Routledge, 2000). Francesco Cacciatore, *Living the Boundary: Twelve Houses by Aires Mateus & Associados* (2018); Francesco Cacciatore, *The Wall as Living Place: Hollow Structural Forms in Louis Kahn's Work* (2016); Paola Leardini and Adrian Lo, "Living in the Edge," in *The City and the Skin*, ed. Mickeal Milocco Borlini, Lelio di Loreto, and Carlalberto Amadori (Florence: Urban Corporis, 2020).
31. Poe, *The Black Cat.*

REFERENCES

Annett, Sandra. "The Nostalgic Remediation of Cinema in *Hugo* and *Paprika*." *Journal of Adaptation in Film and Performance* 7, no. 2 (2014): 169–79.

Benjamin, Andrew E. *Blurred Zones: Investigations of the Interstitial: Eisenman Architects, 1988–1998*. New York, NY: Monacelli Press, 2003 (in English).

Cacciatore, Francesco. *Living the Boundary: Twelve Houses by Aires Mateus & Associados*. Siracusa, Italy: Lettera Ventidue, 2018 (in English).

Cacciatore, Francesco. *The Wall as Living Place: Hollow Structural Forms in Louis Kahn's Work*. Siracusa, Italy: Lettera Ventidue, 2016. (in English).

Clair, René. *Sous Les Toits De Paris (Under the Roofs of Paris)*. 1930.

Collins, Neil. "19th Century Architecture." visual-arts-cork. www.visual-arts-cork.com/history-of-art/nineteenth-century-architecture.htm.

Danly Walther, Susan. *The Railroad in the American Landscape, 1850–1950*. Wellesley, MA: Wellesley College Museum, 1981.

Davidson, John E. "Industry in Idealized Form: The Work of Movies in Film's First One Hundred Years." *PMLA* 127, no. 4 (2012): 879–89.

Deleuze, Gilles. *The Fold: Leibniz and the Baroque*. Minneapolis, MN: University of Minnesota Press, 1993.

Deleuze, Gilles. *Foucault*. Collection "Critique". Paris: Editions de Minuit, 1986.

Downing, Crystal. *Salvation from Cinema: The Medium Is the Message*. London: Routledge, 2016 (in English).

Eisenman, Peter. "Zones of Undecidability: The Interstitial Figure." Paper presented at the Anybody, Buenos Aires, Argentina, 1996.

Eisenman, Peter. "Zones of Undecidability: The Processes of the Interstitial." Paper presented at the Anyhow, Rotterdam, Holland, 1997.

Higgins, Scott. "3d in Depth: *Coraline*, *Hugo*, and a Sustainable Aesthetic." *Film History: An International Journal* 24, no. 2 (2012): 196–209.

Hitchcock, Alfred. *Vertigo*. United States: Paramount Pictures, 1958.

Kennedy, Ian, and Julian Treuherz. *The Railway: Art in the Age of Steam*. Hardcover ed. New Haven, CT: Yale University Press, 2008.

Kent Peterson, Steven. "Space and Anti-Space." *Harvard Architecture Review* 1 (1980): 89–113 (in English).

Leardini, Paola, and Adrian Lo. "Living in the Edge." In *The City and the Skin*, edited by Mickeal Milocco Borlini, Lelio di Loreto, and Carlalberto Amadori, 62–71. Florence: Urban Corporis, 2020.

Lumière, Auguste, and Louis Lumière. *L'arrivée D'un Train À La Ciotat*. New York; Chatsworth, CA: Kino on Video; Image Entertainment [distributor], 1896.

Méliès, Georges, director. *Le Voyage dans la Lune (A Trip to the Moon)*. Johannesburg: Star Film Company, 1902.

Newmeyer, Fred C., and Sam Taylor. *Safety Last!* 1923.

Pauer, Lukas. "Spatial Efficiency on the Edge: On Formal Excess and Surface Strategies in Boundary Conditions." *Very Vary Veri*, no. 1 (2014): 11.

Poe, Edgar Allan. *The Black Cat*. Carlisle, MA: Applewood Books, 2016 (in English).

Porter, Edwin S. *The Great Train Robbery*. 10 min. *10 min*. USA: Edison Manufacturing Co., 1903.

Renoir, Jean. *La Bête Humaine*. Irvington, NY: Criterion Collection, 1938.

Robertson, Barbara. "Visual Effects Artists Push Deep into Cinema History to Help Martin Scorsese Create Hugo Magic Man." 20–24. *Computer Graphics Magazine*, 2011.

Rose, Ted. *In the Traces: Railroad Paintings of Ted Rose*. Railroads Past and Present. Bloomington, IN: Indiana University Press, 2000.

Rowe, Colin, and Fred Koetter. *Collage City*. Basel: Birkhäuser, 2009 (in German).

Ruttmann, Walter. "Berlin: Die Symphonie Der Grossstadt (Symphony of a Metropolis)." 1927.

Scorsese, Martin. *The Aviator*. Sydney, N.S.W.: Gem, 2013.

Scorsese, Martin, and Michael Henry Wilson. *The Century of Cinema: A Personal Journey with Martin Scorsese through American Movies*. London: British Film Institute, 2000.

Scorsese, Martin, director. *Hugo*. Los Angeles, CA: Paramount Pictures, 2011.

Selznick, Brian. *The Invention of Hugo Cabret: A Novel in Words and Pictures*. London: Scholastic, 2008 (in English).

Selznick, Brian, Martin Scorsese, David Serlin, and Jaap Buitendijk. *The* Hugo *Movie Companion: A Behind the Scenes Look at How a Beloved Book Became a Major Motion Picture*. New York, NY: Scholastic Press, 2011 (in English).

Trancik, Roger. *Finding Lost Space: Theories of Urban Design*. New York, NY: Van Nostrand Reinhold, 1986 (in English).

Turner, Victor Witter. *The Forest of Symbols: Aspects of Ndembu Ritual*. Ithaca, NY: Cornell University Press, 1967 (in English).

Unwin, Simon. *Analysing Architecture*. London: Routledge, 2014 (in English).

Unwin, Simon. *An Architecture Notebook: Wall*. London: Routledge, 2000 (in English).

Weinthal, Lois. *Toward a New Interior: An Anthology of Interior Design Theory*. New York, NY: Princeton Architectural Press, 2011 (in English).

4

Horrific Transitions

James F. Kerestes

Exploring the liminal realms of horror films

Horror films may not be for everyone. It is unsettling to think of supernatural forces haunting your home or a scenario where you are running away from an unknown killer in the woods. But if you look a little closer, you will find that the genre offers more than just jump scares and depictions of alternate realities. These films introduce objects, characters, and settings that stand in contrast to, or provide new relationships between, our environments. Horror movies provide another way of viewing and rationalizing the world around us by challenging and questioning our perception of comfort and familiarity. A way of exploring this concept is by eliminating the sense of safety and security one has within the confines of their living space. The boundaries and enclosures of these sanctuaries are meant to be safe and secure, so when these conditions are infiltrated, questions arise about the presence of other vulnerable locations. The existence of latent or hidden spaces, typically uninhabitable cavities, become possible passageways for interlopers to threaten those occupying nearby areas.

Depictions of the unknown and fantastical imagery have been a staple of the genre since its early beginnings. One of the first to introduce audiences to representations of the macabre and the unimaginable was director George Méliès. His short film *Le Manoir du Diable* in 1896,[1] scared viewers with state-of-the-art special effects creating scenes of magical cauldrons, disappearing furniture, and a skeleton transforming into a bat. The short film centers on a cross-wielding cavalier protecting a castle and its occupants from a mysterious being who can conjure spells. In the end, the cavalier is successful in defending the grounds and chases the evil being away. In this early genre example, the antagonist is refrained from seeking refuge within the building. This is the objective of most antagonists in scary movies, to infiltrate a private, hidden space in order to inflict harm on its inhabitants.

The horror genre reveals alternative ways to occupy and inhabit unseen architectural conditions and interstitial spaces within the built world. For instance, the cavities within a wall or floor that are not intended to be occupied or do not have a prescribed use, routinely become an area of refuge for a film's antagonist or a gateway to an impossible world. The representation of these unstructured spaces in architectural drawings have traditionally been to hide or redact the contents in a floor plan or building section drawing with solid black fills. Known within the discipline of architecture as poché, this convention of drawing conceals the contents in a wall, ceiling, or floor to focus attention to the adjacent, inhabited zones. Horror films illustrate that occupying unstructured, latent spaces can offer alternative ways in how to design and inhabit buildings. For the genre, the motivation behind activating these conditions is to create a feeling of fear and uncertainty in the audience. Removing the ability to seek refuge eliminates any thoughts of wellbeing that is typically found in a familiar environment, such as a home.

The genre also reveals to audiences that the unseen cavities of a building may not have the expected spatial relationship with the overall structure and can range in scale, shape, and methods for connectivity. The interior layout and configuration of inhabitable spaces misalign with the silhouette or figuration of its container, the building envelope.[2] In this scenario, the space in-between the visible surfaces has the potential to be activated and inhabited. Typically, a structure's poché is revealed only in a few locations, such as at door or window openings and thresholds.[3] The full extent and distribution of poché is often unknown to building occupants.

Some filmmakers utilize unstructured spaces to support the tension and motivation within the story, where architectural conditions contribute either directly or indirectly to the plot, taking the form of an active or passive character. For instance, in the film *Black Christmas* (1974),[4] a slasher movie where an intruder terrorizes the occupants of a sorority house, the building serves as a backdrop for the narrative. The architectural conditions of the sorority house operate as a passive witness to the events unfolding within. In order to stay hidden and anonymous, the antagonist takes up residence in the attic and moves through the walls in order to attack his victims.

Alternately, in the supernatural thriller *A Nightmare on Elm Street* (1984),[5] the primary protagonist's home is an agent to the plot, an intermediary between the real and the dream world. In this scenario, the structure has agency within the story yet still passively participates in the events of the film. At moments in *A Nightmare on Elm Street*, the architecture is prompted to act. The staircase unexpectedly breaks or disintegrates underfoot as the protagonist tries to escape during a chase scene, or the base of the bathtub becomes suddenly open to a hollow void during another climactic interaction, sucking the bather into its depths. In these examples, the architecture does not behave as is expected but also harbors no malicious intent of its own. The architecture becomes a tool of the antagonist.

Finally, architectural conditions can serve as a perpetrator, an active participant assisting or executing goals within the plot. This can be seen in *Relic* (2020),[6] a film where an elderly woman's home physically and continuously reconfigures to trap her granddaughter within a maze of dead-end hallways. The granddaughter is literally trapped within the interstitial or liminal space of the home, a physical allegory for the grandmother's decaying mental state. Throughout the film, the extent of the home's poché is difficult to comprehend holistically by the viewer as it morphs and readjusts over time, sometimes in reaction to an event and sometimes arbitrarily. The constant changes to the structure disrupt the nostalgic memories the occupants shared with the home.

Utilizing cinematic spaces in this manner can be an effective tactic for scaring audiences because the viewer is unable to determine the scale or location of the space depicted within the larger composition of the set. In this uncanny environment, a house turns into a maze with no logical exit, or a room with seemingly viable boundaries can suddenly exceed its spatial capacity, growing or shrinking on a whim. These solid structures are built conditions which we expect to keep us safe, surrounded, and sheltered, yet they instigate fear by defying logic and changing unpredictably.

Betwixt and between

The reading and interpretation of poché can be evaluated beyond the space in-between two rooms or as impermeable. It can be a point of transition, an in-between space defined by thresholds, a betwixt and between condition. Anthropologist Victor Turner refers to "betwixt and between" as the transitional period between two fixed points, or states, in response to Arnold van Gennep's *Les Rites de Passage*.[7] Van Gennep identifies three distinct phases within rituals or rites of transition in a given society: separation, margin, and aggregation.[8] At separation, a ritual subject is removed from a previous status, or place and time, to transition toward becoming a different kind of person. The ritual occurs during the transition, or margin phase, and leads to the ritual subject's reintegration into society in a changed state.

Turner reflects upon the "margin" or "limen" phase as a process of "becoming" or "transformation" from one state to another.[9] This period of transition has no predetermined or prescribed limits, boundaries, or time constraints. It is an intermediate position that is "neither here nor there." Turner refers to the ritual subject as an ambiguous passenger passing through a realm with little to no attributes of its past or coming future state.[10] He goes on to emphasize, "The subject of passage ritual is, in the liminal period, structurally, if not physically 'invisible.'"[11] Given that the liminal beings are hidden, they are, in turn, the embodiment of the in-between.[12]

In an architectural context, transitions and hidden conditions can manifest in several ways. For instance, liminal spaces such as hallways, corridors, vestibules, stairways, and front porches all fall into this category within the built environment. These examples do not have a defined program, rather they are absent of an identity until engaged and activated by an occupant. These conditions routinely serve as mere connections between inhabited zones. *41 Cooper Square*, an academic building designed by Morphosis Architects for the Cooper Union in New York City, is an example of conceiving the expanded possibilities of a liminal space. The entire building utilizes a stairway to "foster collaboration and cross-disciplinary dialogue among the college's three schools."[13] Described by the design firm as a "vertical piazza," the main stair transforms beyond a vertical means of circulation and transitions into a social condenser for people and activities.

The exploration of in-between space is not only an architectural condition for exploration; artist Rachel Whiteread highlights the existence of liminal space by physically constructing the "transition." Whiteread has produced a number of artifacts reimagining the liminal space in architecture as a solid object. For example, her work "Untitled (Stairs)" from 2001 objectifies the void and volumetric space surrounding a stairway by casting the negative condition with plaster.[14] Solidifying the liminal space creates an impenetrable representation of an otherwise withdrawn, unnoticeable spatial volume. Whiteread's work has the capacity to be seen as a physical representation of poché.

There are additional examples of forgotten spaces within a building that are withdrawn and go unnoticed, such as areas between inhabited zones inside the walls and floors that are available for occupation. Architect Rem Koolhaas has long sought to address various examples of liminal space in his architectural practice and writings. Developed as a large-scale speculative project, *Exodus, or the Voluntary Prisoners of Architecture* is an example of occupying the interstitial space between two walls. Conceived along with Madelon Vreisendorp, Elia Zenghelis, and Zoe Zenghelis, the proposal tells the story of a divided London. Presented with images and text that read as storyboards supporting a screenplay, the zone, or "Strip," is inhabited by "voluntary prisoners." The inhabitants have agency to adhere to or modify the programmatic intentions of the architectural condition, where "the most contradictory programs fuse without compromise."[15] The "Strip" can be seen as an occupied zone of permeable poché that is subdivided into a series of sections.

The depiction of poché as a black void in architectural drawings communicates a sense of impermeability and calls attention to the availability of occupiable space. The early introduction of the representational technique responded to the materials utilized in the construction process. The design group of Lewis Tsuramaki Lewis (LTL architects) comprehensively covers representational techniques in architectural visualization, including the presence of poché, in the book *Manual of Section*. They point out that "constructions produced through the seventeenth century consisted of space circumscribed by masonry mass, resulting in section depictions in which exterior profile and interior space were closely interrelated through the thickness of poché."[16] Poché conveys a sense of structural integrity and stability. LTL go on to remind us that by "the eighteenth and nineteenth centuries, the solid wall of load-bearing masonry architecture was challenged by an increasingly layered set of conditions, reflecting new structural technologies associated with the emerging materials of cast and wrought iron."[17] However, an update in construction technologies did not result in the elimination of poché as a representational technique. The use of poché today continues to assist in the reading of space, highlighted as a solid to void condition. Consequentially, the depiction of poché misrepresents and hides the building components existing within the areas between occupied zones.

Including poché within representations that do not reflect the true existence of a building material or construction lends itself to ranging speculations as to what occupies the black fill. For example, the existence of poché deceives the viewer to the reality of the built condition. John Ruskin's *The Seven Lamps of Architecture* speaks of the existence of "Architectural" and "Structural Deceits" within the built environment. Ruskin asserts that a structural deceit is "the determined and purposed suggestion of a mode of support other than the true one."[18] The suggestion of a mode of support in section depictions that are very much occupiable, rather than a perceived impenetrable mass, is a deceitful representation. If, according to Turner, the subject of the liminal is hidden, what might be lurking in the poché: a hidden space housing hidden elements built upon layers of hidden purpose and meaning? This question is fundamental to understanding the narrative motivations behind horror films.

The betwixt space of Hellraiser

Betwixt space is where the horror genre shows the potential within the poché of buildings. These mysterious, hidden, and unstructured conditions are infiltrated, occupied, and activated in many films, ranging from a closet becoming the portal to a supernatural realm as seen in *Poltergeist* (1982)[19] or the concealed circulation system utilized in *The People Under the Stairs* (1991).[20] However, the first two entries in the *Hellraiser* film series discussed in this text[21] introduce audiences to a betwixt space depicted as a boundless labyrinth of liminality. The massive structure is an endless composition of repetitive, ambiguous spaces.

The *Hellraiser* franchise begins with the screen adaptation of the book *The Hellbound Heart* by author and director of the first film, Clive Barker.[22] The mythology of the films focuses on a puzzle box, the *Lament Configuration*, that unlocks an entry to a realm where unimaginable experiences of pleasure and pain coexist as one.[23] The first film in the series, *Hellraiser* (1987),[24] follows Frank Cotton, who purchases a puzzle box that he believes will lead him to a dominion that can satisfy his most insatiable desires. Frank seeks separation from his current place and time in hopes of transitioning to a state of ecstasy and pleasure, to become a different kind of person upon completing the ritual of solving the puzzle box.

The site for the film is Frank's unoccupied family home in London where he returns after obtaining the puzzle box. He chooses the empty and bifurcated space of the attic to solve the box, a process that entails reconfiguring the box from a cube to a complex, geometric object through a series of manual manipulations. The film depicts Frank, sitting in the center of a dilapidated room which has clearly been unoccupied for quite some time, surrounded by candles. The structure has deteriorated to the point where holes can be seen in the walls where plaster has fallen away from the wooden lath, setting a scene that is foreboding while also suggestive of the many layers of detritus beneath the walls. Upon each successful move, the space slowly begins to glow as a blue light radiates from the fissures in the walls. The wooden structure of the house can be heard adjusting and creaking as if physically transforming. A breeze can also be heard emanating from the cavities in the walls.

Upon solving the *Lament Configuration*, the box opens, releasing several chains adorned with hooks that pierce Frank's body. The camera momentarily cuts away, only to return to the room in a transformed state. Like Frank, the room has undergone a transition as a result of the ritual. The audience rediscovers the room as a dominion for torture, with chains and rotating, rectangular black boxes hanging from the ceiling alongside the brutalized remnants of Frank's body scattered across the wooden floor. It is at this time the audience is introduced to the overseers of the hidden realm, figures known as Cenobites. As they retrieve the box from Frank, the room returns to its original state.

By initiating the ritual, Frank has entered the "margin" or "limen" phase, a period of "betwixt and between" as defined by Turner. Frank can now be identified as a neophyte, experiencing the conditions of the realm for the first time where he is, as Turner describes, "neither living nor dead from one aspect, and both living and dead from another."[25] The film, unlike the novel, does not reveal or explain much of his experience in this in-between realm; however, the text discloses that Frank has become trapped within the poché of the attic room. He "lingered in the wall"[26] with no concept of time, "overdosing on sensuality" and "incalculable suffering."[27] Turner refers to this condition as "one of ambiguity and paradox, a confusion of all the customary categories."[28]

> There was a further sophistication to the torture, devised by a mind that understood exquisitely the nature of suffering. The prisoners were allowed to see into the world they had once occupied. Their resting places—when they were not enduring pleasure—looked out onto the very locations where they had once worked the Configuration that had brought them here.[29]

As the film progresses, Frank's brother Larry and his wife Julia return to the family home. Larry accidentally cuts his hand and drips blood upon the floorboards of the attic room resulting in Frank being birthed by the structure, ending his stasis trapped within the interstitial spaces of the attic. Frank rises from the poché of the floor, returned to reality as a skinless, grotesque figure, in a changed state. Absent of skin, Frank's birth back to the real world is as paradoxical as his time trapped in the liminal realm. He is both newborn and corpse, alive but unable to feel. Frank has passed through the three distinct phases within a ritual: separation, margin, and aggregation.[30] The house, more specifically the interstitial zones of the structure, has served as a mediator and an agent, during the three phases. Frank both exits and is reintegrated into the world through the poché.

Little is shown of the impossible realm within the poché. Our first and only view into the liminal realm reveals a limitless corridor, supported and organized by a series of repeated arches. The banal, repetitive condition encapsulates what one would expect an architectural "betwixt and between" space to resemble; an ambiguous architectural style with no clear attributes referring to a particular time in architectural history.

Hellraiser (1987) concludes as the Cenobites return to the family home to retrieve Frank and imprison him in the liminal realm. Before his capture, Frank accidentally kills Julia and leaves her lying on a blood-stained mattress. Frank's niece, Kirsty, solves the puzzle box and closes the threshold between the real world and the in-between. As the configuration sequence is completed, the house begins to crumble and violently shakes in response, further emphasizing the connections between the structure, the box, and the liminal dominion.

Labyrinth of the in-between

Following the theatrical success of *Hellraiser* (1987), a sequel, *Hellbound: Hellraiser II*, was released in 1988.[31] In the follow-up, the audience is shown the compositional and spatial language of the in-between realm, where we learn more about its prisoners and the multiple thresholds linking the realm with the real world.

Dr Philip Channard is presented as the antagonist early in the film. He is a doctor at the Channard Institute, a mental institution, and, like Frank in the first film, desires to unlock the puzzle box configuration along with the otherworldly knowledge and experience it contains. Unquenchable desire and exotic experiences are recurring themes in these two films. Michel Foucault speaks of experience from the points of view of Nietzsche, Bataille, and Blanchot by stating that through experience, there are moments in life where one can achieve both the possible and the impossible simultaneously, gathering the maximum amount of intensity and impossibility at the same time.[32] Frank speaks of this extreme, paradoxical experience while imprisoned within the poché of the attic in the first film. He states that the Cenobites gave him an experience beyond any conceivable limit, where pain and pleasure were indivisible. The representational technique of poché has the capacity to operate in this area of ambiguity by inviting speculations as to what may occur in the black fill. Is the condition solid or void? What are the spatial qualities and limits of the area? What are the materials and construction methods being used to support the adjacent inhabitable spaces and how were they informed? Through the lack of embellishment, poché becomes all encompassing.

The in-between realm is revealed for the first time through the poché of Dr Channard's home. The doctor utilizes the puzzle-solving skills of a young patient, Tiffany, to unlock the threshold to the liminal zone. Channard and Julia, returned to the real world by the doctor, secretly watch Tiffany solve the configuration from within a brick cavity in the wall of the doctor's office. Multiple thresholds emerge as the walls enclosing the office split open in a series of layered sliding doors. The scene echoes Kirsty's experience in her hospital room from the first film. While Tiffany sits within the office, two thresholds appear behind her and one behind Julia and Channard within the wall cavity. The openings reveal entry to an impossible space via hallways (see Figure 4.1). These passageways should be intersecting the rest of the home and extending beyond the enclosure of the house. Rather the architectural conditions of Channard's home are operating as a perpetrator in the film, participating in the advancement of the story by becoming an active gateway to impossible spaces. Dr Channard, Julia, and Tiffany all pass through the poché and into the other realm. Not far behind is Kirsty from the first film, intent on protecting Tiffany and guiding her back to the real world.

FIGURE 4.1: Entry to an impossible realm through the poché of Dr Channard's home office. *Hellbound: Hellraiser II*. Tony Randel (1988).

The slender, stone-lined hallway connections are organized by a series of redundant arches. The poché of the liminal realm is solid and impenetrable, a callback to the origins of the representational technique. An aerial view of the dominion reveals a seemingly endless, constructed composition of pathways and layers with no clear perimeter or horizontal boundary (see Figure 4.2). The overall pattern is orthogonal in nature, an irregular grid of intersecting, occupiable walls. The view from above reveals that the composition defines a horizon line with a consistent horizontal datum. Walls are either uninterrupted or contain arched openings in the transverse direction. Parallel to the walls are a series of masonry stairs providing additional linkages between the grid lines. The area between the walls within the grid are open volumes leading down to an infinite void.

Levitating above the horizon line and marking a perceived center of the realm is a large, rotating octahedron, a supersized version of a puzzle configuration. This hovering object is referred to as "Leviathan, Lord of the Labyrinth" by Julia. Although called a labyrinth in the film, the constructed landscape does not contain all the characteristics indicative of the origins of the spatial concept. Original labyrinths up to the Renaissance only consisted of one circuitous path that was not intersected. There was only one opening along the perimeter into the composition and it ended at the center so that the inhabitant could trace their steps back to the perimeter opening.[33] The film version includes aspects of a maze, with intersecting paths that cause its inhabitants to meander.[34] In the film, the protagonists and antagonists traverse within, and on top of, the corridors of the horizontal composition.

FIGURE 4.2: Comprehensive view of Leviathan. *Hellbound: Hellraiser II.* Tony Randel (1988).

Labyrinths can have many possible meanings due to contradictory and incomplete historical records.[35] For instance, the Labyrinth concept can be discussed in three forms: as a literary motif, a pattern of movement, or as a graphic figure.[36] The first mention of the term labyrinth is thought to be found on a Mycenaean clay tablet where the script refers to offerings to the gods and the Mistress of the Labyrinth.[37] In the *Hellraiser* franchise, when the puzzle box is solved, the Cenobites retrieve and deliver souls to the impossible dominion within the poché as offerings to the God of the labyrinth, Leviathan.

Hermann Kern refers to one interpretation of the labyrinth in the context of initiation, death, the underworld, and reincarnation stating, "The interior space is filled with the maximum number of twists and turns possible — meaning the greatest loss of time and the most physical exertion for the walker on his or her way to the goal, the center."[38] He continues by saying "A walker leaving the labyrinth is not the same person who entered it, but has been born again into a new phase or level of existence; the center is where death and rebirth occur."[39] The labyrinth structure in the *Hellraiser* franchise films consists of various types of inhabitants or walkers; those who are imprisoned with no prospects of leaving, temporary visitors with the capacity to enter and exit, and the overseers of the realm who move freely between the real world and the in-between. Each of these inhabitants experiences the structure differently, but the consistent mediator between all of these constituents is poché and the threshold it defines between the two worlds.

The second film provides additional insight on the experiential conditions of the labyrinth. At the conclusion of the first film, Frank is imprisoned yet again within the liminal realm and it is implied that each prisoner is provided their own section of the grid to occupy. Frank resides in a large, symmetrical room reminiscent of a small-scale Roman aqueduct structure. The side walls are comprised of layers of masonry, slightly offset from one another. Each layer consists of a series of arched openings leading to unknown spaces beyond the visible limits of the room. Periodically extending and recessing back and forth into the wall along the bottom layer at each opening are white slabs. A human figure is lying on each slab, draped in a sheet. This performative condition is a component of Frank's endless torture, rooted in sadomasochism and occupies the poché of the labyrinth structure. This space illustrates that within the redundancy of the labyrinth infrastructure lies unexpected and unseen spaces that do not align with the overall composition of the grid.

The conclusion of the second film finds Tiffany once again solving a puzzle box that enables her and Kirsty to exit the liminal realm and return back to the real world. Although entry to the labyrinth began at the home of Dr Channard, their return is through a threshold at the Channard Institute. The interconnectivity of the liminal realm reaches beyond the poché of one singular structure and extends to multiple locations of an unknown scale.

Revisiting Victor Turner's position on the concept of the "betwixt and between" as it pertains to the *Hellraiser* films, the identification of "ritual subject" can be assigned to the following characters: Frank Cotton, Dr Channard, Julia, or even the physical structure of the liminal realm, the labyrinth. All of these subjects possess a degree of ambiguity, a "neither here nor there" moment, after going through a transition. For the main antagonists, this comes from the ritualistic practice of solving the puzzle box configuration. As prisoners within the liminal zone, each character loses a sense of time, place, and awareness of their past, or future prospects. The same can be said for the architectural language of the labyrinth. Reading more like a large-scale piece of infrastructure, this manufactured landscape lacks a legible vernacular language. The ambiguous qualities of the composition are due largely to the repetitive and redundant distribution of solid to void geometry. Passing through the corridors, it is difficult for an occupant to discern their position within the overall field or to differentiate between inhabitable spaces versus uninhabitable. Alternatively, the banal characteristics of the labyrinth can prompt and empower its occupants to activate areas in the grid as they see fit. Similar to the occupants of the *Exodus, or the Voluntary Prisoners of Architecture* project, the prisoners of the labyrinth can obtain agency over the liminal zone by determining a wide range of programmatic activities throughout the field.

The capacity for poché to be inhabited and reimagined as a functional space can present alternative design possibilities to existing and new construction. Injecting program elements in existing, unstructured spaces would lead to a disruption of the adjacent areas. Similar to the centralized stairway in the *41 Cooper Square* academic building, this disruption can lead to unexpected social interactions between complimentary or opposing programmatic elements. Providing agency to inhabitants to curate the areas they occupy allows for flexibility in adhering to preconceived formal and programmatic typologies of architecture.

Lasting impressions

The history of horror films and their impact on popular culture can be traced back to the 1890s and the work of director George Méliès. The genre has evolved over time with the rapid development of technology and alongside ever-changing social and cultural norms. During this adaptation, horror films consistently make use of atmosphere and setting to challenge our understanding of comfort and safety. Mundane spaces such as a bedroom closet in *Black Christmas* (1974) or an ominous, exterior stairway like the one seen in *The Exorcist* (1973),[40] significantly contribute to the advancement of a film's plot. Often times, these recognizable locations and environments are remembered by audiences long after viewing the movies.

The *Hellraiser* films effectively acknowledge the existence of poché within our living spaces, calling attention to an otherwise withdrawn component of the built environment. Awakening these latent conditions raises questions as to how these zones may be inhabited, who or what may occupy them, and the connections to other places they may lead to. Human psychological idiosyncrasies allow us to enjoy horror films while simultaneously finding comfort in the same spaces that are interrogated and manipulated within the genre. By drilling down into the connection between structural components, unconscious behavior, popular cultural media, and contemporary domestic practice, new architectural methodologies and philosophies can be conjured and harnessed as tools for design.

NOTES

1. *Le Manoir du Diable* (1896), director Georges Méliès.
2. Robert Venturi, *Complexity and Contradiction in Architecture* (New York, NY: The Museum of Modern Art, 1977), 70–87.
3. Ibid.
4. *Black Christmas* (1974), director Bob Clark.
5. *A Nightmare on Elm Street* (1984), director Wes Craven.
6. *Relic* (2020), director Natalie Erika James.
7. Victor Turner, *The Forest of Symbols: Aspects of Ndembu Ritual* (Ithaca: Cornell University Press, 1967), 97.

8. Ibid., 94.
9. Ibid.
10. Ibid.
11. Ibid., 95.
12. Ibid., 98.
13. "41 Cooper Square," Morphosis Architecture. Accessed January 22, 2022. https://www.morphosis.com/architecture/4/.
14. "Untitled (Stairs)," Rachel Whiteread. Accessed January 22, 2022. https://www.tate.org.uk/art/artworks/whiteread-untitled-stairs-t07939.
15. Rem Koolhaas and Bruce Mau, *S, M, L, XL* (New York, NY: Monacelli Press, 1995), 9.
16. David Lewis, Paul Lewis, and Marc Tsuramaki, *Manual of Section* (New York, NY: Princeton Architectural Press, 2016), 31.
17. Ibid.
18. John Ruskin, *The Seven Lamps of Architecture* (London: Smith, Elder & Co., 1849), 30.
19. *Poltergeist* (1982), director Tobe Hooper.
20. *The People Under the Stairs* (1991), director Wes Craven.
21. The *Hellraiser* film franchise consists of ten installments as of the end of 2021.
22. Clive Barker, *The Hellbound Heart* (New York, NY: Harper Collins, 2007 edition). The horror novella was first published in 1986 as part of an anthology series titled *Night Visions 3* by publisher Dark Harvest Books.
23. Ibid., 60–61. The *Lament Configuration* is also known as *Lemarchand's Configuration*, named after its designer, the craftsman Lemarchand. Solving the complex device summons beings referred to as Cenobites, theologians of the Order of the Gash.
24. *Hellraiser* (1987), director Clive Barker.
25. Victor Turner, *The Forest of Symbols: Aspects of Ndembu Ritual* (Ithaca: Cornell University Press, 1967), 96.
26. Clive Barker, *The Hellbound Heart* (New York, NY: Harper Collins, 2007 edition), 57.
27. Ibid., 62.
28. Victor Turner, *The Forest of Symbols: Aspects of Ndembu Ritual* (Ithaca, NY: Cornell University Press, 1967), 96.
29. Clive Barker, *The Hellbound Heart* (New York, NY: Harper Collins, 2007 edition), 62–63.
30. Victor Turner, *The Forest of Symbols: Aspects of Ndembu Ritual* (Ithaca, NY: Cornell University Press, 1967), 94.
31. *Hellbound: Hellraiser II* (1988), director Tony Randel.
32. Jay Martin, "The Limits of Limit-Experience: Bataille and Foucault," *Constellations* 2, no. 2 (April 1995): 158.
33. Herman Kern, *Through the Labyrinth: Designs and Meaning over 5,000 Years* (Munich, London, New York, NY: Prestel Verlage, 2000), 23.
34. Ibid., 26.
35. Ibid., 30.

36. Ibid., 27.
37. Ibid., 25.
38. Ibid., 30.
39. Ibid.
40. *The Exorcist* (1973), director William Friedkin.

REFERENCES

Barker, Clive. *The Hellbound Heart*. New York, NY: Harper Collins, 2007.

Barker, Clive, director. *Hellraiser*. UK: Entertainment Film Distributors, 1987.

Clark, Bob, director. *Black Christmas*. Burbank, CA: Warner Bros. Pictures, 1974.

Craven, Wes, director. *A Nightmare on Elm Street*. USA: New Line Cinema, 1984.

Craven, Wes, director. *The People Under the Stairs*. New York, NY: Universal Pictures, 1991.

Friedkin, William, director. *The Exorcist*. Burbank, CA: Warner Bros. Pictures, 1973.

Hooper, Tobe, director. *Poltergeist*. Beverly Hills,CA: MGM/UA Entertainment, 1982.

James, Natalie Erika, director. *Relic*. New York, NY: IFC Midnight, 2020.

Jay, Martin. "The Limits of Limit-Experience: Bataille and Foucault." *Constellations* 2, no. 2 (April 1995): 155–74.

Kern, Hermann. *Through the Labyrinth: Designs and Meanings over 5,000 Years*. Munich, London, New York, NY: Prestel Verlage, 2000.

Koolhaas, Rem, and Mau, Bruce. *S, M, L, XL*. New York, NY: Monacelli Press, 1995.

Lewis, David, Paul Lewis, and Marc Tsuramaki. *Manual of Section*. New York, NY: Princeton Architectural Press, 2016.

Méliès, George, director. *Le Manoir du Diable*. Gauteng: Star Film Company, 1896.

Morphosis Architecture."41 Cooper Square." Accessed January 22, 2022. http://www.morphosis.com/architecture/4/.

Randel, Tony, director. *Hellbound: Hellraiser II*. Atlanta, GA: New World Pictures, 1988.

Ruskin, John. *The Seven Lamps of Architecture*. London: Smith, Elder & Co., 1849.

Turner, Victor. "Betwixt and Between: The Liminal Period in *Rites de Passage*." In *The Forest of Symbols: Aspects of Ndembu Ritual*. Ithaca, NY: Cornell University Press, 1967.

Van Gennep, Arnold. *Les Rites de Passage*. Chicago, IL: University of Chicago Press, 1960.

Venturi, Robert. *Complexity and Contradiction in Architecture*. New York, NY: The Museum of Modern Art, 1977.

Whiteread, Rachel. "Untitled (Stairs)." Accessed January 22, 2022. http://www.tate.org.uk/art/artworks/whiteread-untitled-stairs-t07939.

5

Liminal Mies

Beatriz Colomina

Betwixt the lens and the building

A photograph taken during the construction of the Neue Nationalgalerie in Berlin shows Ludwig Mies van der Rohe looking through the window of a white car as the massive one-piece 1250-ton steel roof of the building was raised into position (see Figure 5.1). According to Dirk Lohan, his grandson, collaborator, and the driver of the car,

> When the roof was at a level of two meters, Mies determined to walk under it to see if the space emerging corresponded to his idea of what it should look like. I accompanied him as he walked with great difficulty beneath the floating roof.[1]

FIGURE 5.1: Ludwig Mies van der Rohe on the day of the raising of the roof of the Neue Nationalgalerie, April 5, 1967. Credit: Landesarchiv, Berlin, no. 0119286/Ludwig Ehlers.

It was April 5, 1967. Another photograph on the same day shows the figure of Mies with a coat and a hat on, propped with two canes and holding a briefcase as he appears to prepare to cross the street to see the building from the other side. This was his last view of the building. Mies had traveled to Berlin for this occasion but was too fragile to come back again for the festivities of the ceremonial opening on September 15, 1968. He died on August 17, 1969, without seeing the building completed.

Or had he seen it completed already? Seen, that is, the key polemical statement—the space between the two massive horizontals that would eventually be lightly contained by huge panes of glass yet barely transformed by them, as if emptiness had been placed in a vitrine, a kind of display case, offering it to the city in a dramatic gesture of exposure. So exposed, in fact, that the building at first does not seem to have an inside. Even from a distance, there is the uncanny sense that what normally would be an inside is oddly bigger than the outside, that Berlin has expanded, as if through a lens. The Neue Nationalgalerie is not so much a building in Berlin as a way of seeing Berlin and of becoming yourself the exhibit. Transparency here is, anyway, never simple.

The photographs of the Neue Nationalgalerie under construction recall the image of Mies around 1949 in front of the structure of the Farnsworth House in Plano, IL, where his lonely figure appears to somberly appraise the empty frame (see Figure 5.2). His enormous stature cuts a black silhouette into the frigid land scape. With his coat and hat on, and his back to the camera, he stands like one of Caspar David Friedrich's figures confronting the sublime. Here, again, there is the uncanny sense that the landscape has been expanded by an almost nothing lens of two horizontal planes that will receive only the most delicate shimmery distortions of the barest glass curtain to mark the limit of an occupiable viewing instrument. This is a house not a museum and yet there is a palpable sense of exhibition. First, the house itself is on exhibit—shockingly different from everything around it, just as the Neue Nationalgalerie defines itself in opposition to the city around it. Second, the smooth, perfected floating geometry of both buildings suggests that they have just landed from outer space and paradoxically render everything around them as an exotic captivating landscape on exhibit. Third, everything seen within the spaces is on show. But the ultimate exhibitionism is the combination of all three: the view through the building. The eye passing through the structure is aware that the lens is there, but it focuses only on the distant landscape. Mies's architecture is never simply an object sitting there in its perfection, waiting for us to look at it. It waits to be looked through and, in that moment, becomes out of focus, even ghostly. When Mies looked through a building, and when we, too, look through it, then we complete the work, even become a part of it.

FIGURE 5.2: Ludwig Mies van der Rohe on the construction site of the Farnsworth House, 1950. Credit: Mies van der Rohe Archive, Museum of Modern Art, no. MMA14216.

Seeing through architecture

This is the effect that Mies tried to produce in the work—the effect that, again and again, he checked in buildings under construction but also in the models. For example, in the glass models, he built of the Glass Skyscraper project of 1922 where he realized that the important thing in glass architecture "is the play of reflections and not the effect of light and shadow, as in ordinary buildings."[2] He repeatedly photographed these models in a garden in Berlin before arriving at the few canonic images he finally released. During the opening of his first solo exhibition, at MoMA in 1947, before the Farnsworth House was completed, Mies is seen in a photograph bending over a pedestal, looking intently through the model of the house on exhibit. Not at the model but through it, as if to demonstrate what is important, or even to check the optical effect (see Figure 5.3).

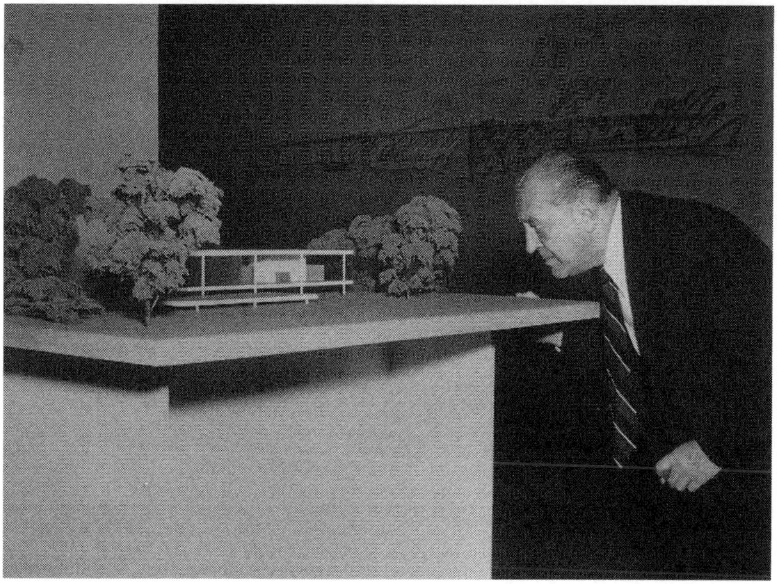

FIGURE 5.3: Ludwig Mies van der Rohe looking through the model of the Farnsworth House at the Museum of Modern Art exhibition of his work, 1947. Credit: The Art Institute of Chicago, no. 198602. 081216-03.

Architecture is a lens through which to see the world, and therefore it has to almost disappear in order to give way to this view. In the Neue Nationalgalerie, all of the elements of the building are thinned down or buried in the plinth so that the structure offers the minimum definition and the works of art displayed will define a different architecture for each temporary exhibition. Depthless collages of suspended panels communicate the essence of the building even though the building itself does not appear in the collages, except for the most delicate grid lines The collages stage an act of looking through the volume to the courtyard and the trees beyond. Even the art is seen not directly but off to the side of an eye that is uninterrupted as it moves through and out. The architecture is not even a frame. Or at least not a frame for art. Photographs show, even before the first exhibition was hung, the plain white panels suspended from the ceiling, designed to support paintings, acting in fact as minimalist paintings in their own right but not blocking the eye that can keep moving under, over, or past them.

But if looking through is what makes the building, then the opening that Mies missed was the inauguration of this unique way of viewing. In the photographs, the visitors spread out to the edges of the site, moving restlessly and looking at everything except the architecture and the art. They look through the spaces at each other, from the plinth through the main gallery, from the gallery to the courtyard, and so on. They go into the building only to pass through and look back through.

Liminal domesticity

Looking at the photographs of the opening, I am touched by the sense of domesticity. This was not the usual stiff affair of a museum opening with people gravely observing the artworks or the building, but an almost wild party with guests dancing to the beat of live music of the Dixieland band in the courtyard (see Figure 5.4). Bodies moving in space, close together, drinking, talking, laughing, some dancing, others perched on the edge of the plinth looking down to the party in the courtyard

FIGURE 5.4: Opening Ceremony of the Neue Nationalgalerie, September 15, 1968. Credit: Staatliche Museum zu Berlin/Zentralarchiv/Reinhard Friedrich.

below (see Figure 5.5). The museum feels like a big house with a patio. The view through, the feeling when architecture goes out of focus, produces a new sense of shared release.

In the Neue Nationalgalerie, Mies's logic of exhibiting without foregrounding—as if teasing the view with what is just off to one side or a kind of mirage in the distance—becomes everything in the most public of buildings, but at the same time, it retains its domesticity. The building is a hybrid of the glass house and the courtyard house. In the photographs of the opening, people are behaving as if in the garden of a big house. And they, too, are on exhibit. Upstairs in the pavilion they float in space like the paintings, and the walls hold them lightly, even tenderly. The miracle of Mies's architecture is that you are continuously framed and reframed in different ways. From the front, the side, just your legs ... And the reverse is also true. The art seems a visitor as well, one that may leave before you do.

The Neue Nationalgalerie in Berlin, now in the 53rd year of its life, is Mies van der Rohe's last building and in a sense also his first. It is as if Mies only ever had one project, reworked endlessly on different sites, a single experiment with a new kind of transparency, a new way of exhibiting the world—an experiment that began and ended in Berlin. When making a gallery, Mies was not simply making a space for exhibitions. All his work is exhibitionist. Mies was incubated in the

FIGURE 5.5: Opening of the Neue Nationalgalerie, 1968. Credit: Staatliche Museum zu Berlin/ Zentralarchiv/Reinhard Friedrich.

immaterial space of exhibitions and he ultimately absorbed the logic of exhibition into the very material of his architecture.

The exhibitionist house

If the Neue Nationalgalerie is a big house, then Mies van der Rohe and Lilly Reich had repeatedly stretched the concept of exhibition into that of the house since the 1920s. For example, when the German Glass Industry commissioned a display of their products for the exhibition *Die Wohnung* (The Dwelling) in Stuttgart in 1927, the two architects turned their *Glas Raum* (Glass Room) display into a house, a flowing space subdivided into a dining room, living room, and workroom by freestanding glass walls. The illusion of a ceiling was produced by strips of stretched fabric; the floors were covered with white, gray, red, and black linoleum areas that produced a sense of movement by not quite coinciding with the rooms; the walls were of etched, clear, and gray opaque glass; the chairs were covered in white chamois and black cowhide; and the bench table was in rosewood.[3] Even a sense of the outside was produced by placing plants and a sculpture of a woman on the other side of one of the glass walls. This strategy anticipates the Barcelona Pavilion, Mies's most famous project.

When commissioned to build the German Pavilion for the Barcelona International Exposition in 1929, Mies asked the Ministry of Foreign Affairs what was to be exhibited. "Nothing will be exhibited," he was told, "the pavilion itself will be the exhibit."[4] In the absence of a traditional client or program, Mies was able to take his work to new limits and one of the most influential buildings of the century emerged. Once again, Mies and Reich, who collaborated on the project, had taken the opportunity to make a proto-house. Defined by the strategic placement of sensuous materials, its flowing space continued the investigations started with the Brick Country House and the Glass Room in Stuttgart. Even the presence of a Georg Kolbe sculpture of a nude woman in the Glass Room would reappear in the *Deutsche Bauausstellung* (German Building Exhibition) in Berlin two years later, when the experiment continued.

Exhibitions in the twentieth century acted as sites for the incubation of new forms of architecture that were sometimes so shockingly original, so new, that they were not even recognized as architecture at all. Think, for example, about the Barcelona Pavilion, widely understood in the architectural world today as the most influential building of the twentieth century. It was in fact seen by "nobody." Despite its prominent location in the layout of the 1929 *Exposición Internacional de Barcelona,* even journalists sent by professional architectural magazines passed it over entirely, unable to detect its significance. Local journalists provided the only testimony to its existence. They commented on the "mysterious" effect,

> because a person standing in front of one of these glass walls sees himself reflected as if by a mirror, but if he moves behind them, he then sees the exterior perfectly. Not all the visitors notice this curious particularity whose cause remains ignored.[5]

It is necessary to go back to these kinds of statements to understand the surprise that a glass building produced in 1929, something that, as Alison Smithson put it, a generation that has grown up around glassy Hilton International hotels may have difficulty imagining.

The permanent beauty of the ephemeral

It was only in the 1950s, in the aftermath of the 1947–48 exhibition *Mies van der Rohe* at the Museum of Modern Art in New York, that the Barcelona Pavilion burst into every architectural publication.[6] As glass architecture became dominant, the pavilion was hailed as the most beautiful building of the century, exemplifying the cult of transparency. A building that was known only through magazine images (it was dismantled at the closing of the exhibition in Barcelona and its fragments misplaced during its return trip to Germany) became the most significant monument of modern architecture. Retroactively, the pavilion is seen to exemplify the new optical and spatial freedom embodied in Mies's houses and exported to all building types.

What is crucial about the Barcelona Pavilion is that it was both real, a one-to-one structure that existed for a time, and an image, a media construction. All we knew about it, before its reconstruction in 1986, were the photographs. It lived in the photographs. The images capture the sense of looking through, from outside to inside to outside. The plan seems to multiply the opportunities for views through. The photographs are not simply of an object, but of a way of viewing supported by an object. The ambiguities produced by the reflections in the glass extend to the object. Even when the looking through does not pass through glass, the seemingly sharp forms are softened by our concentration on the spaces in the distance.

House as lens

Again and again, Mies constructs an object that is ultimately meant to give way to the view it makes possible. Take the Tugendhat House (1928–30), for example, which sits on a sloping site. The house blocks the view from the street, except for an opening which frames a small fragment—a postcard view—which both lures you in and keeps you at a distance with the railing (see Figure 5.6). This framed picture defines the entrance space of the house. It protects you, encloses you, as much as the overhang does, by keeping the "outside" at a distance. And it is only when already inside the house, having passed down the spiral staircase, that the panoramic view finally becomes possible through a glass wall, which can be made to disappear into the floor with the help of a complex machine. Shelter in Mies's houses, protection from the outside, is provided by a window's ability to turn the threatening world outside the home into a reassuring picture. The inhabitant is enveloped, wrapped, protected by the pictures. These perspectives are not simply neutral views of the outside world. The world is at once turned into an outside and interrogated, intensified, transformed, by being framed. As Mies puts it: "When one looks at Nature through the glass walls of the Farnsworth House it takes on a deeper significance than when one stands outside. More is asked for from Nature, because it becomes part of a greater whole."[7] The glass house doesn't simply expose the exterior world. It actively turns the world into a highly composed display. Symptomatic in that respect is Fritz Tugendhat's response to the architectural critic Justus Bier, who had polemically asked the question "Is the Tugendhat house habitable?" in the pages of the journal *Die Form*:[8]

FIGURE 5.6: Ludwig Mies van der Rohe, Tugendhat House, Brno, Czechoslovakia, 1930. Credit: Mies van der Rohe Archive, Museum of Modern Art.

> After almost a year of living in the house, I can assure you without hesitation that technically it possesses everything a modern person might wish for [...]. On clear and frosty days, one can lower its windows, sit in the sun, and enjoy the view of a snow-covered landscape, like Davos.[9]

The house itself has disappeared. What makes the Tugendhat habitable is the view through it. Habitation means occupying this view.

Floating space

The glass house represented the realization of the century-old dream of a transparent house. This dream extended from the science-fiction-like quality of Paul Scheerbart's images of glass buildings in an ideal future in his novels and in his 1914 collection of aphorisms *Glasarchitektur* (Glass architecture) dedicated to Bruno Taut, to Taut's own *Glashaus* (the pavilion for the glass industry in the German Werkbund exhibition in Cologne of 1914), to Mies van der Rohe and Lilly Reich's Glass Room in Stuttgart of 1927, and to Mies's German Pavilion at the International Exposition in Barcelona of 1929 and his project for a Glass House on a Hillside of 1934. By 1949, this dream of a house defined only by glass walls—or, we could even say, the absence of walls—was fully realized in the Farnsworth House. The spaceship had landed or rather was floating just above the ground as if coming in to land. What had been experimented with in drawings, models, writings, and pavilions in fairs had finally become useful.

Already in 1947, in his book on Mies accompanying the exhibition at the Museum of Modern Art, Philip Johnson had described the Farnsworth House as "a floating self-contained cage"[10] and Henry-Russell Hitchcock described it as a "beached yacht" with no provisions for outer living beyond the very confined space of the fly-screened "deck" and the small travertine "dock" below it.[11] The idea of floating can already be found in early articles in the popular press, as when *House & Garden* magazine calls the house a "glass shell that 'floats' in the air."[12] It is this floating, disengaged quality that allows the house to take the logic of the exhibition out into the landscape. The house exposes everything, turning everything into a display, including itself. The house literally stages an exhibition for its occupants and becomes part of the show. The house turns the exhibition gallery inside out. The world itself is put on exhibit. This all-pervasive logic of the exhibition was a part of Mies's project from the beginning, which was always the attempt to assemble a house through an act of collection and exhibition.

Client as collector

Not by chance, many clients of Mies were prominent art collectors: Hugo Perls, for whom Mies built a house in Berlin in 1911–12, collected Pablo Picasso, Henri Matisse, and Edvard Munch; Helene Müller, who commissioned the unrealized project for the Kröller-Müller Villa in the Netherlands in 1912–13, was a formidable art collector (50 Van Gogh paintings alone had to be accommodated in the plans of the project); Eric Wolf, the client of Mies's first modern house, had a great collection of Caspar David Friedrich, Adolph von Menzel, and German Expressionist art; Hermann Lange, who commissioned Mies to do a house for him in Krefeld, was a collector of Cubist and German Expressionist art; Karl Lemke, the client of Mies's only completed court house, was a printer and art collector. But perhaps the most paradigmatic of Mies's client/collectors was Eduard Fuchs, the protagonist of Walter Benjamin's essay "Eduard Fuchs, Collector and Historian" (1931), who bought the house of Hugo Perls in 1927 and commissioned Mies to do an extension to accommodate his collection.

In fact, most of Mies's clients—whether bankers, lawyers, or industrialists—were amateur art collectors, and Mies always made proposals for how to hang their art, considering the placement of works of art as part of the house design. It is important to remember that Mies himself was also an amateur art collector who acquired, over the course of his life, more than 40 works of art (22 by Paul Klee, 14 by Kurt Schwitters, and some by Max Beckmann, Wassily Kandinsky, and Pablo Picasso).[13] Most of the works in his collection were small, and he used them in his domestic settings. Not having any savings, Mies used to say that his collection was his life insurance.

It was yet another art collector, Helen Resor, who brought Mies to the United States. She was a trustee of The Museum of Modern Art (MoMA) who was introduced to Mies's work by the museum's director, Alfred H. Barr. In the controversy over who should design the new MoMA, Barr was in favor of Mies, while Nelson Rockefeller preferred Philip Goodwin and Edward Durell Stone. Resor was on Barr's side despite the fact that she was a client of Goodwin's, who had already built a small guest cabin at Resor's ranch in Jackson Hole, Wyoming. In support of Barr, she fired Goodwin and commissioned Mies to do a house at the ranch.[14]

Resor was a force. She was the director of the world's largest international advertising agency (the J. Walter Thompson Company) and a legendary copywriter, famous for coining the phrase "A skin you love to touch" for the advertising campaign of Woodbury's Facial Soap. She was also innovative with images that transformed the look of advertising. She hired Edward Steichen, later the director of MoMA's photography department, on an exclusive contract in 1924. She put together innovative advertising campaigns introducing new products to American consumers (Cutex nail polish, Lever Brothers' Lux soap, etc.). If MoMA was trying to repackage modern architecture for an American audience, then Helen Resor had all the expertise to do it. Mies was simply the next product to be imported, displayed, and promoted.

Resor was a brilliant fundraiser at MoMA and made a financial agreement with Barr so she could buy art in Europe for MoMA without restrictions. She would keep whatever MoMA didn't take on the understanding that the museum could buy it later at the original price. Even the importing of Mies seems to have followed that pattern. In the end, MoMA went for Goodwin and Durrell Stone, while Resor kept Mies. She even personally brought Mies over from Europe, traveling back to the United States with him by ocean liner, arriving in New York in August 1937. Resor wanted to fly to her ranch in Wyoming (United Airlines being one of her advertising clients) but Mies refused, preferring to take the train via Chicago.[15]

Back in New York, Mies worked for six months on the design of the house, producing over 800 drawings. The basic idea was to create a bridge with the sense of an open box floating in the air. Goodwin had already decided the location over a small river and installed a set of concrete piers to support the house. Mies's project used the same piers and thinned all the elements down to create a large glass room suspended in the air (see Figure 5.7). Much of the endless redrawing of the project attempts to position floating walls in the space, culminating in a famous collage where the view through the expansive glass wall is transformed into a new kind of space (see Figure 5.8). The deep view toward the distant mountains that the site makes available has been replaced with a still from a Western movie facing a steep hillside. It reads like a depthless flat screen with a set of floating panels in the foreground. One of the panels, an enlarged reproduction of Paul Klee's *Bunte Mahlzeit* (Colorful Meal)—a painting in Resor's collection, purchased during

FIGURE 5.7: Ludwig Mies van de Rohe, Resor House, view out into the surroundings, collage 1937–38. Credit: Mies van der Rohe Archive, Museum of Modern Art.

FIGURE 5.8: Ludwig Mies van der Rohe, Resor House (unbuilt). Graphite and collage of wood veneer and cut-and-paste reproductions, 1937–41. Credit: Mies van der Rohe Archive, Museum of Modern Art.

Mies's stay in New York and probably with his advice—becomes a freestanding element, juxtaposed with a wood veneer panel in the foreground that has the same proportions as the landscape view. The view offered by the house is no longer a direct exposure to the outside. Rather, the outside is reframed, brought inside, and transformed into a large painting or, more precisely, a cinematic frame. The collages are again polemically sharp, but the building is almost out of the picture, and even the artworks are to the side of the view that passes through. Mies produced high-resolution images of a way of blurring both architecture and art in favor of a sensuous encounter with the distance. The interior is a landscape that gives way to the extended landscape beyond.

The pivotal project was canceled in 1938, but Mies kept working on it, presenting new models and drawings of the house in his 1947 exhibition at MoMA. The concept of transforming the status of both art and architecture led directly to his Museum for a Small City (1942), a project which stands with Le Corbusier's Museum of Unlimited Growth (1931) as the two most significant proposals for museums of the modern movement.

Barely delineated

The Museum for a Small City was the result of a commission from the journal *Architectural Forum* to design a church for a special issue of the magazine dedicated to "New Buildings for 194X" to be published in 1943. Mies, who had been tutoring George Danforth, a student doing a museum thesis, suggested to *Architectural Forum* that instead of a church he would design a museum. Danforth had worked on the Resor collages and was testing the same strategy on a larger scale.[16] The collages of the museum are very similar to those of the Resor house. Paintings and sculptures are used in the museum as if they were walls and columns defining a space with the feeling of the outdoors. For Mies, the main point was not to contain the art within the architecture but to use the art to create architecture. In his text for *Architectural Forum*, Mies wrote:

> The first problem is to establish the museum as a center for the enjoyment, not the internment of art. In this project the barrier between the artwork and the living community is erased by a garden approach for the display of sculpture. Interior sculptures enjoy an equal spatial freedom, because the open plan permits them to be seen against the surrounding hills. The architectural space, thus achieved, becomes a defining rather than a confining space. A work such as Picasso's *Guernica* has been difficult to place in the usual museum gallery. Here it can be shown to greatest advantage and become an element in space against a changing background.[17]

Art for Mies was a spatial element, but once again supporting a way of viewing rather than simply being viewed. In the Museum for a Small City, *Guernica* becomes a freestanding wall. As in the Resor House, in collages and similar images for the earlier Court House projects, all of the traditional elements of architecture—floor, walls, ceilings, and columns—are barely delineated or simply invisible. It is the unrestrained art that takes over in constructing a visual depth. The works on exhibit generate the real architecture that is occupied. Mies's architecture had been incubated in the gallery space from the beginning. His work is an optical instrument, born in temporary display spaces, then unleashed in different landscapes around the world.

One notices, when looking again at all of Mies's canonical works, that they are exhibitionistic in character. It is not just that they are designed to be published or designed to photograph well. Rather, they are concerned with new forms of exposure, new forms of display, new forms of transparency. The object has been deeply affected by the fact that it is both constructed in the media and infiltrated by the media. Always on show, it has become thoroughly exhibitionist.

This relentless strategy continued in the project for the unbuilt Bacardi headquarters in Santiago, Cuba (1957–60), which became the final model for the Neue Nationalgalerie in Berlin (1962–68). Mies's one extended project finally returned to Berlin as the ultimate statement of an architecture designed to be looked through—a new kind of transparency where the object slips out of view in the very moment that it supports the view that passes through.

NOTES

1. Dirk Lohan, "Skizzen der Erinnerung," in *Neue Nationalgalerie Berlin: Dreißig Jahre*, eds. Paul Kahlfeldt and Andres Lepik (Berlin: XX, 1998), 11. Quoted in Joachim Jäger, *Neue Nationalgalerie Berlin* (Ostfildern: Hatje Cantz, 2011), 67.
2. Mies van der Rohe, *Frulicht* 1, no. 4, 1922, quoted in Philip Johnson, *Mies van der Rohe* (New York, NY: MoMA, 1947), 187.
3. Franz Schulze, *Mies van der Rohe: A Critical Biography* (Chicago, IL, London: University of Chicago Press, 1985), 141–42. Matilda McQuaid, *Lilly Reich: Designer and Architect* (New York, NY: The Museum of Modern Art, 1996), 25.
4. Julius Posener, "Los primeros años: de Schinkel a De Stijl," *A&V: Monografías de Arquitectura y Vivienda* 6, special issue on Mies van der Rohe (1986), 33.
5. A journalist from Barcelona reviewing the pavilion, quoted in Josep Quetglas, *Der gläserne Schrecken: Imágenes del Pabellón de Alemania* (Montreal: Editions b, 1991), 48. Published in English as: Josep Quetglas, "Fear of Glass: The Barcelona Pavilion," in *Revisions* 2, ed. Beatriz Colomina (New York, NY: Princeton Architectural Press, 1988), 130.
6. Juan Pablo Bonta, *Architecture and Its Interpretation: A Study of Expressive Systems in Architecture* (New York, NY: Rizzoli International, 1979), 131–74.
7. Ludwig Mies van der Rohe in conversation with Christian Norberg-Schultz, in *Baukunst und Werkform* 11 (November 1958).
8. Justus Bier, "Kann man im Haus Tugendhat wohnen?," *Die Form*, October 15, 1931, 392.
9. Fritz Tugendhat, *Die Form*, November 1931, 437–38.
10. Philip Johnson, *Mies van der Rohe* (1947; repr., New York, NY: MoMA, 1978), 162.
11. Henry-Russell Hitchcock, "The Current Work of Philip Johnson," *Zodiac* 8 (1961), 66.
12. "A Glass Shell that 'Floats' in the Air," in *House & Garden*, February 1952.
13. For a detailed account of Mies's collection, see Vivian Endicott Barnett, "The Architect as Collector," in *Mies in America*, edited by Phyllis Lambert (New York, NY: Harry N. Abrams, 2001), 90–131.
14. See Cammie McAtee, "Alien #5044325: Mies' First Trip to America." In Lambert, *Mies in America*, 132–91.
15. Ibid.
16. For a year or so, George Danforth had been experimenting with collages of large artworks defining a public gallery. One day, says Danforth, he walked into the office and Mies was smiling with a telegram in his hand. "He said: 'Ja, shall we do it?' And that stopped my work on the thesis." Kevin Harrington in conversation with George Danforth, quoted in Phyllis Lambert, "Space and Structure." In *Mies in America*, 426.
17. Ludwig Mies van der Rohe, "Museum for a Small City," *Architectural Forum* 78, no. 5 (1943): 84–85. Reprinted in Fritz Neumeyer, *The Artless Word: Mies van der Rohe and the Building Art* (Cambridge, MA: MIT Press, 1991), 322.

REFERENCES

"A Glass Shell that 'Floats' in the Air," in *House & Garden*, February 1952.

Barnett, Vivian Endicott. "The Architect as Collector." In *Mies in America*, edited by Phyllis Lambert. New York, NY: Harry N. Abrams, 2001.

Bier, Justus. *"Kann man im Haus Tugendhat wohnen?" Die Form*, October 15, 1931.

Bonta, Juan Pablo. *Architecture and Its Interpretation: A Study of Expressive Systems in Architecture*. New York, NY: Rizzoli International, 1979.

Hitchcock, Henry-Russell. "The Current Work of Philip Johnson," *Zodiac* 8 (1961): 64–81.

Joachim, Jäger. *Neue Nationalgalerie Berlin*. Ostfildern: Hatje Cantz, 2011.

Johnson, Philip. *Mies van der Rohe*. New York, NY: MoMA, 1947.

Lambert, Phyllis. "Space and Structure." In *Mies in America*, edited by Phyllis Lambert. New York, NY: Abrams 2001.

Lohan, Dirk. "Skizzen der Erinnerung." In *Neue Nationalgalerie Berlin: Dreißig Jahre*, edited by Paul Kahlfeldt and Andres Lepik. Berlin: Paul Kahlfeldt, 1998.

McAtee, Cammie. "Alien #5044325: Mies' First Trip to America." In *Mies in America*, edited by Phyllis Lambert. New York, NY: Abrams 2001, 132–91.

McQuaid, Matilda. *Lilly Reich: Designer and Architect*. New York, NY: The Museum of Modern Art, 1996.

Mies van der Rohe, Ludwig. "Two Glass Skyscrapers." *Frulicht*, no. 4 (1922): 122–24.

Mies van der Rohe, Ludwig. "Museum for a Small City." *Architectural Forum* 78, no. 5 (1943): 84.

Neumeyer, Fritz. *The Artless Word: Mies van der Rohe and the Building Art*. Cambridge, MA: MIT Press, 1991.

Norberg-Schulz, Christian. "A Talk with Mies van der Rohe." *Baukunst und Werkform* 11, no. 11 (1958): 615–18.

Posener, Julius. *"Los primeros años: de Schinkel a De Stijl." In A&V: Monografías de Arquitectura y Vivienda* 6, special issue on Mies van der Rohe, 1986.

Quetglas, Josep. *Der gläserne Schrecken: Imágenes del Pabellón de Alemania*. Montreal: Editions b, 1991.

Quetglas, Josep. "Fear of Glass: The Barcelona Pavilion." In *Revisions* 2, edited by Beatriz Colomina. New York, NY: Princeton Architectural Press, 1988.

Schulze, Franz. *Mies van der Rohe: A Critical Biography*. Chicago, IL, London: University of Chicago Press, 1985.

Tugendhat, Fritz. "Die Bewohner des Hauses *Tugendhat* äussern sich." *Die Form VI*, no. 11 (1931): 437–38.

6

Varda Makes Her *Pointe*

Maria Sieira

There is no better example of the liminal than filming on location. An existing architecture, streetscape, or landscape is released from its daily functions and transformed into some invented space. While the actors prepare and the crew sets up the shot, the space is both actual and fictional, both a popular neighborhood diner and the site of an FBI operation.[1] But most local details are framed out, and our attention is redirected so that we are too concerned with the fate of a character to notice a Brooklyn street sign in what is supposed to be Washington, DC. Even the most painstakingly framed camera view will capture serendipitous details of the existing space, but in most films this liminality disappears in the finished film. One filmmaker, the French Nouvelle Vague pioneer Agnès Varda, courts and keeps this liminal quality. She delights in what bits of daily life the camera might happen upon and allows the reality of the existing spaces to show through the finished films.

Space and time constructs in Cléo de 5 à 7

The title character in Varda's *Cléo de 5 à 7* (1962)[2] is surrounded by actual Parisians going about their day.[3] A review at the time dismissed this context as mere atmospheric detail,[4] but in a more nuanced reading of a film's space, those cafe and street environments are the cinematic foil to Cléo's unease about an impending medical test result. Varda exploits what the early film theorist Rudolph Arnheim called film's simultaneous two- and three-dimensionality; a train moving from the back to the front of the film's space is also moving from the upper right to the lower left of the screen.[5] In *Cléo*, Varda takes us into Parisian space by using two-dimensional camera frames to compress all that detail-filled three-dimensional quotidian life around the central character. Varda takes us into Parisian time too. The film is called "*Cléo de 5 à 7*" and we accompany the title character from 5:00 p.m. to about 6:30 p.m. By making this space and time construct, Varda and anchors us to the realities of the existing space we see in the film. Varda does this for the same reason that the Italian neorealists of the late 1940s sought to show the reality of daily life; if a film has a sociopolitical agenda, filming in existing spaces gives veracity to the story. The neorealists filmed among bombed buildings to narrate the impoverished conditions of post-war.

Italy. They frame their scenes so that the real space informs our understanding of the protagonists and their stories. In a well-known scene in Vittorio De Sica's 1948 *Ladri di biciclette*, or *Bicycle Thieves*,[6] we see a boy and his father underemployed sitting together on the curb. Behind them, we see just the legs of people walking who, unlike them, have somewhere to go. Framing this scene at the eye level of the curb, from a literally low space, reiterates the low social strata the father and son occupy and cannot escape. Like the Italian neorealists, Varda uses existing spaces to address socio-economic or sociocultural issues. She also frames her Cléo, who is fretting about a cancer diagnosis, with the hustle and bustle of cafes and shops brimming with quotidian life. As in the De Sica film, the veracity of a real environment informs our understanding of the fictional protagonist, the vitality of a living city contrasting with Cléo's prospects of illness and death.

But Varda differs from the neorealists in how she makes the space and time constructs in her films. She uses film's simultaneous two and three dimensions to experiment with figure–ground ambiguity. The statuesque Cléo is momentarily the figure against the pictorial ground of Cafe Dôme, but neither is subservient to the other and soon she recedes into the context, and we focus on the waitstaff and other patrons swarming around her. Our attention alternates between the figure of Cléo and her environment. She stands out with her polka-dotted dress and dramatic gestures or blends into the café context as she quietly sips from her cup. Cléo's figure comes forward or recedes in the same way that a patch of black in a Léger painting can be perceived as both void and solid. Then when Cléo and her immediate environment appear misaligned in mirror reflections, Varda plays with picture plane fragmentation on film the way Picasso and Braque did on canvas. She also lets serendipitous events, like a street performer eating frogs, show through the final film, like bits of unpainted canvas showing through a Matisse painting.

Early critics chided Varda for what was deemed unnecessary formalism in her films, but recently scholars like Rebecca DeRoo have reassessed Varda's work in an expanded critical context that includes the visual arts. DeRoo's 2018 book on Varda, benefiting from research in Varda's archive, demonstrates the depth and breadth of her films' intellectual and artistic references. wto offer;

she studied at the Sorbonne and L'École du Louvre, and had several centuries' worth of pictorial knowledge at her disposal. By using a new critical lens that includes the visual arts, DeRoo counters those that would call Varda's formalism extraneous. Painterly sources are core to Varda's filmmaking; she "references Renaissance painting techniques to draw attention to the construction of depth of field and the cinematic illusion."[7]

Here we expand the field of reference for Varda's work by looking at her films through an architecture lens. Popular film criticism often defaults to assessing how well the story is directed and acted, with the occasional comment about the cinematography. Scholarly writing often focuses on what happens in the story. And yet what Varda calls her *cinecriture* or "writing with cinema" approach to filmmaking runs counter to this. For Varda, the film is not defined by the script alone. Rather, each component of filmmaking is a fresh opportunity to rewrite it; all elements of cinema, including the spaces in which the plot unfolds, contribute equally to its making. What if we looked at Varda's work as ghostly architecture that exists only while the film plays? The difference is subtle but significant. Rather than assessing the film as a script that has been enacted, we engage Varda's space and time constructs as a matter-of-fact, albeit immaterial, film architecture. The neurobiologist Antonio Damasio has found that human brains experience the space of stories and actual space in similar ways, so when we watch a film, we are mentally inhabiting its space.[8]

Early unfavorable reviews of *Cléo* and other Varda films criticizing her extraneous stylization of spatial contexts were biased toward the script and expected adherence to one or another film genre. But by looking at the films as space and time constructs, what we will term here Varda's *cinearchitecture*, we are able to better comprehend how she masterfully blends realism and artifice to create artistically powerful films that are also socially relevant. Varda uses the Parisian spaces she captures in her camera frames to examine the role of women in French society. A passerby ogles Cléo on the street, shopkeepers and assistants dress her like a doll, and she symbolically removes her wig and feathered robe to stop being the focus of everybody's gaze and start doing some gazing of her own. By setting up this character in a quotidian environment we can mentally inhabit, Varda implicates us all in Cléo's vanity and self-absorption; we too are part of the sociocultural community that puts undue emphasis on the appearance of women.

In sum, there are a number of liminalities in *Cléo*: the existing spaces in 1960s Paris both maintain their non-fiction veracity and are reframed as part of Cléo's fictional story, the film space we mentally inhabit is the result of visual constructs that rely on both two- and three-dimensional formal structures, and the film has both social and artistic intent. These apparent both–and contradictions are reconciled through an architectural reading of the film.

The theatricalized social portrait of La pointe courte

In her first film, *La pointe courte* of 1955,[9] preceding *Cléo* by seven years, Varda builds a film space, a cinearchitecture, that represents the French Mediterranean fishing village of the same name. We come to know this geographically and culturally unique place through alternating segments of two distinct stories, a couple taking some time out of their Parisian lives to talk through the aftermath of an affair, and the village residents' efforts to preserve their way of life in the face of financial struggles and unfavorable government regulations. Varda has maintained in several interviews that the idea for the film came from the two parallel stories in William Faulkner's 1939 novel *The Wild Palms*.[10] She was interested in how two separate narratives presented side by side could have an effect on each other just by virtue of their juxtaposition. But Faulkner may have had significance for Varda beyond a structural idea. He was rooted in the American South and an attentive documenter of the rural vernacular. Varda too is attentive to the social and cultural space of her own French South, and like Faulkner, she captures people and place so vividly it feels as if we are there. Young Varda had spent her summers in La Pointe Courte as a child, learning to mend nets well enough to get a summer job, and returns with a camera to document their specific economic and political struggles they face.

Varda makes a portrait of a place that has personal meaning for her, so *La pointe* could have easily become a poetic reminiscence of her childhood complimented with a more sober adult understanding. As a *cinéma vérité* exercise, for example, a camera would have jauntily recorded the streets of La Pointe as villagers looked up from their tasks to smile at lovely Arlette, all grown up (Varda legally changed her name to Agnès when she was 18 years old). Instead, she made extensive preparations prior to shooting the film. She took countless still photographs in order to determine how the town's spaces and their inhabitants would be framed. She wrote their linguistic expressions into the script to be repeated later in front of a rolling camera. Then she shot over 30,000 feet of film, an amount on par with the 30,000 feet of film that the early American filmmaker Robert Flaherty shot in the Canadian Arctic 40 years before.[11] Varda relentlessly catalogs the familiar the way others catalog the exotic.

This seemingly excessive thoroughness in researching and documenting a place is the foundation on which Varda builds her work betwixt the socially minded and the formally ambitious. Because her *cinecriture* approach makes each subsequent step in the filmmaking process a new opportunity to redefine the project, every aspect of the film must be diligently researched. At each stage, from planning what to frame and script, to post-production addition of narration and music, Varda takes the opportunity to rewrite the film a little, and to inextricably dovetail the ethical and the aesthetic.

If the formalisms in *Cléo* allude to women's position in French society, *La pointe* is an exquisitely framed and stylized social portrait. Varda rejects documentary objectivity because "you'd have to put fifteen cameras in one place and just let them film by themselves for five years; but even then the editing would be subjective."[12] While she revels in the real-life bits that slip into her camera frame, the film is always constructed. Even when in *Cléo* she brought us into the real space and time of a 90-minute Parisian afternoon, it was not a found space and time; rather, it was painstakingly constructed using both realism and artifice. This is Varda's position on technology, that the responsibility of the representation lies with the filmmaker and not with the camera's mechanical recording, no matter how ingenious or extensive; this approach that served her well later when she started working with digital cameras. *La pointe* employs formal-aesthetic means to achieve the social-ethical task of making a portrait of the villagers' plight.

The real spaces of La Pointe lend veracity to the film, make it easier to enter the story's mentally inhabitable spaces, and conversely, the story's constructed cinearchitecture reframes the existing spaces of the town. A liminal condition emerges from the doubling in *La pointe*, the filmic spatial construct, assembled through visual and narrative frames of La Pointe, the fishing village, which is now forever changed by the film. We see evidence that a film's story has real-life effects in its reframing of a place when tourism-dependent cities like New York dedicate resources to facilitate on-location filming; people want to visit the exciting, romantic, mesmerizing places they have seen at the movies. For Varda, the task in La Pointe, the place, was to uncover and document all its real-life details and squeeze out all its formal potential so that the resulting *La pointe*, the film, had both ethical and aesthetic value.

She builds the cinearchitecture of *La pointe* with a series of tableaux showing residents in direct and purposeful interaction with their environment, be it sitting around a lunch table, net-mending in a workshop, setting out in boats, sorting shellfish on the docks, hanging laundry in the wind, hiding the day's takings from government watchdogs, discussing political strategies, or gathering in a spot of shade for rest and conversation. The villagers and their quotidian activities are filmed as if framed by an imagined proscenium. There is often a wall in the space that is parallel to the picture plane of the film, with figures compositionally arranged in front of it, talking to each other using theatrical conventions, with heads turned but with the rest of their bodies facing more or less forward. Sometimes that wall has an opening that frames what is inside, and we see figures looking in or in the perspectival depth of the interior space. When the two-dimensional frame of the film is divided by an architectural element that extends beyond the top and bottom extents of the screen, like a column or the outside corner of a structure, one side of frame recedes and accordingly figures move forward and backward in that space. Making the edge of the dock parallel to the edge of the screen reframes the harbor into a kind of stage too. A documentation of the villagers' struggles could have simply involved recording their spontaneous utterances and aiming the camera at each person that speaks, without concern for the framing of the space. Varda assembles these staged quotidian lives into the film's cinearchitecture and theatricalizes the social portrait.

Varda made *La pointe* after working as a professional theater photographer and pays the same attention to the spatial framing and portraiture of the villagers as she had to the portraits of actors in leading roles. She ennobles every villager as an individual with a distinct body and life story. In this and other films, Varda uses formal techniques to elevate protagonists with beauty and grace, no matter their socio-economic standing. The theater where she worked, run by Jean Vigo, was also known for introducing French audiences to the alienation techniques of Bertold Brecht and *La Pointe* too is somewhat Brechtian.[13] After first extensively researching and documenting their daily life, Varda had the villagers themselves dramatize the scripted and framed representation. They repeat for the camera their own linguistic expressions reconfigured into a story and pose motionless in their living spaces, as if standing for a daguerreotype, in scripted arrangement. Varda forgoes the spontaneous utterance caught on camera for the highly stylized re-statement.[14] In the spirit of Brecht, we witness the social plight before us while remaining aware that we are seeing a fastidiously designed construction. Far from compromising the *verité* of the film, Varda's stylization is a kind of truth telling because it is being honest about the film's artifice.

The couple visiting from Paris, the only two professional actors in the film are also framed in staged tableaux. Unlike the residents, however, they are disengaged from their environment. They are too involved with each other to meaningfully engage the context around them, and as if to illustrate their mutual enmeshment, Varda shows us their two faces, the front view of one precisely aligned with the profile of the other, blending into one monstrous hybrid [predating similar shots in Ingmar Bergman's 1966 film *Persona* by more than a decade]. The couple wander through the center of town briefly but spend most of their time in the deserted outer reaches. They float through La Pointe's industrial landscape as if inside their own private psychological bubble, engaging in the existing conditions only when they are looking at where to step next. As they talk through their conjugal travails they are on literally shaky ground, navigating the obstacles of a working harbor in dress clothes and shoes. We follow them to the end of jetties and we linger with them inside an unfinished ship's hull, a whale-like interior that appears to have swallowed them up.

As with the residents' retelling of their own story, this too is a Brechtian representation of the relationship as Varda directs them to use monotone voices devoid of emotion. She shows us a couple's realistic impasse and not the facile romantic plots familiar from movies. There is no dramatic rupture or reconciliation, only two people trying to make sense of what they feel, and this lack of theatrics has the effect of calling attention to the spaces framed around them. But although the couple seem oblivious to La Pointe, La Pointe is not oblivious to them. It frames them in wood and steel, revealing as much about the relationship as the couple's dialogue. Varda frames their figures with La Pointe's industrial spaces so that protagonists and environment are fused in one inhabited spatial construct.[15] Perhaps we are privy to the couple's struggles in the context of workspace because, well, relationships need work.

Varda assembles the cinearchitecture in *La pointe* from staged tableaux that correspond to the two parallel stories in the film, the community's economic struggles and the relationship struggles of the couple; the film, like all of Varda's work, is positioned between the socially minded and the formally precise. Fellow French *Nouvelle Vague* figure André Bazin was instrumental in bringing *La pointe* to the 1955 Cannes Film Festival, and the film was also shown in Paris to critical acclaim. But because it was never distributed, until recently few people knew about it, and those who did logged it as the curious work of a naïf. For a long time she was considered peripheral to the *Nouvelle Vague* movement because she had not studied film. Varda herself promoted the perception that she was an inexperienced filmmaker until her 2008 autobiographical *Les plages d'Agnès*.[16] When she repeats her customary "I didn't study film," the cartoon cat Guillaume, representing her friend and fellow filmmaker Chris Marker, rolls his eyes. She may not have had specific experience in the industry when she directed *La pointe* in 1955, but the film already evidences a sophisticated understanding of cinema's visual and narrative structures. It is important to recognize Varda's sophistication and that *La pointe* is an artistic and intellectual achievement, rather than a lucky amateur effort. Besides her arts and humanities degrees from Sorbonne and L'Ecole du Louvre, Varda had professional photography experience and was highly trained in both its technical and artistic aspects. Chris Marker as Guillaume the cat rolls his eyes because Varda may not have studied film, but she studied everything else. With *La pointe* Varda started a filmmaking career that lasted six decades, and she now occupies her rightful place as a pioneer in the *Nouvelle Vague* cannon.

Food politics in Les glaneurs et la glaneuse

Diametrically opposed to *La pointe* is her 2000 film *Les glaneurs et la glaneuse* or "The Gleaners and I,"[17] as it was translated for English-speaking audiences. It is in color instead of black and white, shot with a portable digital camera that Varda carries in one hand instead of a cumbersome film camera that requires a crew to maneuver. She is the film's narrator and one of its protagonists, and the film is generally classified as a documentary instead of fiction, although as we have been arguing, all of Varda's film spaces combine reality and artifice. Still, if *Cléo* and *La pointe* are fictions with documentary elements, *Les Glaneurs* is a documentary with fictional elements.[18] What remains the same is Varda's commitment to addressing serious social issues with formal sophistication.

Les Glaneurs is arguably her most important project because its popularity and immediate critical acclaim prompted a reevaluation of her previous work, and because it initiated a new kind of Varda films. We are referring here to *Les plages d'Agnès*, *Visages villages* (2017),[19] and *Varda par Agnès* (2019),[20] all of which use cinematic-spatial approaches that were first used in *Les Glaneurs*. This and later films still build, frame by frame, what we are calling here a cinearchitecture, a complete environment that viewers mentally inhabit while the movie plays, but with some differences. The formal control is less overt, the presentation of real-life protagonists is more direct, and there is an added self-reflective examination of Varda's social and artistic intent.

Les glaneurs started in the fourteenth *arrondissement*, where Varda lived and worked all her life, at the *marché*, the heart of French food culture. Every arrondissement in Paris has an outdoor market serving the culinary needs of the neighborhood's residents with proper fish, meat, and cheese mongers. The market grocers will ask "*pour aujourd'hui?*" when they choose tomatoes for you that are ripe now or in a couple of days. On market day Parisians go home with select ingredients and perhaps a bit of gossip from their neighbors, so when Varda invites us to linger after the market closes and watch people of all ages scour discarded boxes for salvageable produce, she is pulling back the curtain on French food politics. The social commentary here is the revealed imbalance between an excess of food and those who rummage through the discards.

To capture this post-market scene, Varda propped her now inconspicuous digital camera on a sidewalk barrier and initially filmed the urban gleaners at a distance. These are not the composed tableaux of *La pointe* in part because digital filmmaking shifted the financial burden from shooting and developing the film to post-production. With a film camera the commitment to the shot happens at the time of filming whereas with a digital camera there is no cost until the final version of the film is transferred to physical film for theatrical projection. In *Les glaneurs*, Varda lets the camera roll to see what it could capture in its memory card. She still composes her formally eloquent cinearchitecture, but instead of meticulously staging shots as she does in *La pointe*, she does her compositional work afterwards, editing the footage into a choreography of bodies stooping, and adding music and narration that complete the construction of a very specific film space. These urban gleaning cinearchitectures bring the audience a visceral understanding of what it might be like to be in those spaces, bending over to pick up discarded produce; this is, after all, the power and promise of film, to transport us somewhere else, in this case a space that is physically adjacent but socially distant from the Parisian market day.

The shift to digital filming in this and her subsequent films allowed Varda to film more and in more places and this led to new kinds of liminality. One of the most referenced shots from the film is the camera's inadvertent recording of the lens cap as it hangs from its strap. Varda edited this aleatory moment into the film and called it a "dancing lens cap." We find the shot endearing because we recognize the moment of leaving some personal device running, but Varda is also saying something about our escalating entrenchment in all things digital. During the 1990s images became increasingly malleable. The Y2K scare that came to nothing nevertheless inspired great dystopian films by Catherine Bigelow and Wim Wenders, and the mostly northern European founders of the Dogme95 movement,[21] who set limits for themselves within the suddenly limitless possibilities of digital filmmaking. In this context, Varda's whimsical dancing lens cap is a comment on the discombobulation that at the time surrounded the making of images, and for that matter, the making of space too. The rogue camera disengaged from the eye keeps documenting, seemingly out of control, but all is well because the artist still gets to reframe it within a narrative—it's a dancing lens cap. At one point in *Les glaneurs* Varda stands still facing us and methodically brings the digital camera up to her eye. The shot is reminiscent of David Lynch's Mystery Man character doing the same motion in *Lost Highway* (1997).[22] The character in Lynch's film presents us with liminalities between physical and digital presences whereas Varda instructs us on the reflexivity of the gaze, here I am looking at you looking at me. Varda's cinearchitecture, the space we mentally inhabit as we watch the film, continues to be the result of reassembled pieces of reality, but in *Les glaneurs* and subsequent digital film work, we see more layered narratives that discipline the potential rampancy of digital film. There is also a larger scale range of film subjects, from lens caps to landscapes.

Before *Glaneurs*, Varda had made two other films about the Parisian market and food scene. In *L'opéra Mouffe* (1958), she places us inside the market crowd with a sequence of faces filmed at eye level and in *Daguerréotypes* (1975),[23] we spend time with a baker, a butcher, a hairdresser, and other shopkeepers, learning about their craft and standing with them at their counters as they wait on customers. Both films intimate that food in Paris has everything to do with the state of agriculture in the provinces, but *Les glaneurs* takes us to this vitally important part of French cultural identity. We spend time in the French countryside with rural gleaners, on post-harvest potato farms where Varda finds her now famous heart-shaped potatoes. Farm fields stretch in our visual field long and wide, brown blankets occupying most of the two-dimensional frame, and we linger there, unhurriedly. Then, we see performances on these earth stages, from a farmer who permits gleaning, from a lawyer who in full robes reads what the law allows, and from a dog that curiously has a red boxing glove around its neck.

Viewers that only know Varda's twenty-first-century work appreciate *Les glaneurs* for its light documentary style and playful asides, Varda filming one aging hand with the other or cupping it around a freight truck on the highway. But as with the dancing lens cap, there is significance behind the playfulness. Looking at her aging hand leads her to contemplate her own mortality, and those freight trucks bringing Parisians produce from the countryside represent the vicissitudes of French farming. When the trucks escape Varda's grasp, we are reminded that although an artistic practice gives us the power to see and show, effecting change may initially elude us.

The status of French farming is always a serious concern for Varda. Already in *Daguerréotypes* she muses how the shop keepers in rue Daguerre have family roots in rural France, and later, in *Visages villages* (2017), she is pensive about the farmer mainly works alone thanks to advances in farming equipment. As for her documentary light-handedness, compared to her earlier work, there is a more direct presentation of the people she meets; she is no longer pre-scripting what the gleaners or farmers say as she did for the villagers in *La pointe*, and she is less conspicuous about the tableaux she sets up. She continues, however, to very consciously build, frame by frame, a visually specific cine-architecture for us to inhabit, one that in *Les glaneurs* includes landscape space. shot of the painting of three gleaners by the nineteenth-century realist painter Jean-François Millet is a literal frame of reference. Varda's low to the ground shots fill up the screen with brown earth, making it possible for us to experience the expansive French countryside, and placing us alongside the gleaners, the potatoes seemingly within arm's reach. This is the low-framing viewpoint Millet uses in his painting to show the faces of the stooping gleaners. Varda continues to use pictorial references for spatial effect with the digital camera the way she had with a film camera.

In *Les glaneurs et la glaneuse*, Varda includes herself in the title as "*la glaneuse*," the specific feminine gender French word for gleaner, and when she looks through her camera right after posing as one of Jules Breton's *glaneuses* with a bundle of wheat on her back, she reminds us she is a gleaner of images. But why a gleaner and not a harvester of images? Are her leftover images like those leftover heart-shaped potatoes? There is nothing inherently ethical or aesthetic about the heart potato, but Varda makes it beautiful and denotative with her visual and narrative frames. The unusually shaped tubers are left in the field, exposed to sunlight, becoming inedible because they fall outside the size range requirements for shipment and sale. Food, and interesting food at that, is left to rot because industrialized contemporary food production and distribution functions best when everything is the same shape and size. Movies are similarly cranked out of studios, are they not? One after the next follows the same formulaic plot that producers believe is sure to please audiences. So yes, hers are gleaned images because they fall outside the expected range. With her heart-potato narrative, she transforms what does not fit the norm into something with unique aesthetic worth, and in the process she checks in on the agricultural heart and soul of France. That many a blog has been written about those wrinkly "eye" sprouting brown hearts affirms Varda's ethic-aesthetic liminal intent, that her place in the world as an artist is one of power because she can bring attention to issues of social importance.

Varda's stakeholders

The word "stakeholder," used in architecture to give inhabitants political agency, has an etymology that relates it to putting down stakes and defining a territory. In Varda's film spaces, the protagonists, whether real or fictional, help map out the ethical and aesthetic territory she covers. The Varda scholar Delphine Bénézet has argued that the marginalized who populate Varda's films, whether fictional or real, remain puzzling and difficult to categorize so that they are empowered through their newly bestowed singularity.[24] One such character central to Varda's oeuvre is Mona in the 1985 film *Sans toi ni loi*.[25] She is a homeless and angry young woman who is introduced to us through the people she encounters on the road, making us all collectively responsible for her position, just as we were complicit in Cléo's superficiality.

We enter the cinearchitecture of *Sans toi* through a broad view of vineyards in winter where the burning canes evoke funeral pyres. Almost immediately we come upon Mona's motionless body. Farmers and policemen stand around her for a while speculating about the cause of death, the conversation occasionally interrupted by the sight and sound of brushes cleaning wine stains off the town walls, ones that match those on Mona's clothes and face. Then we are in the ditch again, close enough to Mona's body to hear the sound of the zipping body bag, not unlike the sound of the missing sleeping bag that would have kept her warm and alive.

Then the narrator resets time, Mona emerges, as if born, from a bath in the ocean, and we begin retracing her steps through villages and countryside. Varda uses several structuring elements that anchor this film's cinearchitecture. Every so often we are in a tracking shot, Mona coming in and out of view. These walking sequences are linked with a soundtrack, like a rail running continuously underneath whatever else is going on in Mona's travels, keeping us cognizant of her ongoing journey. In this "*sans toi*" space, without a roof over her head, her space is an endless strip of road, landscape, and sky, with the occasional respite on a curious found object or sign. When she finds food and shelter, we enter with her into spatial constructions of partially built or partially accessible versions of home. The resultant cinearchitecture is a horizontal, open-air, continuously slipping space punctuated by fractional pockets of domesticity to which Mona only forms tenuous attachments and in which her presence is a temporary disruptor. This spatial construct allows Varda to present Mona without judgment or introduction. We only learn about Mona through the people she encountered who after her death, speak of the effect she had on their lives. Varda asks what collective behavior led to a 17-year-old freezing to death in a field.

Cinephiles might recognize this ploy from Orson Welles's (1941) *Citizen Kane*.[26] Both films begin after the title character dies alone, and both to puzzle who they were through those who knew them. But whereas Welles gives us Kane, the wealthy, powerful old man in a mansion, Varda gives us a penniless, disenfranchised young woman in a ditch. Varda's choice to tell us from the start that Mona is dead eliminates any hope that she might be saved, forcing us to reckon with the day-to-day reality of Mona's life. Varda the filmmaker is always challenging her audience, poking at biases, and piercing pieties by, for example, confronting us with a character like Mona who is both very much in need of help and very difficult to help.

The two wives in the 1965 film *Le bonheur* or "Happiness,"[27] possibly Varda's most controversial film, are compliant and domestic. They are opposite to lawless, roofless Mona but just as marginalized. In *Le bonheur*, François is married to Thérèse and has an affair with Emilie, who, after Thérèse dies, takes her place as wife and mother to his children. Varda has described this film as a perfectly ripe fruit with a worm in the middle because it is a feminist critique, but at the time audiences were unhappy that the cheating husband went unpunished. In another of Varda's films, *L'une chante, l'autre pas* (1977),[28] the two main characters are women and their respective romantic relationships are secondary to their friendship, exactly the kind of plot that offers women primary roles to play. But talking about it in a 1981 interview, Varda "always feel[s] betwixt and between," because the film "wasn't feminist enough for the feminists and too feminist for the others."[29] Recent scholarship, however, has recognized the nuances of the feminist arguments Varda makes with her work. *Le bonheur* is now understood as a critique of domestic bliss as women's highest aspiration.[30]

Varda bookends the cinearchitecture for this apparent happiness using two sharply defined seasons, one associated with the first wife Thérèse, and one with the second wife Emilie. Seasons figure prominently in Varda's films and provide spatial specificity to her narratives. *Sans toi ni loi* is set in winter, *Cléo de 5 à 7* is set in spring about to turn into summer, and *Le bonheur* is set in summer turning to autumn. We enter *Le bonheur* at the start of summer with the first wife Thérèse surrounded by luscious vegetation, tall grasses, and bunches of flowers. We leave the film in autumn, with Emilie, a former lover and now second wife, walking under old-growth tree canopies shading a brown and bare ground. In-between we follow François move with ease from his family life to his carpentry shop, from work to play, and from one wife to the next.

But perhaps the most defining element of *Le bonheur's* cinearchitecture is one added in post-production. As in *Sans toi ni loi*, Varda superimposes music over the footage for spatial and narrative effect. The Mozart pieces she chose lend the film an assertive rhythm to which all else must conform, just as everyone must conform to François's relentless and sure-footed patriarchy. His two wives, first Thérèse and then Emilie, inhabit a domestic space that is as perfectly orchestrated as the music. It is a picture-perfect happiness because with François at its center there are no competing demands. The word "*bonheur*" is appropriately a masculine noun in the French language because what we experience here is his happiness.

We go through a domestic sequence twice, the doubling creating one of the most interesting liminal conditions of Varda's oeuvre. The first time, with Thérèse, takes longer. It is already dominated by the rhythm and phrasing of Mozart's music, but it occasionally includes some dialogue. The second time, with Emilie, is much faster, with no dialogue; it is a balletic composition of household duties set to music. Emilie can slot into the role of wife and mother because Thérèse's participation in the household had less to do with who she was as a person and more with the service she provided. DeRoo has also noted how, copying magazine ads of the time, both Thérèse's and Emilie's hands are framed out from the rest of their bodies, emphasizing the two women's interchangeability and defining their value according to the household tasks they can perform.[31] Varda is critiquing the systemic patriarchy that defines the value of women by how smoothly they can provide for everyone's needs. Defined in this way, women's personhood is essentially denied. The worm in the fruit is not the extramarital affair; the tragedy here is the effective elision of women's individuality for the sake of a well-orchestrated life.

Between aesthetic and socio-political space

Today there is no question that Varda is a feminist filmmaker, just as there is no question that she is a leader of the French *Nouvelle Vague*. She made her first film in 1955 but it was only with the advent of digital technology that she was able to make the later audacious work, starting with *Les glaneurs et la glaneuse* in 2000. Varda took it upon herself to educate us about the tremendous design complexity involved in the making of her films in *Les plages d'Agnès*, made as she was turning 80, in *Varda par Agnès*, her final film released a few months after her death in March of 2019, as well as in the numerous interview videos and talks with live audiences recorded in the intervening decade. These are heuristic films and videos in which she reiterates, over and over, how her films address sociopolitical issues, yes, but always with aesthetic intent; what is beautiful is true and vice versa.

Digital technology makes it possible for old film stock to be restored and digitized, making all her oeuvre, at last, accessible around the world. Streaming services as well as the *Tout(e) Varda* DVD box, first assembled in 2012 but now including all her films, gives her work the distribution and viewership she never received when her films were made. "Look at that box," she says in a 2018 TED Talk, walking over and lifting *Tout(e) Varda* with both hands, "it's full of DVDs of all my films and other things. Sixty years of creation, not even four pounds."[32] The box is a body of work, but also the weight of a body in ashes for a smallish five-foot person like Varda. Was the director that in *Les glaneurs* filmed one aging hand with the other thinking about her own mortality again?

Finally, given that Varda feminizes "*tout*" in her DVD set as "*Tout(e) Varda*," and given that she calls *La pointe courte* "a film to read," one that "makes more of an impression retrospectively than while you're watching it,"[33] perhaps "*La pointe*" is a fortuitous title with which to start making a life's worth of films that say quite a bit about social and political conditions, and about the meaning and making of art. In French, the masculine "*le point*" is the word meaning purpose or objective, whereas the feminine "*la pointe*" refers to the physically shaped tip of something. This is what Varda is all about, making her *pointe*, using the tactile and the physical to anchor the conceptual.

NOTES

1. This writer was delighted to notice in a *Blacklist* episode that a site purportedly in Washington, DC was instead the Del Rio Diner in the Brooklyn neighborhood of Bensonhurst ("Marvin Gerard [No. 80]," Season 3, Episode 2, 2015).
2. *Cléo de 5 à 7* (1962), director Agnès Varda.
3. The status of Varda in the French *Nouvelle Vague* has been reassessed in recent years and speaks to the funding inequity that existed in France at the time that Varda started making films. She funded her 1955 film *La pointe courte* with a small inheritance she received at the time, money she borrowed from her mother, and the "sweat equity" of actors and crew members willing to work on her film for little or no compensation. The film was a critical success but never distributed widely and she was not able to obtain proper funding to make a film like *Cléo* until many years later. For a contemporary assessment of Varda's rightful place as a leader of the French *Nouvelle Vague*, see Scott, A. O. "Agnès Varda: The Filmmaker as Rigorous Friend." *New York Times*, March 29, 2019. Accessed December 20, 2021. https://www.nytimes.com/2019/03/29/movies/agns-varda-appreciation.html.
4. The reviewer incorrectly calls this Varda's first feature. She had already made *La pointe courte* in 1955 to critical acclaim at the Cannes Film Festival and in Paris, but the film was never widely distributed until much later. Bosley Crowther, "A French New Wave Drama: Cinema II Introduces *Cleo From 5 to 7*, Agnes Varda Describes Two Anxious Hours," *New York Times*, September 5, 1962. Accessed December 22, 2021. https://www.nytimes.com/1962/09/05/archives/screen-a-french-new-wave-dramacinema-ii-introduces-cleo-from-5-to-7.html.
5. See Rudolf Arnheim, *Film as Art* (Oakland, CA: University of California Press, 1968). Also, Sergei Eisenstein's work on film that encouraged contrasting diagonal compositions is an example of early twentieth-century theory that saw the simultaneous two-dimensionality and three-dimensionality of film. See Sergei Eisenstein and Jay Leyda, *Film Form: Essays in Film Theory* (San Diego, CA: Harcourt, Brace, Jovanovich, 1977).
6. *Ladri di biciclette (Bicycle Thieves)* (1948), director Vittorio De Sica.

7. Rebecca J. DeRoo, *Agnès Varda Between Film, Photography, and Art* (Oakland, CA: University of California Press, 2018), 30.
8. See for example Antonio Damasio, *The Self Comes to Mind: Constructing the Conscious Brain* (New York, NY: Vintage Books, 2010).
9. *La pointe courte* (1955), director Agnès Varda.
10. Also known as *If I forget Thee, Jerusalem*, the novel's chapters alternate between two separate stories, one about a man and woman fleeing her husband to live together as lovers, and one starting ten years earlier about an escaped convict. William Faulkner, *The Wild Palms* (New York, NY: Random House, 1939).
11. The project eventually resulted in the groundbreaking film *Nanook of the North* (1922). See Erik Barnouw, *Documentary: A History of the Non-Fiction Film* (Oxford: Oxford University Press, 1993).
12. From an interview with Pierre Uytterhoeven in 1962, as reproduced in T. Jefferson Kline, *Agnès Varda: Interviews* (Jackson, MI: University Press of Mississippi, 2014).
13. The early twentieth-century playwright Bertold Brecht developed an approach to theatrical productions that kept the audience from becoming emotionally involved in what they were watching on stage. He wanted his audience to respond rationally to his plays. His fellow Marxist and German political exile Walter Benjamin outlines the characteristics of Brecht's "Epic Theater" in an essay collected in *Illuminations*, Hannah Arendt, ed. (New York, NY: Schocken Books, 1968), 147. Contemporary artists continue to employ Brecht's methods to remind the audience that what they are seeing is an illusion. In film, an unscripted street event and a sudden break in the soundtrack remind us that what we are watching has been framed through a camera and edited in post-production.
14. The Brechtian alienation in the film is additionally emphasized by superimposing, in post-production, voices from actors over the video footage of the residents.
15. If the discipline of architecture is to learn from Varda's betwixt position, ably straddling ethics and aesthetics, it would behoove us to consider how her cinearchitecture indelibly joins the protagonists with their space.
16. *Les plages d'Agnès* (2008), director Agnès Varda.
17. *Les glaneurs et la glaneuse* (2000), director Agnès Varda.
18. For example, the online film database imdb.com https://www.imdb.com/name/nm0889513/. Accessed January 5, 2022.
19. *Visages villages* (2017), director Agnès Varda.
20. *Varda par Agnès* (2019), director Agnès Varda.
21. Richard Kelly, *The Name of this Book is Dogme95* (London: Faber and Faber, 2000).
22. *Lost Highway* (1997), director David Lynch.
23. *L'opéra Mouffe Daguerréotypes* (1975), director Agnès Varda.
24. Delphine Bénézet, *The Cinema of Agnès Varda: Resistance and Eclecticism* (New York, NY: Wallflower Press, 2014), 122–23.
25. *Sans toi ni loi* (1985), director Agnès Varda.

26. *Citizen Kane* (1941), director Orson Welles.
27. *Le bonheur (Happiness)* (1965), director Agnès Varda.
28. *L'une chante, l'autre pas* (1977), director Agnès Varda.
29. "Interview with Philippe Carcasonne and Jacques Fieschi" as reproduced in T. Jefferson Kline, *Agnès Varda: Interviews* (Jackson, MI: University Press of Mississippi, 2014), 107.
30. Susan Felleman, "'Show the Clichés:' The Appearance of Happiness in Agnès Varda's *Le Bonheur*," Acta Universitatis Sapientiae: *Film and Media Studies* 19, no. 1 (March 1, 2021): 17–34.
31. DeRoo, 53.
32. Agnès Varda, "Inspiration and good mood: THAT'S CINEMA!" TEDxVeniceBeach, February 23, 2018. Accessed July 16, 2021. https://www.youtube.com/watch?v=HmGap7-RxdA.
33. Interview with Michel Capdenac as reproduced in T. Jefferson Kline, *Agnès Varda: Interviews* (Jackson, IL: University Press of Mississippi, 2014).

REFERENCES

Bénézet, Delphine. *The Cinema of Agnès Varda: Resistance and Eclecticism*. London: Wallflower Press, 2014.

Bergman, Igmar, director. *Persona*. Copenhagen: AB Svensk Filmindustri, 1966.

Damasio, Antonio. *The Self Comes to Mind: Constructing the Conscious Brain*. New York, NY: Pantheon Books, 2010.

De Sica, Vittorio, director. *Ladri di biciclette (Bicycle Thieves)*, 1948.

DeRoo, Rebecca J. *Agnes Varda Between Film, Photography, and Art*. Oakland, CA: University of California Press, 2018.

Faulkner, William. *The Wild Palms*. New York, NY: Random House, 1939.

Felleman, Susan. "'Show the Clichés:' The Appearance of Happiness in Agnès Varda's *Le Bonheur*." *Acta Universitatis Sapientiae: Film and Media Studies* 19, no. 1 (March 1, 2021): 17–34.

Kline, T. Jefferson, ed. *Agnès Varda: Interviews*. Jackson, MI: University Press of Mississippi, 2013.

Lynch, David, director. *Lost Highway*. London: October Films, 1997.

Varda, Agnès, director. *La pointe courte*, 1955.

Varda, Agnès, director. *L'opéra Mouffe*, 1958.

Varda, Agnès, director. *Cléo de 5 à 7*, 1962.

Varda, Agnès, director. *Le bonheur*, 1965.

Varda, Agnès, director. *Daguerréotypes*, 1975.

Varda, Agnès, director. *L'une chante, l'autre pas*, 1977.

Varda, Agnès, director. *Sans toi ni loi*, 1985.

Varda, Agnès, director. *Les glaneurs et la glaneuse*, 2000.

Varda, Agnès, director. *Les plages d'Agnès*, 2008.
Varda, Agnès, director. *Visages villages*, 2017.
Varda, Agnès, director. *Varda par Agnès*, 2019.
Welles, Orson, director. *Citizen Kane*. Los Angeles, CA: RKO Pictures, 1941.

7

A Cross-Temporal Standstill

Michael Young

Film as a technological medium relies on the rapid substitution of still images to create illusions of movement and distortions in duration. These effects of montage often operate below thresholds of consciousness, altering perception and rewiring the human sensorium. Within the aesthetic manipulation of temporality lies important questions regarding attention, questions which bind cinema and architecture in unique ways. Walter Benjamin famously claimed that architecture prepared the human sensorium for cinema, as it is the "work of art the reception of which is consummated by a collectivity in a state of distraction."[1] It is only natural to ask how cinema has returned the favor.[2]

Examples abound comparing the experience of the modern metropolis to the shock juxtapositions of cinematic montage. Montage has been deeply influential on image making over the past century providing a conceptual and technical mechanism for the reuse of cultural detritus. Architecture itself is increasingly designed as a montage of predefined elements and programs, be they given by history, industry, or media. One does not have to look far to find the jump-cut implications in Rem Koolhaas's description of the effects of the elevator in *Delirious New York*,[3] Bernard Tschumi's reframing of architecture as ruptures and juxtapositions in sequences of programmatic events,[4] and the impossible spatial speculations of Giovanni Battista Piranesi notated as montaged sequences by Sergei Eisenstein and then theorized by Manfredo Tafuri.[5] This list could go on, and it has not even broached how photomontage radically transformed architectural image making to the point where it became the dominant mode of assembling images over the past half-century.

What follows in this chapter however is not focused on programmatic, spatial, or formal juxtapositions, instead attention will be given to the seamless sequences that create and distort sensations of movement and time.

There is no literal mechanism in architecture that directly parallels the reversal of motion in cinema. Instead, the connection is analogical. The experience of duration within a city or a piece of architecture is variable in its intensities. Much of this has to do with our own inner moods and movements, but a significant amount also has to do with how attention is manipulated—architecture's "state of distraction." As we will see, when cinematic motion is reversed, or in some instances crossed, the results are not simply things moving backward, but instead a redirection of attention to details, behaviors, and qualities that operate typically outside of or below conscious attention. Reverse motion releases a plethora of aesthetic effects that range from the uncanny to the humorous, the enchanted to the possessed, yet continually tie back to questions of realism even when they are incredibly strange. The chapter concludes with a suggestion for how cross-temporal montage—that is motions in two temporal directions simultaneously—can induce an aesthetic of standstill. This is not motionlessness, but an experience of multi-temporality as an acknowledgment of the random noise of the everyday. It is not static, but precarious, and through this, proposes an alternate relation to our environment that does not privilege an alienating distancing of critique, but instead includes us in the constant flux of interactions. Attention shifts into the mediated noise of the background, that is towards architecture.

Reversed processing

Media theorist Friedrich Kittler postulated that all technologies of mediation involve the storage, transmission, and processing of information, and it is through these three aspects that they can properly be differentiated.[6] Furthermore, "media" is in a constant process of combining prior technologies into new assemblages increasing storage, extending transmission, and expanding processing, all of which aim toward higher realism in "real time." Cinema is, and always has been, a multimedia apparatus. Let us pull apart a few of the elements. First, of course, is photography. At a material level, a photograph is the interaction of luminous energy with a chemically sensitive emulsion. This reaction is held on a film positioned to receive a pattern of light focused by a spherical lens and exposed through the timing mechanisms of a shutter. Mechanics, optics, and chemistry are coordinated in the apparatus of the camera, resulting in the storage of patterned intensities of light: photographs.

E. J. Marey and Eadweard Muybridge would use the sequential capture of rapid exposures uniformly spaced over time in their analytical studies of motion.[7] To achieve their studies, the photographic camera joined with an expanded set of components: multiple cameras linked to timed clocks, stroboscopic flashes, light reflective and absorptive materials, interior and exterior stage sets, industrially standardized mechanisms such as the revolver—all assembled to transform the continuous into the discrete, to stop time.[8] The desire to stop motion and the desire to animate motion are driven by different objectives yet require the same apparatus. Concurrently during the late nineteenth century, questions regarding time and motion were being approached from another direction. That is, at what rate, at what speed, is the human sensorium deceived into thinking that a series of still fragments is animate with continuous motion. These studies occurred at the intersection of the psychology and physiology of perception. Their focus: the persistence of vision in afterimages.[9] The questions are of no less importance than the relations between sensation and cognition; in other words, how is reality sensed? Machines such as the zoetrope and the praxinoscope would spin sets of slightly different still images persuading the viewer's sensorium that what they witnessed as occurring was not what they knew to be true.[10] Cinema married the rate of deception to the rate of capture to create the illusion of motion and time. The playback machine of the projector re-presented image sequences 24 frames per second by shooting electric light through constantly replaced photographic images stored on reels of translucent film.

Cinematic projections were consumed by large groups of people in darkened halls, a reuse of the architectural typology of the theater. The backdrop screen of the stage set was brought forward to become flush with the plane of the proscenium, the background now occupying the entire field of attention. These public performances were an important condition for early cinema both economically in terms of paid attendance and psychologically as the socially shared experience legitimized and verified communal hallucination. "Cinema" is this entire technological, perceptual, psychological, and sociological apparatus colluding to convince the human sensorium that it is seeing movement and experiencing time in a manner akin to natural embodied sensations. The motion of "motion pictures" is, however, not natural. Cinema as a technology of mediation is a series of frozen instances sequenced, shuffled, sped-up, slowed-down, and sometimes even reversed.

The illusions of cinematic movement are tied to cognitive experiences of duration and conceptual ideas of time. Although cinema is tuned to simulate stimulations to the human nervous system, it also alters how these systems attend to the world. Aesthetics is never simply a question of subjective taste regarding the evaluation of visual appearances; it also transforms neurological structures and processes of attention.[11] Cinema entwines the virtual with the real.[12] In other words, what constitutes reality includes the spatial and temporal experiences of technological mediations. This produces a fair amount of anxiety, but we should remember that the fear of deception through artifice has always been part of discussions regarding images. Typically, the focus has been on problems of verisimilitude, with the primary fear being that we would not be able to tell a real perception from an artificial simulation. This fear of "realism" is focused on questions of mimesis, but as Paul Virilio observes with cinema,

> The problem of the objectivization of the image thus largely stops presenting itself in terms of some kind of paper or celluloid *support surface*—that is, in relation to a material reference space. It now emerges in relation to time, *to the exposure time that allows or edits seeing.*[13]

Time within cinema can be considered as part of a post-Enlightenment ideal of rationalized regulation; a homogenous, objective, uniform, mechanized succession of 24 frames per second measuring the world as a steady click of a clocklike tick. However, this aspect only reflects the mechanisms of capture and projection—the experience of cinematic temporality is much more malleable. The montage techniques of jump cuts, cross-fades, speed dilations, and reverse motion produce what film theorist Andrew Tohline describes as film's "temporal plasticity."[14] These effects have a broad range of impacts on the viewer, from magical gasps to emotional reverie, from fantasy spectacles to uncanny realism.

The first noted reversed motion is almost mythological in its attributions of accidental discovery. The story goes that in 1896, the film clip for the Lumière Brothers' "Demolition of a Wall" was mistakenly fed into the projector backwards, and at this moment, conceivably, the handful of people present became the first humans to witness motion move in the opposite temporal direction.[15] This must have been quite a startling experience, for reverse motion is not something that our cognitive abilities can initially account for. The inverted "Demolition of a Wall" is also prescient given that over a century later it is often the destruction and reconstruction of architecture that fascinates filmmakers using reverse motion.[16]

Although it is tempting to slip into conundrums and contradictions raised by the notion of "time" moving backwards, reverse motion cinema is not the reversal of time. Time still moves in the same direction; a sequence of static images is seen at 24 frames per second. The difference is simply that the images are played back in the opposite sequence of their capture. The reversal is perceptual. Motion, and with it the experience of time in film, is what happens "between" images, in the blank black absences. Stillness is required before a sequence of images can create forward or backward motions.[17]

Montage exchanges

Montage is a spatial and temporal question. The selection of an image, and its placement in relation to another image, engages questions of order and original, sequence and adjacency, and the assumptions of how reality is assumed to proceed through time. How a series of fragmented images are stitched together can radically alter the associations and interpretations that a viewer will make.[18] Like collage, when two or more elements of disparate origin are brought together, the status of the seam conditions the effects that will be generated by the artwork. These seams can clearly express their artifice, or they can disappear into continuity. Discussions of montage in film are typically dominated by the techniques and concepts of sharp disjunctive cuts, but as important as editing is to any film, this bias overlooks the fact that the illusion of motion is created by montages with only slight differences, seamlessly accommodating retinal afterimages below thresholds of conscious attention.

Montage also occupies a prominent position throughout the twentieth century in art, architecture, and philosophy, its effects establishing key concepts for critical theory and discussions related to notions of the avant-garde in art, particularly those of estrangement, defamiliarization, appropriation, the death of the author, the shock of the new, and technologies of reproduction.[19] Underlying most of these discussions is the assumption that to reveal the seams of a montage is to raise awareness of the medium's artifice inviting viewer participation in the construction of potential meanings, the politics of montage requiring a clear dialectical tension between images. This terrain has been discussed so frequently over the past century that it will not be the focus in what follows. Instead, we will look at techniques that operate through seamless distraction to manipulate temporal perception.

When a film is run backwards, the ontological status of the reality represented is not immediately questioned. Stated more simply, the viewer accommodates what is seen as potentially real, only its sequence has been reversed. Our senses are constantly trained to distinguish sensorial information that feels "real" from something that feels "fake," a term that for all intents and purposes simply means that the artifice is noticed. Most special effects in movies attempt to remove the appearance of the artifice as they seek to embed the viewer in an alternate reality. When we notice these effects, we describe the scene as not "feeling" real. Reverse motion is a kind of special effect that is typically obvious; we understand its origin and can assign its cause. In other words, we know the object is not moving backwards, the film is. Most of the time.

Some usages of reverse motion, however, are not so easily reduced. They produce affects in excess of their technical explanation. They are strange, awkward, and often funny. They present startling experiences where some things seem to be moving forward in time while others are moving backwards simultaneously. A well-known recent example is Christopher Nolan's film *Tenet* (2020). Early in the film, a character offers this advice, "Don't try to understand it, feel it." This quote provides a clue as to what is at stake when temporal direction is variable, and causality undermined. Our senses engage the imagery and its motion, but our cognitive capacities cannot fully comprehend what is happening. The human sensory apparatus, neural processes, and conceptual logics are formed through perceptions and thoughts occurring always in the same forward temporal direction. Filmed sequences which present multiple temporal directions can be incredibly frustrating for some viewers and engrossingly pleasurable for others, but regardless, it demands modes of attention not present in our daily non-cinematic existence. Although one cannot experience reverse motion in "natural" unmediated perception, these scenes do not necessarily seek to alienate the viewer by pulling her out of the cinematic experience for a distanced critical judgment. Instead, the viewer can be fully enmeshed, yet also sense that there is something precarious, something not quite "right" regarding the reality they are perceiving.

"The Man from Another Place" is a character in David Lynch and Mark Frost's television series *Twin Peaks* (1990–92, 2017). He is an occupant of the red curtained room in the Black Lodge. He also has a very particular way of moving and speaking. The movements of walking, winking, smiling, clapping, snapping, and dancing are made uncanny. This is not a magical escape into the impossible, it is a strange realism. This affect continues with verbal speech. Phonics are in the right order, but the pronunciation, delivery, and clarity of linguistic content are disturbed. What is going on is most likely known to many readers already—the actors are performing backwards, including their dialogue. These sequences are then reversed so that in playback the action appears to run forwards.

Within the *Twin Peaks* storyline, the Black Lodge is not posited as part of the normal physical world in the Pacific Northwest where the story takes place. Yet it is also not quite allocated the status of fantasy. Instead, the best explanation is that it is a parallel reality, another dimension interfering with our world. As an architectural analogy, it exists within the pockets of the poché, swollen and withdrawn between the interior and exterior, between time as variable internal duration and shared external measurement. Importantly for these scenes, things do not appear temporally reversed. Actions are imbedded in moments that move forward, but there is something off, something wrong with the movements, and it is this tension that creates the strangeness.

In the film *Tenet*, some things proceed in a forward motion while other objects and actions are "inverted." For these, not only are their motions and behaviors reversed, but they are also moving backwards in time. Importantly, the two temporalities interact with each other as they cross. Objects and characters may be moving in one direction, but they are affecting, and are affected by, things moving in the opposite temporal direction. *Tenet* wants both temporal motions to appear equally real, together. The interaction means that they share a series of temporal instants. This requires the montage seam as a technical artifact to disappear, yet the tensions between distinct temporal trajectories remain. The rupture, the seam, and the disjunction are not on the visual surface but instead conceptually created as the viewer attempts to understand what it is that they are experiencing.

This conceptual tension between two temporalities holds several interesting possibilities for architectural aesthetics. The first is perhaps the most obvious that all buildings are at some level an assemblage of materials, techniques, and articulations that have disparate temporal origins. How these are held together to create a coherent reality is part of architecture's aesthetic responsibility. But the analogy can be pressed further. Objects could be conceived of as having their own temporality, that they interact with each other constantly, and that these interactions form the appearance of the background of reality, the majority of which the human sensorium is not attuned to and treats as random noise. It is common for architects to talk about the aesthetics of a project through allusions to other practices—art and technology two of the most dominant. But what would be an aesthetic that instead is completely non-referential, and considers architecture as something that senses and is sensed by its environment? This is not to locate sentience in the building, it is a suggestion that the aesthetics of any building are created by the effects recorded in its material assemblies of multiple temporal crossings. To speculate on this further, we need to unpack some of the differences between species of temporality in montage.

Four possible motions

I propose four categories for the relations between cinematic motion and temporal montage: Forward, Reverse, Reversed-Forward, and Cross-Temporal.

Forward Motion: 24 still images per second are captured, stored, and then played back in the same order. Their playback typically approximates the perception of normal visual motion but can also be slowed or sped up to elongate or compress the experience of time. Slow motion was originally achieved by adding duplicate frames into the sequence, while fast motion was achieved by removing frames. The rate of image projection is still at 24 frames per second, variability of motion speed is perceptual and its temporal plasticity cognitive.

An example of temporal plasticity in forward motion is Douglas Gordon's *24-Hour Psycho* (1993). The "film" is exactly what its title says—Alfred Hitchcock's film slowed down to occur over 24 hours. Static frames of high horror and drama are equalized with frames of the mundane and uneventful, dismantling the temporal tension of the original film and creating an alternate tension between the experienced time of viewing the work and the delayed progression of "movie" images no longer moving.

Another example is Chris Marker's *La Jetée* (1962).[20] Composed (almost) entirely of photographic images, the narrative of time travel is provided by the sound of a voice-over and the leaps of association that the viewer makes between still images. This is until the "moment" when an eye blinks to life compressing the past and future into the present. This is the only sequence in the film when motion is animate. It is in a way the opposite of conventional techniques of critical montage where cinematic motion is revealed to be an artifice of still images by emphasizing disjunction. This moment of perceived movement in *La Jetée* shocks not through the sharp jump of the cut, but because the viewer realizes that perceived motion happens beyond conscious control, one cannot help being deceived.

Reverse Motion: 24 still images per second are captured, stored, and then played back in the reversed order.[21] A film strip can only run in two directions, so it would seem obvious that one of the easiest manipulations is to play it back in the other direction. Reverse motions are the technological side-effects of the medium itself, in a way more basic than editing and splicing. In principle reverse motion seems self-evident, but in practice, there are some complications to note. There are two primary ways to produce reverse motion. One is to literally run the film backwards as the actions are captured. The second is to use an optical printer to copy a piece of film shot "normally" in a reversed sequence with the last image first and the first image last.[22] Although both achieve reverse motion, the first happens in the mechanics of capture, while the second is post-processed at the stage in which other visual effects are brought into the film. Post-processing has been present in cinema and photography throughout their entire history, the rise of digital technologies expanding the capacities and range of effects.[23]

As stated above, if a film sequence is simply reversed, the viewer is apt to treat it as a record of reality, the only difference is that it is played backwards. Somehow, we can tell ourselves that backwards and forwards are just directions for the playback of the same "faithfully" captured images. There are, however, important differences in the affective response to reverse motion that are worth noting. One is humor. Normal motions look funny in reverse, and this aspect has been taken advantage of quite often in comedy.[24] A simple reversal can redirect attention toward aspects of everyday bodily motion so internalized that we no longer see them.

Reversed-Forward Motion: This effect occurs when motion is reversed but is perceived to be temporally proceeding in the normal forward direction. This may seem like a subtle distinction, but its difference is important. In typical reverse motion, as discussed in the previous category, image sequences are clearly understood as normal action played backwards. Reversed-forward motion, however, progresses within the same timeframe shared by the characters and the viewer. The reversed sequence does not broadcast itself as a reversal. The easiest way is to splice a reversed montage next to a scene with normal motion, but sometimes these effects require certain things to be performed backwards so that when sequenced in the opposite order they appear to move forwards. In reverse-forward motion, the response is closer to enchantment or the uncanny. Petals return to a flower, objects leap off the floor as if under the influence of magnetism, cars stop on a dime, guns catch bullets, explosions contract. This is the world of *Twin Peak's* Black Lodge where the "The Man from Another Place" is also from another time.

One of the most provocative uses of reversed-forward motion is practiced by the artist William Kentridge. His medium is ostensibly "drawing," but what is under investigation is closer to how temporal erasure is shared between drawing and film. For Kentridge, drawing becomes the animate accumulation and removal of lines over time. The startling innovation is that in reversed-forward motion, erasure creates lines by withdrawing them. When these effects are combined seamlessly with normal forward motion, we have an aesthetic where the indexical traces of time are continually placed in doubt. This variability of temporal directionality allows Kentridge to explore issues of personal memory and cultural amnesia extended into political abuses that draw and erase lines between fiction and reality.

Cross-Temporal Motion: Cross-temporal motion requires that some things be perceived as moving forward in time while others are temporally inverted. There are three ways this has been explored in cinema. One, everything is normal, except a single object is reversed and behaving strangely. Two, the subject's point of view is reversed, which means that perceptually everything is backwards, yet you appear to be moving forwards within this reversal. Three, half the objects of the world are moving in one temporal direction, the other half is moving in the opposite, thus there is no clear frame to reference things against. There are important differences between these three versions of cross-temporal motion, but they all share one trait in common. The different temporal directions interfere and affect each other, thus they should both be considered real.

Tenet has scenes that qualify for each of these expressions of cross-temporality. In fact, the film is structured to walk the viewer through each level of complexity, in a way educating the audience on how they can understand what is being shown on the screen. Early in the film, bullets and other small objects are inverted to demonstrate the idea that a single object can be temporally reversed. One of the scenes has two of the actors "playing" with a bullet moving backwards in time. The bullet is "caught" by dropping it and passed back and forth between the characters as they learn to interact with the inverted object. It looks fun. The audience and the actors engage with this object as a magically enchanted curiosity, yet it requires a significant restructuring of assumptions regarding the categorical framework of time. This sequence implies that temporality could be in the objects themselves, not given *a priori* as a universal container or frame of reference. Objects share "instants" as they proceed in opposite temporal directions.

The second level is best presented when the primary protagonist of the story—known as "The Protagonist"—becomes inverted himself. In these scenes, the audience is brought with the character and immersed in what he experiences. The initial effect is that everything besides the protagonist appears to be moving backward, but it quickly becomes clear how incredibly disorienting it must be to be temporally inverted. Puddles splash up to meet your foot before it hits them. Driving a car requires your foot catch the acceleration pedal after it catches the break. An explosion of heat causes hypothermia. This is a strange world where everything is temporally turned upside down. The oddities of behavior are no longer isolated or attributed to small objects in the world; instead, "you" are the object behaving strangely.

The third level occurs when there appears to be equal parts moving forward and backward in time. In *Tenet*, this is best exemplified by the battle scene at the end of the film where half the soldiers are moving forward in time and the other half are moving backwards. This results in moments where the viewer sees the same thing twice, but from different temporal perspectives. The epitome occurs exactly halfway through the scene when a building is imploded and exploded simultaneously as one rocket is caught and another is fired. The building is a pile of material rubble on both sides of the explosions, just not the same pile. Matter and energy exist in a temporal flow where entropy increases regardless of the direction. Stability of the environment is a momentary instant temporarily assembled to appear coherent to the human sensorium.

The questions for architecture to gleam from reverse motion and cross-temporal montage are not that time can run backwards; it is the ways in which attention is directed and diffused. Cross-temporal montage displaces the hierarchical biases for what we should pay attention to, details begin to equalize and exchange relative importance depending on which temporal direction is attracting attention. The overall effect is an intensity of distraction—everything is potentially important or randomly meaningless. Minor things in the background become major events when inverted. Linear causality is dismantled as future events effect the past and vice versa. In painting this would amount to a fluctuation between figure and ground, but here it is the fluctuation of temporal directions that creates the inability to know where and to what one should attend. Since both directions are montaged together as equally real, the status of what is real and what is "effect" cannot be determined by an external reference frame. Each object brings its own temporal reality with it, its own importance as a random accidental occurrence in the world. The aesthetics are noisy, dense with information that eludes clear meaning, importance, or intent. The effect is akin to a flattening of causal relations between objects, everything is happening together all the time, attention to the temporal interactions is intensified, elongated, in a way, it stands still—which should seem a rather odd effect when talking about a climactic battle scene with exploding buildings.

Ontology and cinema

The aesthetic discourse on realism first emerges in nineteenth-century European painting and literature. Philosopher Jacques Rancière identifies this as a break with previous conventions regarding the relations between art and life.[25] Fundamental to Rancière's thought is the idea that aesthetics redistributes the sensible and through this opens political implications. An aesthetics of realism redirects attention toward the accidental, toward the interactions of daily life. The valuation of the paintings of Gustave Corbet, Édouard Manet, and others is not determined by the content described, but by the aesthetic qualities of the description. This not only shifts attention to the noise of the background, but also to such mundane things as the materiality of pigment, the patterns of brush strokes, or the flatness of the supporting canvas. These attributes are commonly associated with twentieth-century abstraction, yet they are initiated in nineteenth-century realism. The fundamental questions are the relations between art and life. Realism, as an aesthetic, puts into tension the relations between reality and representation. It is one thing to speak about what is real vs. what is fantasy for the characters within a film. It is another thing to speak about how the world depicted aligns with assumptions by the viewer. And it is another issue entirely to suggest that a movie can redistribute external qualities in the world, for example, in the realm of architecture. These three levels—one, the logic internal to an artwork; two, the relation between an artwork and an observer; three, the effects of an artwork on the reality of daily life—have been crucial questions for art over the history of Western culture. Many arguments for or against certain expressions, mediums, or practices depend upon linking or breaking relations between art and reality.

> The everyday is the fictional frame within which the truth of the experience of time must be manifested: the truth of the coexistence of this multiplicity of miniscule events that, produced at one and the same time, interpenetrate one another without hierarchy, outlining improbable arabesques that the novelist must transcribe as they occur and not as they *can* occur. But the principle of coexistence is also the

> principle of a sensible continuum shared by subjects of experience, the principle of this common world [...] is announced in the *random occurrence*.[26]

This quote is how Rancière explains Enrich Auerbach's insistence that the most abstract modern literature is also the most radical regarding realism.[27] The abstractions of twentieth-century literature of James Joyce and Virginia Woolf are seen as developments from the nineteenth-century realism of Gustave Flaubert and Émile Zola.[28] These works dismantled the linear narratives of plot by intensifying the focus on the details of random distractions in the background, which in effect, changed the way in which people paid attention to the world around them. This writing suspends time, disrupting the apparent organic relations of causal actions, and instead posits events, characters, thoughts, and objects that "glide over one another, penetrate into one another."[29]

The term "realism" is especially loaded in film studies given the presence of both documentary filmmaking and the influential movements of the French *Nouvelle Vague* and Italian Neorealism in post-World War II cinema. The film critic Andre Bazin was one of the leading proponents of both these movements and his writing often discussed notions of ontology in film and photography. Daniel Morgan describes Bazin's arguments as invested in realism, but not in the naturalism of a simple memetic resemblance between image and reality; instead the film image has its own ontology. He quotes Bazin, a "'photograph is not an image of reality ... There is ontological identity between the object and its photographic image'. Neorealism, then, constitutes a particular mode of responding to and articulating facts while respecting the reality of objects in the image."[30] Morgan continues,

> It is not about reflecting the world, but taking its reality and using sound and image to give it meaning. Bazin often describes this as a dialectic between the concrete and the abstract, the physical level of reality and the style that gives it meaning.[31]

Morgan positions Bazin's "realism" through the concept of "acknowledgment," for a film to engage realism it must acknowledge the reality conveyed through its medium and construct an aesthetic that directs attention to this as its specific style.[32]

Bazin is grappling with the intersection of different understandings of realism. Consider the qualities that are attributable to the Neorealism of post-war Italian cinema: light is natural daylight, sets are real city streets and building interiors, actors are often not "professional." Now, let us list some qualities attributable to French New Wave cinema: fragmentation through jump-cuts, sound disconnected from image, and actors directly addressing the camera. These would seem to be non-compatible notions of realism in cinema—one attempts to remove artificial stylistic fabrications, while the other makes the artifice of the medium painfully evident. Regardless of these clear differences, there are some important shared concerns. For example, minor details are as important as key narrative events, the events are the every-day and familiar, the camera is often hand-held, framing feels incidental and accidental, portions of dialogue and action are improvised, and the movements of the plots do not feel predetermined, they are open, random, like life. That they use different methods is of course important, but for both movements, the filmmaking techniques direct attention to the overlooked; both acknowledge the reality of the world and the reality of the image. Neither sees cinema as a neutral medium, but as an aesthetic tension between reality and its representation. To quote Morgan again,

> The open-endedness of acknowledgement means that it avoids being defined as a particular set of terms, emphasizing instead the process by which a relation between style and reality is generated. It does not specify the content in the relation so much as the specific mechanism that produces it.[33]

Aesthetics intersects with ontology in philosophical questions that ask how reality is made available to the senses. The philosopher Graham Harman claims aesthetics is first philosophy, for the sensible qualities of an object initially determine how we evaluate that object's ontological status.[34] This would seem to suggest that reality is fully dependent on the human sensorium, a popular theme revisited throughout the history of cinema from Georges Méliès (1861–1938) to *The Matrix* (1999),[35] but this is not Harman's argument. Instead, for Harman, sensual qualities are simply how objects relate to each other, the human as one object among many without hierarchical privilege.[36] What becomes compelling in the propositions of cross-temporal montage is that ontological status is not determined by *a priori* categories. One object may be moving forwards, the other backwards, but at the instant they interact, they are real for each other. Furthermore, this is an aesthetic relationship, for what any two objects share are the ways they are sensible to each other, how they attend to each other. This relation does not exhaust their reality—they are moving in opposite temporal directions after all—but it does locate ontology within the objects themselves as opposed to overarching relational constructions such as "nature," the subjectivity of an individual, or even assumed universal categories such as "time."

Aesthetics is fundamentally about how the world is sensed, focusing on the qualities available to a particular entity that is doing the sensing. Eyal Weizman and Matthew Fuller argue that

> aesthetics does not exclusively refer to a property or capacity of humans. It equally refers to other sensing organisms, such as animals and plants, which themselves

apprehend their environment. Further, we argue that sensing is also found in material surfaces and substances, on which the traces of impact or slower processes of change are registered, including in digital and computational sensors, which themselves detect, register and predict in multiple novel ways.[37]

The precarity of standstill

The effects of cross-temporal montage, such as the intensification of miniscule details to the point of distraction, the dismantling of cause-and-effect sequence, the loss of hierarchy between what should and what should not be attracting attention, can be likened to a standstill of temporality where an excess of ideas, perceptions, ruminations, allusions all happen simultaneously. The effect is a diffusion of attention, where objects interact and exchange value in a constant churning dynamic, precarious in its inability to predetermine causal relations. To quote the philosopher Martin Seel,

> Not just art, but also elsewhere, aesthetically perceived standstills enable an exciting self-engrossment with otherwise inconspicuous, concealed, or suppressed interrelations of change and persistence. Here, standstills become an event of examination and understanding in a special way. One fundamental phenomenon of aesthetic standstill is noise: the sensorily perceptible process of something happening without a clearly identifiable sense of what is happening. [...] With artistic objects, the time of their actual presentation interacts with the time presented through or in them.[38]

There is a phenomenological aspect that comes with this use of the word "standstill," so I want to be clear that I am not implying some transcendental timelessness achieved through an ethos of embodied experience. Nothing could be further from the case, as these effects in cinema, literature, and architecture are achieved through an extreme mastery of a technological media where visible artifice is concealed in the name of a conceptual paradox. What is important is how the mediation redirects attention to the world, sensing the environment as the accrual of traces of random occurrence. There is a range of possibilities for how these aesthetics manifest. Three that follow from the discussions above are: the awe of the enchanted, the strangeness of the uncanny, and the precarity of standstill.

When architecture enchants, it behaves like a special effect. This can be done with such expertise and subtlety that the result is astounding. These are the spatial experiences that reawaken a joy for being in the world. However, when done poorly these buildings possess a hubris of the heroic that can quickly descend into the effects of a gimmick. When architecture is uncanny, the familiar is made strange. At its best this leads toward a curiosity for a deeper involvement in the world, as what was thought to be the everyday holds something in reserve outside of initial assumptions. These moments can be very humbling, totally creepy, or utterly sublime. Eventually, however, we become accustomed to the effects and require new modes of engagement. On the one hand, this is good in that it keeps open desires for ever-changing aesthetic investigations. The problem though is that this can also become weird for weird's sake, effective but quickly digested.

Finally, what would an architecture of diffused attention, an aesthetics of standstill be? At one level, it is potentially meaningless, just another object in the environment. This initially sounds banal, which should not be completely discounted for the utmost banality is not without interest. However, a more productive implication may be that architecture does not need to define itself as meaningful or important by claiming difference from the mundane objects of culture and nature. Its provocations can instead erode ingrained hierarchies between foreground and background, context and causality, what we should and should not pay attention to. An aesthetic of precarity requires greater care within the environment, and this attitude seems to offer insight as to how architecture can involve itself in important ways with ever-accelerating ecological and social emergencies. An acknowledgment of coexistence is here preferred to that of critical alienation. This is a distinctly different starting point when asking how architecture can engage the crises it is constantly affecting and being affected by. As an aesthetics of standstill, architecture hurtles forward and backward simultaneously, asking us to attend to aspects typically ignored yet constituting what often is understood as the reality of the environment. The key questions shift away from which aesthetics an architecture should use—a style question—to how the aesthetics of architecture fluctuates attention—a temporal question.

NOTES

1. Walter Benjamin, "The Work of Art in the Age of its Technological Reproducibility" (1936), in *The Work of Art in the Age of Its Technological Reproducibility, and Other Writings on Media* (Cambridge, MA: Harvard University Press, 2008), 40.
2. "Let's Rock!" (The Man from No Place). It will be helpful if the reader has familiarity with several films before reading this essay. The two most important being Christopher Nolan's *Tenet* (2020) and the scenes in the Black Lodge from David Lynch and Mark Frost's *Twin Peaks* TV Series (1990–92, 2017).
3. Rem Koolhaas, *Delirious New York* (New York, NY: Monacelli Press, 1994).
4. Bernard Tschumi, *Architecture and Disjunction* (Cambridge, MA: MIT Press, 1994).

5. Manfredo Tafuri, *The Sphere and the Labyrinth* (Cambridge, MA: MIT Press, 1990).
6. Friedrich Kittler, *Optical Media: The Berlin Lectures*, trans. Anthony Enns (1999; Cambridge, MA: Polity Press, 2010), 26.
7. Friedrich Kittler, *Gramophone, Film, Typewriter*, trans. Geoffrey Winthrop-Young and Michael Wutz (Stanford, CA: Stanford University Press, 1999).
8. Ibid.
9. Jonathan Crary, *Suspensions of Perception* (Cambridge, MA: MIT Press, 1999), 29–30.
10. Ibid.
11. Warren Neidich, *Blow-Up: Photography, Cinema, and the Brain* (New York, NY: DAP, 2003), 25–26.
12. Neidich, 47.
13. Paul Virilio, *The Vision Machine* (London: British Film Institute, 1994), 61.
14. Andrew Tohline, "Towards a History and Aesthetics of Reverse Motion" (PhD diss., College of Fine Arts, 2015), 9.
15. Tohline, 36.
16. *Tenet* (2020), director Christopher Nolan.
17. Andrew Tohline, "Towards a History and Aesthetics of Reverse Motion" (PhD diss., College of Fine Arts, 2015), 13.
18. See Sergei Eisenstein and Lev Kuleshov.
19. This list includes but is not limited to: Bertolt Brecht, Manfredo Tafuri, André Breton, Theodor Adorno, Peter Burger, Walter Benjamin.
20. *La Jetée* (1962), director Chris Marker.
21. Andrew Tohline, "Towards a History and Aesthetics of Reverse Motion" (PhD diss., College of Fine Arts, 2015), 13.
22. https://en.wikipedia.org/wiki/Reverse_motion. Accessed July 30, 2021.
23. A quick note is necessary here regarding digital images. Although there are crucial differences between images as indexed through photochemical reactions and those detected and stored as numeric translations of electromagnetic data, the differences between analog and digital cinema are not primary to the ways in which sequences of still images are perceived temporally. Yes, it is easier to remove the seams of montage between images through digital post-processing. It is also easier to montage elements internally within a digital frame (the prevalence of green screen to CGI, e.g.). These methods of processing digital information alter the ways that movies are produced in significant manners. The perception of motion and its reversal, however, is still conditioned by a sequence of images, regardless of if they are captured and stored through chemical reactions or data signalizations.
24. Andrew Tohline, "Towards a History and Aesthetics of Reverse Motion" (PhD diss., College of Fine Arts, 2015), 32.
25. Jacques Rancière, *The Politics of Aesthetics*, trans. Gabriel Rockhill (London: Bloomsbury Academic, 2006), 16–19.

26. Jacques Rancière, "Fiction at a Standstill" from *Aesthetics of Standstill*, eds. Reinhold Gorling, Barbara Gronau, and Ludger Schwarte (Berlin: Sternberg Press, 2019), 184.
27. Rancière, 175–76.
28. Jacques Rancière, "Fiction at a Standstill" from *Aesthetics of Standstill*, ed. Reinhold Gorling, Barbara Gronau, and Ludger Schwarte (Berlin: Sternberg Press, 2019), 182–83.
29. Rancière, 183.
30. Daniel Morgan, "Rethinking Bazin: Ontology and Realist Aesthetics." *Critical Inquiry* 32, no. 3 (Spring 2006), 463.
31. Morgan, 464.
32. Morgan, 470–72.
33. Morgan, 471.
34. Graham Harman, *The Quadruple Object* (Winchester: Zero Books, 2011).
35. *The Matrix* (1999), director Lana Wachowski and Lilly Wachowski.
36. Harman.
37. Matthew Fuller and Eyal Weizman, *Investigative Aesthetics* (London: Verso, 2021), 33.
38. Martin Seel, "Standstills in Motion" from *Aesthetics of Standstill*, ed. Reinhold Gorling, Barbara Gronau, and Ludger Schwarte (Berlin: Sternberg Press, 2019), 275.

REFERENCES

Benjamin, Walter. "The Work of Art in the Age of its Technological Reproducibility (1936)." In *The Work of Art in the Age of Its Technological Reproducibility, and Other Writings on Media*, edited by Michael W. Jennings, Brigid Doherty, and Thomas Y. Levin, 19–55. Cambridge, MA: Harvard University Press, 2008.

Crary, Jonathan. *Suspensions of Perception*. Cambridge, MA: MIT Press, 1999.

Fuller, Matthew and Eyal Weizman. *Investigative Aesthetics*. London: Verso, 2021.

Harman, Graham. *The Quadruple Object*. Winchester: Zero Books, 2011.

Hitchcock, Alfred, director. *Psycho*, Shamley Productions, 1960.

Koolhaas, Rem. *Delirious New York*. New York, NY: Monacelli Press, 1994.

Kittler, Friedrich. *Gramophone, Film, Typewriter.* Translated by Geoffrey Winthrop-Young and Michael Wutz. Stanford, CA: Stanford University Press, 1999.

Kittler, Friedrich. *Optical Media: The Berlin Lectures*. Translated by Anthony Enns, 1999. Cambridge, MA: Polity Press, 2010.

Lynch, David, director. *Twin Peaks*. CBS Television Distribution, 1990–92, 2017.

Marker, Chris, director. *La Jetée*. Paris: Argos Films, 1962.

Morgan, Daniel. "Rethinking Bazin: Ontology and Realist Aesthetics." *Critical Inquiry*, 32, no. 3, (Spring 2006): 443–81.

Neidich, Warren. *Blow-Up: Photography, Cinema, and the Brain*. New York, NY: DAP, 2003.

Nolan, Christopher, director. *Tenet*. Burbank, CA: Warner Bros. Pictures, Syncopy, 2020.

Rancière, Jacques. *The Politics of Aesthetics*. Translated by Gabriel Rockhill. London: Bloomsbury Academic, 2006.

Rancière, Jacques. "Fiction at a Standstill." In *Aesthetics of Standstill*, edited by Reinhold Gorling, Barbara Gronau, and Ludger Schwarte, 174–190. Berlin: Sternberg Press, 2019.

Seel, Martin. "Standstills in Motion." In *Aesthetics of Standstill*, edited by Reinhold Gorling, Barbara Gronau, and Ludger Schwerte, 270–282. Berlin: Sternberg Press, 2019.

Tafuri, Manfredo. *The Sphere and the Labyrinth*. Cambridge, MA: MIT Press, 1990.

Tschumi, Bernard. *Architecture and Disjunction*. Cambridge, MA: MIT Press, 1994.

Tohline, Andrew. "Towards a History and Aesthetics of Reverse Motion." PhD diss. College of Fine Arts, Ohio University, 2015.

Virilio, Paul. *The Vision Machine*. London: British Film Institute, 1994.

Wachowski, Lana, and Lilly Wachowski, directors. *The Matrix*. Burbank, CA: Warner Bros, 1999.

8

Rituals, Reality, and Its Double

Alican Taylan and Mehmet Şahinler

> *And now, an ending. Where there was once one, there are now two. Or were there always two? What is a reflection? A chance to see two? When there are chances for reflections, there can always be two—or more. Only when we are everywhere will there be just one.*
>
> —Log Lady, *Twin Peaks*, Season 2: "Beyond Life and Death"

Here is an attempt at an anthropological analysis of the Black Lodge, the infamous space of pure evil in the series *Twin Peaks* created by David Lynch and Mark Frost. The analytical framework for this chapter will be the writings on rituals of anthropologist Victor Turner and specifically his essay, "Betwixt and Between." We must first lay some foundations by outlining what is meant by ritual in this text since it has always been difficult to define what a ritual really is.[1] In the famous words of anthropologist Edmund Leach, "even among those who have specialized in this field there is the widest possible disagreement as to how the word ritual should be used and how the performance of ritual should be understood."[2] As Indologist Axel Michaels emphasizes, ever since its emergence in the nineteenth century, the term has been central in defining religious, cultural, and social subject matter. The term was however used in a somewhat pejorative sense until the 1960s.[3] Ritual sounds tribalistic and religious. Yet, behind this ungrounded distinction separating rituals and modern secular life, anthropologist Victor Turner sees an uncanny similarity between some of our daily activities and what has been traditionally called a ritual. He points toward this similarity when he writes,

> Just as when tribesmen make masks, disguise themselves as monsters, head up disparate ritual symbols, invert or parody profane reality in myths and folk-tales, so do the genres of industrial leisure, the theatre, poetry, novel, ballet, film, sport, rock music, classical music, art, pop art, etc., play with the factors of culture, sometimes

> assembling them in random, grotesque, improbable, surprising, shocking, usually experimental combinations.[4]

Ritual, in that sense, is a practice in which reality is somewhat inverted, distorted, changed, or blurred and can be equally observed in premodern and modern societies.

What happens in a ritual is a conjunction of the so-called real and imaginary worlds.[5] The result of this coupling is the creation of what can be called ritualization. Ritualization is a way of distinguishing certain practices from other, mundane practices.[6] With ritualization, real and imaginary are intermixed and thus the ritual is distinguished from other activities.

Rituals, three criteria

The conjunction of real and imaginary alone does not necessarily create a ritual. For instance, in dreams, especially in vivid dreams, real and imaginary are certainly enmeshed. When one dreams, they occupy the real (physical tangible space of the body) and the imaginary (intangible space occupied by the mind). Dreams alone however still lack a crucial aspect of ritualistic practices, for dreams are but a mundane occurrence in daily life. What is then a second necessary condition for a ritual? Dreams can become part of a ritual, but only with the condition that they are somehow performed. For example, Iroquois believed that what people see in their dreams had to be enacted while awake to avoid illness.[7] They created dream-guessing practices, symbolic representations of death, violence, and revelations as performances. Iroquois weaved a ritual around dreams. Without this performative aspect, it would be hard to call them rituals at all. The attribution of meaning to dreams and acting on them systematically appears as an important performative criterion. Another example where dreams play a critical and authoritative role is the rite of passage of Omaha boys into adulthood.[8] Omaha boys, like other North American Indians, go alone into the wilderness to fast and pray.[9] If they dream that they receive a woman's burden-strap, they feel compelled to dress and live in every way as women for the rest of their lives. They are then known as *mixuga*. Here again, it is important to note that it is the contextualization and transubstantiation of dreams that are weaved into the ritual, and not simply the dream itself.

A similar point can be made for hallucinations. When a person hallucinates, it can be argued that real and imaginary worlds are intermixed. A physical condition, toxicity, or a hallucinatory substance can create such conjunctures. It is a distinguished form of perception that can be quite performative.

Still, hallucinating alone does not seem to be a form of ritual. Although hallucinations can certainly be part of a ritual, they alone cannot establish it. Here, old shamanistic practices can present a clue for establishing a distinction between hallucination and rituals. Even when their powers are needed to heal an ill member of society, shamans never perform their healing ritual without the presence of an audience.[10] In a sense, the audience gives the shamans their abilities. Without the audience, the shaman is powerless. This relationship between the performer and the audience, between stage and seats, is an inseparable part of ritualistic practices.[11] In that sense, performances and audiences are unbreakably interconnected. For example, it would be hard to say that what has been called a "prisoner's cinema," "the trains of brilliantly colored and varied hallucinations which come to console or torment those kept in isolation" is a ritual.[12] However, collective practices that cause hallucinations like native American ant ingestion,[13] or Oceanian collective Kava consumption,[14] are undoubtedly some examples of ritualistic practices, because of their performative nature.

We now have three criteria for defining rituals. Ritual, first, is a practice in which reality is somewhat inverted, distorted, changed, or blurred. Ritualization occurs when (1) a mundane practice is transubstantiated, intermixing the real and imaginary; (2) rituals must then have a performative aspect. They must have an enactment, sometimes with life-changing consequences; and (3) they directly or indirectly require an audience.

We need to keep in mind that the real/imaginary conjunction does not necessarily imply a completely fictional narrative. Quite on the contrary, the tie to the real is critical in setting up a ritual. What is imaginary in a ritual can be a set of rules valid for a specific period, in a specific space. For example, board games create imaginary, even magical worlds, with specific rules, patterns of conduct, and norms. They however do not necessarily fictionalize. Players can remain who they are in real life while competing or cooperating during the timeframe and in the space of the game. To borrow and adapt Johan Huizinga's term, a ritual creates a "magic circle" in which social arrangements change.[15] "Within the magic circle," as Katie Salen and Eric Zimmerman emphasize,

> special meanings accrue and cluster around objects and behaviors. In effect, a new reality is created, defined by the rules of the game, and inhabited by its players. Before a game of Chutes and Ladders starts, it's just a board, some plastic pieces, and a die. But once the game begins, everything changes. Suddenly, the materials represent something quite specific. This plastic token is you. These rules tell you how to roll the die and move. Suddenly, it matters very much which plastic token reaches the end first.[16]

Reality and its double

A threshold defines the boundary of the magic circle, the space where the rules of the "real" world are bent and shifted for the duration of a ritual. Not unlike the magic circle that David Lynch's characters must step into in the woods to access the Black Lodge in *Twin Peaks* (1989).[17] Similarly, in Lars von Trier's *Dogville* (2004),[18] lines are chalked on the stage, recreating a village. Or as in Buñuel's *The Exterminating Angel* (1962),[19] characters are stuck in a living room and cannot get past the doorway, an invisible threshold.

Certain filmmakers assume the authority that the "elder" holds in rites of passage. They position their viewers as neophytes for the duration of the film. Turner comprehensively describes the role of the elder in rites of passage in his essay, "Betwixt and Between." He observes that there exists "a set of relations that compose a social structure of highly specific types" between elders and neophytes.[20] Elders are imbued with an absolute authority that is not based on legal sanctions. Instead, the authority is self-evident and represents the absolute, "axiomatic values of society in which are expressed the 'common good' and the common interest."[21] This is very valid for filmmakers who from the twentieth century onward garnered an unprecedented authority over their audience by capturing their attention for prolonged durations (compare the distracted state most people are in when viewing a painting in a museum to the hours spent in front of a screen watching a single film, from a single filmmaker). We chose to watch films. This creates an equalizing effect on all "neophytes," the viewers: "if complete obedience characterizes the relationship of neophytes to elder, complete equality usually characterizes the relationship of neophyte to neophyte."[22] All viewers become equals for the duration of the film, watching in silence the presented work. This equalizing effect extends to both the period before and after the projection. Before the film starts, the theater is typically dimly lit, and people who arrive early speak quietly, if they do at all. After the film, the crowd usually leaves in silence.

Filmmakers who successfully assume this role of the elder will then take on an important responsibility. Turner introduces a concept he calls the "communication of the *sacra*" as the heart of the liminal matter for him. *Sacra* is the cultural component of a ritual. We will see here that the creation of a magic circle is a key component for these filmmakers in communicating the *sacra*. Turner defines and classifies the *sacra* in a rite of passage in three parts: (1) as the exhibition: "what is shown," (2) as actions: "what is done," and (3) as instructions: "what is said." Turner observes that "a striking feature of such sacred articles [what is shown] is often their formal simplicity." He further notes that "it is their interpretation which is complex, not their outward form."[23] In effect, Lynch's portal into the Black Lodge in *Twin Peaks* is a simple circle, Von Trier's village in *Dogville* is made of rectangles, and Buñuel's unleavable space in *Exterminating Angel* is a simple room. In premodern rituals, "the exhibition" includes evocatory instruments and sacred articles such as relics of deities, aboriginal *churingas*, or sacred instruments. Within the ritualized spaces shown by the filmmaker, their characters take actions, communicating the *sacra* of the film.

In *Twin Peaks*, the Black Lodge is a space of sheer evil. It is a space where the actions of all characters are distorted, where their speech becomes robotic, and the rules of physics are bent. The Black Lodge is for Lynch a literary device, a space that distills down the complex personalities of characters in the "real world" into their pure "evil" counterpart. The main protagonist, agent Dale Cooper played by Kyle MacLachlan, along with the neophyte spectator, receives sets of instructions and prophetic statements from the "dark" side. Like the instructions that Turner describes for premodern rituals, Lynch's characters deliver prophecies to the protagonist and subsequently to the viewer, such as "that chewing gum you like is going to come back in style," (humoristically) or "we will meet again in 25 years" (the third season of *Twin Peaks* was filmed 25 years later).

Lynch's spatial ritualization is a complete transfiguration of reality, creating dream-like sequences using jump cuts extensively in a sensorially intense space. Floors have black and white striated patterns, rooms are delimited by red curtains but have no walls, furniture appear and disappear, a jazzy soundtrack is interrupted by screams, etc. Furthermore, the spatial organization of the Black Lodge is incoherent. A corridor does not necessarily lead to the same space twice. Lynch's space is a bodily, visceral experience. His *sacra* adapts archaic ritual artifacts into the modern world: a classical Greek sculpture is placed in the middle of a room or a gold-plated antique vase sits behind two characters where one steals the other's soul.

Lynch, perhaps intuitively, perhaps consciously, further replicates certain tropes that Turner observes in the communication of *sacra* in rites of passage: disproportion/transfiguration, monstrousness, and mystery. For example, the giant played by Carel Struycken is a mysterious and very tall character who inhabits the Black Lodge, with a "real-world" counterpart room service waiter played by Hank Worden, much more "normal" in size. The Black Lodge is hence a space of ritualization, which blurs and distorts reality. Similarly, the character of the Man from Another Place, another inhabitant of the Black Lodge, is a red dwarf who gives clues as to who killed Laura Palmer to the main protagonist agent Dale Cooper through appearances in the latter's dreams. The communication between Dale Cooper and the inhabitants of the ritualized space of the Black Lodge through Cooper's dreams is another element that ties the series to ritual studies. The connections between dreams and monsters have been observed and interpreted through the ages in various ways. A common reading explaining the presence of monsters and humanoid animals in ancient cultures and their rituals relies on the so-called "primitive" societies seeing themselves as part of the animal kingdom. "If the exaggeration of single features," according to Turner, "is not irrational but thought-provoking, the same may also be said about the representation of monsters."[24] According to McCulloch, who wrote the entry for "Monsters" in the *Encyclopedia of Religion and Ethics* (1913 edition), monstrous masks/figures that are often seen in the liminal period of initiations are products of "hallucinations, night-terrors and dreams." "As man drew little distinction (in primitive society) between himself and animals, as he thought that transformation from one to the other was possible, so he easily ran human and animal together. This in part accounts for animal-headed gods or animal-gods with human heads."[25]

Turner however holds the opposite view to McCulloch. He thinks that "monsters are manufactured precisely to teach neophytes to distinguish between the different factors of reality, as it is conceived in their culture." Turner references William James's "law of dissociation" to clarify the problem of monsters. The so-called law of dissociation states that when a variation in an object with *a* and *b* qualities is introduced, say as *ax*, this new combination makes the differences between qualities *a*, *b*, and *x* evident.[26] For Turner, it is not the terrorizing or bemusing qualities of monsters that are supposed to teach the neophytes, by way of submission. Elders, on the contrary, alter, distort, blur, and grotesquely reassemble pieces of reality in totally unique configurations. This incites neophytes into rethinking objects, persons, relationships, and features of their environment they previously took for granted.

Lynch's introduction in *Twin Peaks* of a monstrous, animalized Laura Palmer in the Black Lodge, as opposed to the idealized and cherished young woman she was as perceived by the people of her town, is a perfect example. In the series, the character of Laura Palmer is the epitome of feminine beauty in popular aesthetic standards. At the same time, her personality is rebellious, outspoken, adventurous, and defies mainstream conceptions. She is beautiful and flawless in every way. Once we meet her again in the Black Lodge, she is physically still the same, but everything has changed. Her movements are slow, and her voice is robotic and distorted. In one memorable sequence, her eyes become turquoise, and her stare becomes animal. She transitions from a Greek statue pose into having an animalistic behavior, screaming in a dark room with flashing spotlights on her, and, still screaming, she approaches agent Dale Cooper, who flees the room. If her quality *a* is her charming personality and *b* her seductive appearance, the introduction of *ax*, the animalistic behavior in a distorted reality, dissociates the unity of her real-life character and shows it to the neophyte viewer. Beauty then becomes an object of reflection for the viewer through processes of componental exaggeration and dissociation by varying concomitants.

Questioning reality

To open up the subject by way of conclusion for this chapter, these discussions around the distortion and blurring of reality in rituals and *Twin Peaks*, and the effects of aesthetic manipulations such as rendering something grotesque or monsterly are directly adjacent to prevalent interests in realism within architectural theory today. The didactic processes of disfiguration and deformation deployed by ritual elders interestingly resemble processes of estrangement experimented by certain contemporary artists, architects, and designers. Speculative realism theorizes a flat ontology among objects. Artificial intelligence produces imagery that precisely works through similarity, exaggeration, and dissociation. Photogrammetry makes the manipulation of photographic material easier than it has ever been, blending three dimensional geometries with their surface properties. Big data allows anyone to access a nearly infinite archive of stock imagery and information online, ready to be manipulated. In other words, we live in an age of constant deformation, dislocation, translation, and transubstantiation. The lesson to be learned from Turner is then the critical potential of these processes. His work on liminality creates a continuous thread between premodern ritualistic practices and a contemporary lineage of filmic, architectural, literary, philosophical, and other artistic practices. Turner reads in premodern rituals and the artifacts involved in them a promiscuous intermingling of prevalent norms of a society, experience, and knowledge, always imbued with a pedagogic intention. For him, disfiguration and distortion are methods for placing an emphasis on what is being distorted or disfigured. The sphinx refers to the human head in abstract, specifically because the human head sits on a lion's body and has lost its unity. For Turner, the symbolism of the sphinx emerges from the tension created by "intellect contrasted with brute force."[27]

Lastly, Turner introduces in his essay a special type of *sacra* he calls the *sacerrima*, or "most sacred thing."[28] The *sacerrima* is best described as an artifact of mystery. In ancient cultures, it often references myths about the origins of the world. Turner here quotes anthropologist Lloyd Warner who would call these "nonrational or nonlogical symbols." When they come into play, he suggests, "such factors as data, evidence, proof, and the facts and procedures of rational thought in action are apt to be secondary or unimportant."[29]

The play on non-logical symbols is perhaps Lynch's area of predilection. Throughout the series, the director disseminates large quantities of non-rational elements that the rational-minded viewer tries at first to interpret as scientifically explainable narrative threads. Slowly, they must however give in to the supernatural occurrences of the depicted world. This is precisely when, in Warner's terms, rational thought becomes secondary or unimportant. The very existence of a supernatural order that characters accept as such further consolidates the *sacerrima* in the storyline. Supernatural elements like the Black Lodge have consequently irrational spatial properties. Both in ancient rituals and contemporary artistic practices, the irrational does not necessarily stem from the ignorance of scientificity but can, on the contrary, be a device to emphasize and question factors of culture that are usually taken for granted within a purely rational framework. Ritual studies then become a portal for questioning reality. Understood as a practice in which reality is inverted, distorted, changed, or blurred, rituals and their rich analytical framework studied by anthropologists like Victor Turner open uncharted territory for spatial investigations.

NOTES

1. Many social scientists proposed different definitions, some emphasizing the distinctive character of ritual, others stressing its congruity with almost all kinds of human practice (Bell, *Ritual Theory, Ritual Practice*, 70–71). Some anthropologists like Max Gluckman proposed a necessary differentiation between different kinds of rituals (Max Gluckman. *Essays on the Ritual of Social Relations* [Manchester: Manchester University Press, 1962], 23).
2. Edmund R. Leach, 1968. "Ritual," in *Encyclopedia of the Social Sciences*, vol. 13, ed. David L. Sills (London: The MacMillan Company and the Free Press, 1968), 520–26.
3. Bell, *Ritual Theory, Ritual Practice*, 3; Axel Michaels, *Homo Ritualis: Hindu Ritual and Its Significance for Ritual Theory* (New York, NY: Oxford University Press, 2016), 19–20.
4. Victor W. Turner, *From Ritual to Theatre: The Human Seriousness of Play* (New York, NY: PAJ, 1982), 40.
5. Clifford Geertz points to this relation between the real and imaginary in rituals. He writes, "In a ritual, the world as lived and the world as imagined, fused under the agency of a single set of symbolic forms, turn out to be the same world" (Clifford Geertz, *The Interpretation of Cultures*, 2000 ed. [New York, NY: Basic Books-Perseus Books Group, 1973], 112).
6. Catherine Bell writes,

> In a very preliminary sense, ritualization is a way of acting that is designed and orchestrated to distinguish and privilege what is being done in comparison to other, usually more quotidian, activities. As such, ritualization is a matter of various culturally specific strategies for setting some activities off from others, for creating and privileging a qualitative distinction between the "sacred" and the "profane," and for ascribing such distinctions to realities thought to transcend the powers of human actors.
>
> (Bell, *Ritual Theory, Ritual Practice*, 74)

We agree that a ritual has to be orchestrated in a way that separates it from other activities. But this distinction doesn't necessarily call for another distinction between sacred and profane activities. The sacred and profane are conjured in ritual practices, such as coming of age rituals, marriages, funerals and so on.

7. Anthony F. C. Wallace, "Dreams and the Wishes of the Soul: A Type of Psychoanalytic Theory among the Seventeenth Century Iroquois," *American Anthropologist*, 60, no. 2 (1958): 234–48; David Graeber, *Toward an Anthropological Theory of Value: The False Coin of Our Own Dreams* (New York, NY: Springer, 2001).
8. The Omaha tribe is a Native American tribe that resides in what is now northeastern Nebraska and western Iowa. They were dispossessed of most of their lands by the United States of America through a succession of treaties starting with the Fourth Treaty of Prairie du Chien in 1830.
9. Turner, Victor. *The Forest of Symbols: Aspects of Ndembu Ritual* (Ithaca, NY: Cornell University Press, 2002), 100.
10. Metin And, *Oyun ve Bügü: Türk Kültüründe Oyun Kavramı* (İstanbul: Yapı Kredi Yayınları, 2012).
11. Ronald L. Grimes, *The Craft of Ritual Studies* (New York, NY: Oxford University Press, 2014).
12. Oliver Sacks, *Hallucinations* (New York, NY, Toronto: Alfred A. Knopf, 2012), 97.
13. Jan Dirk Blom, *Dictionary of Hallucinations* (New York, NY: Springer, 2014), 30.
14. Ibid., 297.
15. Johan Huizinga, *Homo Ludens: A Study of the Play Element in Culture* (London: Routledge, 1980).
16. Katie Salen and Eric Zimmermann, *Rules of Play: Game Design Fundamentals* (Cambridge, MA: MIT Press, 2003), chapters. 9 and 3.
17. *Twin Peaks* (1989), director David Lynch.
18. *Dogville* (2004), director Lars von Trier.
19. *The Exterminating Angel* (1962), director Luis Buñuel.
20. Turner, Victor. *The Forest of Symbols: Aspects of Ndembu Ritual* (Ithaca, NY: Cornell University Press, 2002), 101.
21. Ibid., 102.
22. Ibid., 103.
23. Ibid.
24. Ibid., 105.
25. Cited in Ibid.
26. William James (1918), quoted in Ibid.
27. Ibid., 106.
28. Ibid., 107.
29. W. L. Warner (1959). *The Living and the Dead* (New Haven, CT: Yale University Press), quoted in Ibid.

REFERENCES

And, Metin. *Oyun ve Bügü: Türk Kültüründe Oyun Kavramı*. İstanbul: Yapı Kredi Yayınları, 2012.

Bell, Catherine. *Ritual Theory, Ritual Practice*. New York, NY: Oxford University Press, 1992.

Blom, Jan Dirk. *Dictionary of Hallucinations*. New York, NY: Springer, 2014.

Buñuel, Luis, director. *The Exterminating Angel*. Mexico City: Gustavo Alatriste, 1962.

Geertz, Clifford. *The Interpretation of Cultures*, 2000 ed. New York, NY: Basic Books-Perseus Books Group, 1973.

Gluckman, Max. *Essays on the Ritual of Social Relations*. Manchester: Manchester University Press, 1962.

Graeber, David. *Toward an Anthropological Theory of Value: The False Coin of our Own Dreams*. New York, NY: Springer, 2001.

Grimes, Ronald L. *The Craft of Ritual Studies*. New York, NY: Oxford University Press, 2014.

Huizinga, Johan. *Homo Ludens*. London: Routledge, 1980.

Leach, Edmund R. "Ritual." In *Encyclopedia of the Social Sciences*, vol. 13, edited by David L. Sills, 520–26. London: The MacMillan Company and the Free Press, 1968.

Lynch, David, director. *Twin Peaks*. Los Angeles, CA: CBS Television Distribution, 1990–1992, 2017.

Michaels, Axel. *Homo Ritualis: HINDU Ritual and Its Significance for RITUAL THEORY*. New York, NY: Oxford University Press, 2016.

Sacks, Oliver. *Hallucinations*. New York, NY, Toronto: Alfred A. Knopf, 2012.

Salen, Katie and Eric Zimmermann. *Rules of Play: Game Design Fundamentals*. Cambridge, MA: MIT Press, 2003.

Turner, Victor W. *From Ritual to Theatre: The Human Seriousness of Play*. New York, NY: PAJ, 1982.

Turner, Victor W. *The Forest of Symbols: Aspects of Ndembu Ritual*. Ithaca, NY: Cornell University Press, 2002.

Trier, Von, Lars, director. *Dogville*, Columbia: TriStar Film Distributors International, 2003.

Wallace, Anthony F. C. "Dreams and the Wishes of the Soul: A Type of Psychoanalytic Theory among the Seventeenth Century Iroquois." *American Anthropologist*, 60, no. 2 (1958): 234–48.

9

The Sensual Character of the Betwixt

Graham Harman

Phenomenology and the sensual

We begin with a small dose of phenomenology. Edmund Husserl launched this school by calling for a return to "the things themselves."[1] By this, he did not mean Immanuel Kant's "thing-in-itself" beyond all human access, which Husserl viewed as an absurdity.[2] The whole point of phenomenology is to get rid of speculation about what may or may not lie beyond the phenomenal sphere, whether it comes from Kantian philosophy or even from natural science. Instead, phenomenology asks us to focus exclusively on what is directly *given* to thought. Husserl's motto "to the things themselves" means a return to the phenomena, not to the unknowable noumena. This step has led to a predictable controversy that is still with us today. Does Husserl elide reality itself and give us nothing but mere appearances? That is the critique made by object-oriented ontology (OOO), though most Husserlians see no problem here. The phenomenological subject is not limited to appearances to the mind, they say, since we are always already outside ourselves amidst the "intentional objects" that populate the world. This is the only realism we can ever have, they contend, and the only kind worth having.

Often lost in this dispute is Husserl's key insight, which runs diagonally across the realism/anti-realism dispute: the discovery that even if phenomenology limits itself to what is given and rejects any talk of an "external world," there is a new rift *within* appearance that cuts between objects and their own qualities. An intentional object remains self-identical even as its numerous qualities (or "adumbrations") constantly change. Whereas David Hume saw in objects nothing more than "bundles of qualities," with the implication that the slightest change in quality will change the object into something new altogether, Husserl is at pains to emphasize that the object is one thing and its shifting adumbrations quite another.[3] In OOO terminology, this is called the SO–SQ tension, or the rift between sensual objects and their sensual qualities.[4] Yet Husserl takes another radical step that goes beyond the usual dispute over whether he is enough of a realist. Namely, not all of the qualities of an intentional object are dispensable. True enough, the senses give us nothing but accidental adumbrations of any apple, pear, or lamppost. But each of these things must also have some invariant core that makes them what they are since otherwise all things would be identical once we scrape away their sensual qualities. As Husserl sees it, the intellect is able to grasp the underlying real qualities of an intentional object even though the senses cannot. Hence, although Husserl dismisses real objects such as Kant's thing-in-itself, the question of reality emerges in his philosophy anyway, through the back door of qualities. For even the hallucination of a unicorn has a real essence that makes it different from the hallucination of a centaur or anything else. We need only doubt whether Husserl is right to draw a major distinction between the intellect and the senses, with the former aimed at the real or eidetic qualities of objects and the senses only at the sensual ones. This deeply rationalist presupposition seems to grant too much power to the intellect. For as Martin Heidegger later noted, both the intellect and the senses reduce any object to a state of presence-at-hand (*Vorhandenheit*), both of them equally distant from the being of things.[5] In a sense, Heidegger merely repeats the error elsewhere, with his claim that human *practical* activity has a deep relation to things that the intellect and senses do not. But for OOO, praxis reduces objects to a present-at-hand simulacrum no less than other mental activities do.[6] Beyond all such human comportment things simply are what they are, and any human relation to an object will always fall short.

Of course, OOO pushes things another step further than this. It is not only human or animal activity that fails to do justice to the things themselves: objects cannot make direct contact with each other either. Whereas for Kant the noumena were a special burden of finite human beings, OOO treats finitude as lying at the core of every relation, including purely inanimate ones. A strong precursor of this theory is found in the philosophies of Alfred North Whitehead and later Bruno Latour.[7] Yet both of these path-breaking thinkers take this step at the high price of a purely relational theory of entities, treating any non-relational surplus in things as a sad remnant of Aristotelian substance theory: or as a "vacuous actuality," in Whitehead's terminology. But the path opened up by Whitehead enables us to dream once more of a *philosophical* theory of the relations between inanimate entities, one not dominated by the typically modern prestige of natural science as the master discourse on every possible topic. Unless we follow Whitehead here, we will remain within the basic modern outlook that I have called "onto-taxonomy," or the notion that the cosmos consists of two and only two basic kinds of entities: (1) human thought and (2) everything else.[8] Unless we take this step we will remain onto-taxonomists, which means that we will remain modernists. Stated differently, we remain within the familiar permutations of Kant's outlook and its Hegelian or phenomenological modifications, while still unable to take any basic forward step in philosophy.[9]

Art vs. the literal

Unfortunately, most existing proclamations about "the future of philosophy" still operate within an onto-taxonomical framework. Those who say that Jacques Lacan is our best path forward, for instance, are satisfied to reduce "the Real" to an impasse or trauma of formalization, which means that the Real is nothing more than a residue that humans cannot master.[10] Nothing is said, and supposedly nothing can ever be said, about relations between objects in which human thought is not one of the relata. "The future of philosophy" becomes nothing more than a projection of the modern deadlock where most contemporary thinkers remain confined. The future is reduced to a "far-out" version of where we already stand. This holds equally well for two other pre-eminent "philosophers of the future": the German idealist F. W. J. Schelling and the French phenomenologist Maurice Merleau-Ponty, who attempt highly futuristic theories that leave the onto-taxonomy of modernism intact.[11] To repeat, it is not enough to empower the "world" side of the equation in an apparent challenge to idealisms that grant too central a role to thought. What is needed is to discard the presupposition that the thought-world relation provides the two central terms of dispute. Whitehead is much closer to clearing the path for us, though again, his ultra-relational model cannot properly account for the autonomy of individual things. The problem with this outlook is that things are capable of many relations but not reducible to any of them, or even to all of the possible relations that might be imagined. Literary critics have long been aware that a poem cannot be paraphrased by any number of critical assessments of it. This is not just true of poems, but of anything in the world.[12] Rationalism in philosophy is essentially the false doctrine that reality can be paraphrased, replaced by some prose description or other, even if the proviso is added that we can only approach such descriptions "asymptotically."

In any case, sensual reality exists. Note that by this term I do not mean "sensible" reality, as if it were a matter of the senses *as opposed* either to the intellect or to everyday practices. In OOO terminology, "sensual" includes the senses, the intellect, practical comportment, and all other human, animal, or merely causal dealings with the world. Every relation is a sensual relation in which objects do not confront each other directly, but only in the form of translations or caricatures. Sensual reality is thus a kind of universal ether that fills the space between all things, and is the place where all relations must occur. In the terms of the anthropologist Victor Turner, the sensual is "betwixt and between."[13] But we should note further that the sensual ether comes in two distinct forms, both of them crucial. In one sense, the ether is a *medium* in which we stand at any given moment, and is usually not noticed consciously. This is what Marshall McLuhan means by "medium": the fact that we are on social media these days rather than reading newspapers is far more important than any accidental differences in mere *content* between the two media.[14] A Marxist proclamation on Twitter is not the same thing as an identical statement published in a printed gazette. But along with the sensual ether considered as a *medium*, it also takes the form of specific sensual objects, which we might call *mediators*.[15] In the thought of McLuhan, not only is the car a medium that enables most aspects of modern life but it is also a mediator that can trigger what he and his late son Eric called "reversals" or "retrievals," meaning that the car—like all other media—contains the seeds of its own demise, meaning its replacement by new media.[16] A further parallel can be found in Roland Barthes's distinction, in photographs, between the general atmosphere or *studium* of the photo and the *punctum* embodied by a specific element that captures the viewer's attention and can transform our sense of what the photo is about.[17]

It is on this note that we turn to a discussion of art. Let us adopt the currently unpopular word "beauty" as a name for what is produced by art, though not only by art. In everyday speech, the opposite of the beautiful is the ugly. Yet in a deeper sense, beauty and ugliness are not really opposites, but more like a pair of cousins. This is true not only in the sense that something can be "so bad it's good," as when an originally garish pattern of colors, a tasteless building, or a wretched novel is so horrible that it eventually attains a certain degree of charm for the beholder. More importantly, the beautiful and the ugly are united in their ability to make a rupture with average, ordinary entities of daily life that make no strong impression on us one way or the other. Stated differently, beauty and ugliness are joined in opposition to the banal literalism that surrounds most of us at most times. Here there is no aesthetic experience at all, but simply a kind of bland neutrality.

Thus, I would propose that the enemy of art is not the ugly; instead, the enemy of art is *literalism*. The case of Marcel Duchamp is merely the exception that proves the rule: although he inserts a literal urinal or bicycle wheel into a gallery context, their very insertion into this context prevents them from being the literal devices we encounter amidst everyday life.[18] However much we may try to reduce these gestures to social scandals—as my fellow formalists tend to do—there is at least some residual aesthetic effect generated by the clash between the literal and aesthetic gestures in this case.[19] But the really important point here about literalism, which has been universally missed, is that in literal experience an object is no different from its qualities. In other words, literalism mistakes objects for "bundles of qualities," just as Hume does in his philosophy. It was Husserl who drove an initial wedge between the two, despite his ultimately idealist refusal to countenance real objects. The sensual (intentional) object in Husserl—we saw—was characterized by its difference from its own sensual qualities in phenomenal experience and its own real qualities in intellectual intuition. What Husserl shows us so clearly is that Hume is not just an empiricist, but a literalist; this should be no surprise given that empiricists never manifest any special difficulty in describing sense experience in simple prose terms. Since the most obvious opposite to literalism appears in metaphorical language, we should take a quick look at metaphor.

Jacques Derrida is widely known for the thesis that there is no such thing as literal language.[20] The reason he says so is because he is looking in the wrong place when defining what the literal means. For Derrida as for Heidegger, the chief enemy is any form of *presence*, any claim that reality itself can come directly to view; it is seldom noticed that they say so for different reasons. For Heidegger, literalism can be countered by the simple *absence* of something, its withdrawal into an obscurity that no mental act can fathom. Derrida's critique is more radical, though in my view less convincing. Namely, absence for Derrida is never enough to subvert presence, since the absent thing remains "self-identical," which Derrida treats as a form of "self-presence."[21] I hold that no such thing as "self-presence" actually exists, not even in introspection with its famous difficulties. Here Derrida seems to take Hegel's word for it, but OOO does not accept Hegel's identification of substance with subject in the first place and hence does not view substance as the sort of thing that even attempts to become directly present to itself.[22] For this reason, there is no risk of literalism in the sense of direct presence. Instead, literalism comes from the second opposition that is recognized by Husserl but never by either Derrida or Heidegger: the difference between the sensual (intentional) object and its two kinds of qualities. But this is exactly where literalism occurs: in the attempt to deny this difference between objects and qualities, which both Derrida and Heidegger tacitly do. Thus, we have now shifted the terms of dispute: literalism occurs when an object is taken to be nothing more than a bundle, and aesthetics occurs where the split between object and qualities is made overt.

Let us take as our example a simple and pedestrian metaphor drawn from everyday life. My wife Necla and I drive a beautiful red 2017 Mazda CX-5. We are completely satisfied with this car, which has served us well, and would not trade it in for another. Nonetheless, it has not escaped our notice that the CX-5 is sometimes jokingly called "the poor man's BMW." Of course, poverty is surely an exaggeration in this case—the vehicle cost us somewhere in the low $30,000 range, a good bit for a couple of university professors—but all metaphor contains a degree of exaggeration anyway, since otherwise it would be a literal statement instead. In any case, we are all familiar with harmless witticisms of the "poor man's X" type, and at this stage of the phrase's history, it is barely even offensive. In the present case, we might rewrite the statement as follows: "the CX-5 is a BMW without luxury." In this stripped-down form, the statement is barely metaphorical anymore, though we can still catch just a glimpse of an aesthetic structure. First, the remark creates an apparent identity between the Mazda and a comparable BMW, though qualifying it by removing the luxury from the Mazda. Thus, what we initially have in mind is a BMW surrounded by vaguely sensed poverty qualities. But it is difficult to imagine *literally* an impoverished BMW, and therefore this famous German luxury car becomes inaccessible to us. Since the BMW withdraws from direct view, what object remains on the scene to support the poverty qualities that the metaphor invites us to think? It cannot be the Mazda, because then we would simply have a literal experience of the Mazda as a bundle of stipulated pauper's qualities. The only remaining possibility is that I myself, the one who hears and vaguely grasps the metaphor, am the sole real object able to sustain it. In short, I am a theatrical auditor of the metaphor and personally perform the absent BMW while sustaining the supposedly impoverished qualities of the Mazda. The statement is not literal for the simple reason that the usual bonds between Mazdas, BMWs, and their respective qualities have been tampered with to such an extent that there is no possibility of viewing either car in literal terms. Neither can be reduced to a bundle since bundles are precisely what the metaphor dissolves.

There are other things that are true about aesthetic experience, but we can satisfy ourselves here with the following. Whereas literal objects are fully relational beings, existing in relation with those who view and speak about them, the aesthetic object cuts itself off from its context. The mere fact that the BMW "withdraws" from the metaphor, even as it is named, is evidence of this. To withdraw, to use that fabled Heideggerian term means that something secludes itself in its private reality, revoking its place in its previous relations. While this may sound controversial at first hearing, it is nothing more than what Kant already established in the *Critique of Judgment*.[23] In that highly influential work, Kant argues that an artwork is incommensurable with both concepts and personal preferences. Thus, the artwork cannot be reduced to any prose meaning at all. But neither can it be reduced to *utility*, which makes Kant suspicious of the beauty not only of humans and horses (which too often inspire lust and the wish to ride them, respectively) but even of architecture. This great aesthetic discipline is removed by Kant from the sphere of pure beauty for no better reason than its usefulness, which emphasizes his view of the non-relational character of beauty all the more.

A new sense of formalism

Here we encounter the root problem with Kant's theory of art, and indeed with the usual sense of formalism more generally. For what the formalist really detests is not all relations, but a very specific one: the relation between a human and a non-human. It is clear from Kant's discussion of artworks that he primarily wants them to be severed from all links with purely human faculties, despite the odd twist that he is more interested in the universal human faculty of judgment than he is in the works themselves. This orientation is reversed by such formalist critics (and admirers of Kant) as Clement Greenberg and Michael Fried, who ask us to turn attention to the works themselves rather than to the deep structures of our own minds.[24] Yet this reversal merely emphasizes the point that Kantian aesthetics, and the formalism that grew from it, is a basically onto-taxonomical enterprise. According to this attitude there are two great kingdoms in the cosmos, the human and the non-human, and never must the two be conflated. This is the unstated central principle of practically all modern philosophy, of which Kant is obviously among the great heroic figures.

What Kant neglects, and what Latour sees more clearly than anyone, is that many or most objects in the world (Latour would say all objects) are neither purely human nor purely non-human, but *hybrids* composed of elements of both domains.[25] Once we see the ubiquity of hybrids, then the meeting of human and non-human in a new composite object no longer seems especially threatening. For even if the experience of an artwork consists in a relation between the work and a beholder, this relation is not merely a relation, and therefore not merely literal. Instead, one's relation with an artwork is itself a new, third object, one that cannot be exhausted either by ourselves in recollection or in any observer trying to describe our interaction with the work. From this it should be clear that relations can be de-relationized, at least with a bit of work. Hydrogen and oxygen relate to form water, yet this new chemical is not just the sum of its ingredients; instead, it has a new reality and bears new properties not found in either of its constituents. The same holds for any beholder and any artwork—say, Rembrandt's *Nightwatch*—since this aesthetic experience is something more than either of the two terms taken in isolation, and has nothing to do with most of the millions of other properties of both the painted canvas and its human observer. In this sense, contra the principles of the early Fried, *all* art is theatrical; it is to Fried's credit that his historical work on Gustave Courbet and Édouard Manet later led him to the opposite of his initial thesis.[26]

As a further corollary of this discussion, formalism can no longer maintain Kant's favored stance of disinterested contemplation toward the artwork, or indeed toward any sort of beauty. Given the need to fuse beholder and object into a new, third entity, it might even be the case that the more heated our comportment, the better. Or at least this seems to be Dante's conclusion in *The Divine Comedy*, one of the least Kantian works to be found in the entire literary canon.[27] Dante presents an uncompromising cosmos consisting of love and hate, and this seems to be a better match for our new conception of aesthetics than the notion of a calm and skeptical observer. Indeed, it might even have implications for the whole of our lived culture, which grants the highest merit to "cool" disinterest, detachment, and the inability to be surprised by events no matter how extreme. It is high time for passion to rise again on our list of approved modes of comportment. Given that we have managed to rehabilitate the status of relations within a formalist context, at least in so far as they can also be de-relationized, we need not follow the usual formalist path of disdain for the inclusion of socio-political and biographical factors in an artwork. Marxist or feminist thoughts can be de-literalized, and in this way, they have every right to appear at the heart of aesthetics. Needless to say, if they occur there as nothing but a literal statement, then they are better left to pamphlets and speeches; art is not a safe vehicle for direct prose utterance, which easily becomes distorted or redirected under aesthetic conditions. Yet we must also emphasize that every aesthetic phenomenon ought to have strict conditions for entry, and in fact already has such conditions. Even the most emphatically "site-specific" artworks never enter into dialogue with the whole of their sites, but at most with a half-dozen or so. All art is formalist in the sense that all art is anti-literalist, but a broader conception is needed of what counts as "form." In this respect, I am indebted to the work of such literary critics as Anna Kornbluh and Caroline Levine, who show that forms spread well beyond the boundaries of art, and structure politics and society themselves.[28]

As I contended in *Architecture and Objects*, this completely changes the aesthetic status of architecture as well.[29] For Kant, the designer and the builder are destined for a low status in the eyes of the muses, given their regrettable inclusion of "usefulness" among the other, more aesthetic virtues. But again, we have seen that the mere relation of usefulness is not enough to make an object literal. A function can be detached from its relations no less than a beautiful form can be. The term I have used for this is "zero-function," a topic left for the following section of this chapter. But the fact that architecture cannot avoid grappling with this problem, under penalty of becoming just another form of sculpture, entails that architecture is uniquely equipped to lead the way toward a new aesthetics after Kant, the single figure who has most dominated aesthetic thinking in the past two centuries and more.

In keeping with the theme of this anthology, we should also ask what Kant might have thought about two important genres of art that did not yet exist in his time: photography and cinema. My best guess, though it is hardly more than that, is that Kant would have recognized cinema—but not photography—as a legitimate art form. The basis for saying so is that Kant's favorite form of art was literature, and what literature shares most closely with cinema is a temporal element. While it might technically be possible to view different portions of a painting over time to create a synthesis of viewpoints on it, and even more possible to do so in the case of sculpture, there is a sense in which Fried was right to claim that visual art is instantaneously present. We take in a painting—and to some extent even a sculpture—at a single glance, however long it might take our eyes to scan each portion of such works in greater detail. One could never say this about a novel or a film, which are not only temporal, but which compel us to experience their parts in a definite order. There might seem to be an exception in a case like the film *Of Oz the Wizard* (1939),[30] in which the entire original of *The Wizard of Oz* is rearranged in alphabetical order, word by word. But here we have an exception that proves the rule, since the alphabetical order of the film—however novel—is just as compulsory for the viewer as the order employed in the original film. Among architects, the young Peter Eisenman made a similar case for architecture as a temporal art: a building cannot be experienced instantaneously but must string together a series of views, usually anchored in simple geometrical forms as an aid to the inherent feebleness of memory.[31] Of course, in architecture the order of experience is not quite as rigid, aside from the fact that the façade will normally be experienced before the interior. But the relative flexibility in exploring a building is already enough to differentiate architecture from its fellow temporal arts, literature, and cinema. Perhaps a closer analogy would be that aspiring new art form, videogames, in which landscapes are explored as the flow of gameplay allows.

It may be worth asking here about a possible "liminal" experience midway between two genres, one in which the exact genre we are experiencing remains ambiguous. I have already mentioned the need to distinguish between architecture and sculpture by insisting that the former have some sort of use value. Yet in the case of deliberately designed austere monuments, we are frozen somewhere between these two genres. The large size of the Washington Monument, the Gateway Arch in St. Louis, or the Arc de Triomphe in Paris immediately suggests architecture rather than sculpture. And true enough, one can also enter these structures physically in a way that most sculpture does not permit. But in some sense, the fact that tickets are sold for tourists to enter these monuments, just as one can enter and explore a house, is a distraction from their mostly non-architectural character. Insofar as they have a core "function" at all, it is to punctuate the skyline of a city, not to provide an interior space to be occupied. Frequent visitors to St. Louis, for instance, may have gone to the top of the Arch once or twice, but such visits pale in comparison to the hundreds of distant glances they have no doubt taken at its unforgettable form. If we ask about the liminal space between architecture and cinema, videogames again come to mind. Like architecture, a videogame landscape can often be explored in any order of the player's choosing; like film, such a geography is composed of fleeting images rather than bedrock, soil, granite, glass, and sunlight.

In concluding this section, it is worth pointing out that Kant has little if anything to say about comedy and tragedy, both so crucial to Aristotle's meditations at the dawn of Western aesthetics. The possible reason for Kant omitting them is that these two dramatic forms are difficult to describe as forms of disinterested contemplation, Kant's favored mode of aesthetic beholding. As Aristotle notes, drama brings about *katharsis*, a release which implies that our emotions were not yet released before experiencing such works.[32] He adds that tragedy is about those better than us, and comedy about those worse, which implies further entanglement of the beholder's own status in the way such works are experienced. In this sense, we could speak of comedy and tragedy as early forms of second-order formalism, much like architecture itself. All of these genres raise a Kantian-sounding question: "how is de-relationized relation possible?" The previous pages have suggested that something as basic as the part–whole relation teaches us how. For in one sense, everything is a composite formed of relations between its ingredients. But in another, the whole is just a whole, presenting itself as an object partly resistant to all our attempts to relate to it.

Zero-function and zero-form

The architectural concepts of function and form are widely familiar to the general public, and we need not trace their history here. Most important for the present chapter is that both terms are usually interpreted *relationally*. This is clear enough in the case of function, which seems to entail that buildings are not self-contained realities, but are directed toward a particular purpose that goes beyond the building itself: whether it be to house the headquarters of an international bank, to enable air travel, or to seat 60,000 spectators for a football match. Yet form in architecture is no less relational, insofar as it usually refers to the "visual look" of a building, and a look is always a look for some observer or observers. In an age like ours, in which relationality is viewed as a liberating principle wherever it is found, the reader might wonder if there is anything wrong with relational architecture. After all, architecture is supposed to enter into relations with people and with other architectural works, is it not? The problem is that relationality is a form of literalism, and while architecture may have its literal aspects, it is also an important genre of aesthetics, and we have already seen that the relation between aesthetics and literalism is no less dire than that between matter and anti-matter.

Aesthetic experience, I have argued, requires the partial separation of an object from its own qualities. The usual way this happens is that an object becomes distant from us even while its qualities remain palpable and present. We ourselves, as observers or beholders, stand in for the object that has withdrawn into darkness and left its qualities behind like evidence of a criminal act. Aesthetic phenomena entail a de-relationizing of objects in order to draw us into relation with qualities, as a substitute for the suddenly missing objects. But how could one possibly de-relationize function, which by definition is always a relation between at least two terms? Perhaps the best description I have seen of such a thing comes from Jeffrey Kipnis in his article "Recent Koolhaas." In writing about Koolhaas's failed but highly influential entry into the competition for the Tate Modern in London, Kipnis refers to Koolhaas having harnessed the power of "*nonspecific* flows and events."[33] Stated differently, by severing links with any *specific* function, Koolhaas finds his way toward a zeroed or non-relational function. Kipnis speaks further: "More like a sadist than a surgeon, [Koolhaas] has begun to knife the [Tate Modern] brief, hacking away its fat, even its flesh, until he has exposed its nerve."[34] Reduction of this sort is eminently suited to the sphere of function, which suffers in advance from an excess of relations to the various tasks envisaged for any given building. In other words, function always starts off life as much too concrete and specific, and for this very reason, it offers a fertile environment for abstraction.

Another such case can be seen in Aldo Rossi's well-known treatment of monumental buildings in urban settings, a form of architecture in which his native Italy is especially rich.[35] With the benefit of calendar time, working across centuries and millennia, it becomes increasingly clear that no edifice is wedded to its original function: cathedrals can become bookstores (as in Maastricht), and rail depots can turn into architecture schools (as with the SCI-Arc building in Los Angeles). The monumental building is functional in different ways in different historical periods and shapes the urban fabric like a black hole more than being shaped by the needs of the moment. Such monuments are far from being non-functional, but all their specific functions emanate from a deeper proto-functional core that is never fully expressed in any individual moment of history.

In the case of form, something like the reverse seems to hold. If at first, we identify the form of a building with its visual look, it is relatively easy to de-relationize this superficial layer and inquire about its "deep form." The Medieval Scholastics liked to speak of the "substantial form" of objects, which was something deeper than anything that could be seen or said about them: something like the inner animating principle of a thing, rather than its specific physical appearance at any moment of time. Speaking more practically, the substantial form of an architectural work would be the general spirit of a building beyond any of the prose descriptions that can be given of it. The problem, of course, is that we have seen—with reference to the words of the young Eisenman—the degree to which architecture is a temporal genre. The general spirit of a building is not normally something that can be gathered from standing at a single privileged point; simply recall Robin Evans's reflections on the difficulty of locating the center of a cathedral.[36] Instead, a temporal synthesis is required: the deliberate compression of a series of related experiences into each other. This amounts to zeroing in a constructive rather than abstractive sense: by stringing numerous different experiences into a single chain, a new and temporally extended entity is produced that is every bit as foreign a metaphorical hybrid as Homer's "wine-dark sea" or "dawn with her finger-tips of rose."

NOTES

1. Edmund Husserl, *Logical Investigations*, 2 vols., trans. John Niemeyer Findlay (London: Routledge & Kegan Paul, 1970).
2. Immanuel Kant, *Critique of Pure Reason*, trans. Norman Kemp Smith (New York, NY: St. Martin's Press, 1965).
3. David Hume, *A Treatise of Human Nature* (Oxford: Oxford University Press, 1978).
4. Graham Harman, *The Quadruple Object* (Winchester: Zero Books, 2011).
5. Martin Heidegger, *Being and Time*, trans. J. Macquarrie and E. Robinson (New York, NY: Harper & Row, 1962).
6. Graham Harman, *Tool-Being: Heidegger and the Metaphysics of Objects* (Chicago, IL: Open Court, 2002).
7. See Alfred North Whitehead, *Process and Reality* (New York, NY: Free Press, 1978). See also Bruno Latour, *Pandora's Hope: Essays on the Reality of Science Studies* (Cambridge, MA: Harvard University Press, 1999).
8. For a discussion of onto-taxonomy, see Graham Harman, *Dante's Broken Hammer: The Ethics, Aesthetics, and Metaphysics of Love* (London: Repeater Books, 2016). See also Graham Harman, "The Only Exit from Modern Philosophy," *Open Philosophy* 3 (2020): 132–46. Finally, a sophisticated discussion of this theme can also be found in Niki Young, "Only Two Peas in a Pod: On the Overcoming of Ontological Taxonomies," *Symposia Melitensia* 17 (2021): 27–36.
9. Georg Wilhelm Friedrich Hegel, *Phenomenology of Spirit*, trans. Arnold V. Miller (Oxford: Oxford University Press, 1977).
10. Jacques Lacan, *Écrits: The First Complete Edition in English*, trans Bruce Fink (New York, NY: Norton, 2007).
11. F. W. J. Schelling, *First Outline of a System of the Philosophy of Nature*, trans. Keith Peterson (Albany, NY: SUNY Press, 2004). See also Maurice Merleau-Ponty, *The Visible and the Invisible*, trans. Alphonso Lingis (Evanston, IL: Northwestern University Press, 1968).

12. See Cleanth Brooks, *The Well Wrought Urn* (New York, NY: Harcourt, Brace, & World, 1947). For a critical treatment of Brooks's position, see Graham Harman, "The Well-Wrought Broken Hammer: Object-Oriented Literary Criticism," *New Literary History* 43 (2012): 183–203.
13. Victor Turner, "Betwixt and Between: The Liminal Period in *Rites de Passage*," in *The Forest of Symbols: Aspects of Ndembu Ritual* (Ithaca, NY: Cornell University Press, 1970), 93–111.
14. Marshall McLuhan, *Understanding Media: The Extensions of Man* (Cambridge, MA: MIT Press, 1994).
15. Graham Harman, "The Two Faces of Mediation," in *Phenomenology and Realism*, ed. N. Garrera-Tolbert, J. G. Ferrer Ortega, and A. Schnell (Leiden, The Netherlands: Brill, 2022).
16. Marshall and Eric McLuhan, *Laws of Media: The New Science* (Toronto: University of Toronto Press, 1992).
17. Roland Barthes, *Camera Lucida: Reflections on Photography*, trans. Richard Howard (New York, NY: Hill & Wang, 1982).
18. See Gavin Parkinson, *The Duchamp Book* (London: Tate, 2008).
19. See Graham Harman, "Greenberg, Duchamp, and the Next Avant-Garde," *Speculations* V (2014): 251–74.
20. Jacques Derrida, "White Mythology: Metaphor in the Text of Philosophy," in *Margins of Philosophy*, trans. Alan Bass (Chicago, IL: University of Chicago Press, 1982), 207–71.
21. Jacques Derrida, *Of Grammatology*, trans. Gayatri Spivak (Baltimore, MD: Johns Hopkins University Press, 2016).
22. Jacques Derrida, "*Ousia* and *Gramme*: A Note on a Note from *Being and Time*," in *Margins of Philosophy*, trans. Alan Bass (Chicago, IL: University of Chicago Press, 1982), 29–67.
23. Immanuel Kant, *Critique of Judgment*, trans. Werner Pluhar (Indianapolis, IN: Hackett, 1987).
24. Clement Greenberg, *Homemade Aesthetics: Observations on Art and Taste* (Oxford: Oxford University Press, 2000). See also Michael Fried, "Art and Objecthood," in *Art and Objecthood: Essays and Reviews* (Chicago, IL: University of Chicago Press, 1998), 148–72.
25. Bruno Latour, *We Have Never Been Modern*, trans. Catherine Porter (Cambridge, MA: Harvard University Press, 1993).
26. Michael Fried, *Courbet's Realism* (Chicago, IL: University of Chicago Press, 1990). See also Michael Fried, *Manet's Modernism: Or, The Face of Painting in the 1860s* (Chicago, IL: University of Chicago Press, 1996).
27. Dante Alighieri, *The Divine Comedy*, trans. Allen Mandelbaum (New York, NY: Random House, 1995).
28. Anna Kornbluh, *The Order of Forms: Realism, Formalism, and Social* Space (Chicago, IL: University of Chicago Press, 2019); Caroline Levine, *Forms: Whole, Rhythm, Hierarchy, Network* (Oxford: Oxford University Press, 2015).

29. Graham Harman, *Architecture and Objects* (Minneapolis, MN: University of Minnesota Press, 2022).
30. *The Wizard of Oz* (1939), director Victor Fleming.
31. Peter Eisenman, *Eisenman Inside Out: Selected Writings, 1963–1988* (New Haven, CT: Yale University Press, 2004), 9.
32. Aristotle, *Poetics*, trans. Malcolm Heath (London: Penguin, 1997).
33. Jeffrey Kipnis, "Recent Koolhaas," in *A Question of Qualities: Essays in Architecture* (Cambridge, MA: MIT Press, 2013), 115–45. The reference is to page 135, emphasis added.
34. Ibid.,126.
35. Aldo Rossi, *The Architecture of the City*, trans. Diane Ghirardo and Joan Ockman (Cambridge, MA: MIT Press, 1982).
36. See Chapter 1 of Robin Evans, *The Projective Cast: Architecture and Its Three Geometries* (Cambridge, MA: MIT Press, 1995).

REFERENCES

Aristotle, *Poetics*. Translated by Malcolm Heath. London: Penguin, 1997.

Barthes, Roland. *Camera Lucida: Reflections on Photography*. Translated by Richard Howard. New York, NY: Hill & Wang, 1982.

Brooks, Cleanth. *The Well Wrought Urn*. New York, NY: Harcourt, Brace, & World, 1947.

Dante, Alighieri. *The Divine Comedy*. Translated by Allen Mandelbaum. New York, NY: Random House, 1995.

Derrida, Jacques. *Of Grammatology*. Translated by Gayatri Spivak. Baltimore, MD: Johns Hopkins University Press, 2016.

Derrida, Jacques. "*Ousia* and *Gramme*: A Note on a Note from *Being and Time*." In *Margins of Philosophy*. Translated by Alan Bass, 29–67. Chicago, IL: University of Chicago Press, 1982a.

Derrida, Jacques. "White Mythology: Metaphor in the Text of Philosophy." In *Margins of Philosophy*. Translated by Alan Bass, 207–71. Chicago, IL: University of Chicago Press, 1982b.

Eisenman, Peter. *Eisenman Inside Out: Selected Writings, 1963–1988*. New Haven, CT: Yale University Press, 2004.

Evans, Robin. *The Projective Cast: Architecture and Its Three Geometries*. Cambridge, MA: MIT Press, 1995.

Fleming, Victor, director. *The Wizard of Oz*. Beverly Hills, CA: Metro-Goldwin-Mayer, 1939.

Fried, Michael. *Courbet's Realism*. Chicago, IL: University of Chicago Press, 1990.

Fried, Michael. *Manet's Modernism: Or, The Face of Painting in the 1860s*. Chicago, IL: University of Chicago Press, 1996.

Fried, Michael. "Art and Objecthood." In *Art and Objecthood: Essays and Reviews*, 148–72. Chicago, IL: University of Chicago Press, 1998.

Greenberg, Clement. *Homemade Esthetics: Observations on Art and Taste*. Oxford: Oxford University Press, 2000.

Harman, Graham. "Greenberg, Duchamp, and the Next Avant-Garde." *Speculations* V (2014), 251–74.

Harman, Graham. "The Only Exit from Modern Philosophy." *Open Philosophy* 3 (2020): 132–46.

Harman, Graham. "The Two Faces of Mediation." In *Phänomenologie und spekulativer Realismus/Phenomenology and Speculative Realism/Phénoménologie et réalisme spéculatif*, edited by N. Garrera-Tolbert, J. G. Ferrer Ortega, and A. Schnell, 12–15. Blaufelen: Königshausen & Neumann, 2021.

Harman, Graham. "The Well-Wrought Broken Hammer: Object-Oriented Literary Criticism." *New Literary History* 43 (2012): 183–203.

Harman, Graham. *Architecture and Objects*. Minneapolis, MN: University of Minnesota Press, 2022.

Harman, Graham. *Dante's Broken Hammer: The Ethics, Aesthetics, and Metaphysics of Love*. London: Repeater Books, 2016.

Harman, Graham. *The Quadruple Object*. Winchester: Zero Books, 2011.

Harman, Graham. *Tool-Being: Heidegger and the Metaphysics of Objects*. Chicago, IL: Open Court, 2002.

Hegel, Georg Wilhelm Friedrich. *Phenomenology of Spirit*. Translated by Arnold V. Miller. Oxford: Oxford University Press, 1977.

Heidegger, Martin. *Being and Time*. Translated by J. Macquarrie and E. Robinson. New York, NY: Harper & Row, 1962.

Hume, David. *A Treatise of Human Nature*. Oxford: Oxford University Press, 1978.

Husserl, Edmund. *Logical Investigations*, 2 vols. Translated by John Niemeyer Findlay. London: Routledge & Kegan Paul, 1970.

Kant, Immanuel. *Critique of Judgment*. Translated by Werner Pluhar. Indianapolis, IN: Hackett, 1987.

Kant, Immanuel. *Critique of Pure Reason*. Translated by Norman Kemp Smith. New York, NY: St. Martin's Press, 1965.

Kipnis, Jeffrey. "Recent Koolhaas." In *A Question of Qualities: Essays in Architecture*, 115–45. Cambridge, MA: MIT Press, 2013.

Kornbluh, Anna. *The Order of Forms: Realism, Formalism, and Social Space*. Chicago, IL: University of Chicago Press, 2019.

Lacan, Jacques. *Écrits: The First Complete Edition in English*. Translated by Bruce Fink. New York, NY: Norton, 2007.

Latour, Bruno. *Pandora's Hope: Essays on the Reality of Science Studies*. Cambridge, MA: Harvard University Press, 1999.

Latour, Bruno. *We Have Never Been Modern*. Translated by Catherine Porter. Cambridge, MA: Harvard University Press, 1993.

Levine, Caroline. *Forms: Whole, Rhythm, Hierarchy, Network*. Oxford: Oxford University Press, 2015.

McLuhan, Marshall. *Understanding Media: The Extensions of Man*. Cambridge, MA: MIT Press, 1994.

McLuhan, Marshall and Eric McLuhan. *Laws of Media: The New Science*. Toronto: University of Toronto Press, 1992.

Merleau-Ponty, Maurice. *The Visible and the Invisible*. Translated by Alphonso Lingis. Evanston, IL: Northwestern University Press, 1968.

Parkinson, Gavin. *The Duchamp Book*. London: Tate, 2008.

Rossi, Aldo. *The Architecture of the City*. Translated by Diane Ghirardo and Joan Ockman. Cambridge, MA: MIT Press, 1982.

Schelling, F. W. J. *First Outline of a System of Nature*. Translated by Keith Peterson. Albany, NY: SUNY Press, 2004.

Turner, Victor. "Betwixt and Between: The Liminal Period in *Rites de Passage*." In *The Forest of Symbols: Aspects of Ndembu Ritual*, 93–111. Ithaca, NY: Cornell University Press, 1970.

Whitehead, Alfred North. *Process and Reality*. New York, NY: Free Press, 1978.

Young, Niki. "Only Two Peas in a Pod: On the Overcoming of Ontological Taxonomies." *Symposia Melitensia* 17 (2021): 27–36.

10

Fake Architecture, Real Image

Ferda Kolatan

The inescapable strangeness of images

Much has been made of the commonalities between cinema and architecture. To name a few: they are both technologically driven cultural expressions, they rely on medium-specific techniques to achieve these expressions, they deal with time and space sequentially, they affect us materially and viscerally, and they are framed by narratives and fictions. But beyond these perhaps more apparent shared qualities, both fields are also charged with the manifestation and representation of the real through images.

The respective meanings of the terms real and image, how they evolved over time, and the complex interrelations and co-dependencies between them have been essential to the shaping of our understanding of the world and how we participate in it. Our cognitive processes, the ways we communicate with each other, how we express our fears, hopes, and desires, and also how we view nature per se and assert agency and control over it are all contingent on our ability to conjure up images of what we either believe or perceive to be real. After all, to imagine means to "form a mental image" of a possible real, to concretize loose ideas into form, and to make them communicable to others.

The capacity to not only capture the world in images but also to further expand and remake it through pictorial artifacts, and the need to archive these artifacts for posterity, is deeply ingrained in our species. Since the earliest days of human interaction, we find evidence for this proclivity in all the cave paintings, ornamented tools and weapons, and numerous other prehistoric human-made objects that represent something beyond their immediate selves. Through each of these artifacts and the images they project, we can trace a given population's predilections of what "nature" was for them, how they utilized it toward material causes, and what their sentiment was toward an immaterial beyond. The pictorial image—through format, content, and style—maps civilization's millennia-long journey marked by societal transformation, progression, and upheaval. The reliance on images to depict the real makes Homo Sapiens a distinctly aesthetic creature.[1] Culture is unthinkable without images.

Yet, images are profoundly strange. They are allusive in kind and by their very definition as "reflections, copies, facsimiles," cannot ever be the real thing itself. And still, they are things nonetheless and thus, presumably, real in some way. All visual arts have been coping with this dilemma since the days of their inception. In particular, both architecture and cinema have distinct yet intersecting histories in their respective ways of dealing with the contradictions inherent in the image. The reliance of architecture and cinema, as representational mediums, on technology is further complicating the status of the images they produce. By being inseparably tied to various synthetic tools and apparatuses, architecture and cinema can only ever express the real through some sort of machine vision.

The recent advent of digital technology has dramatically accelerated and further interlaced the problem of the image and the real, altering their positioning vis-à-vis each other, and shifting our conception of the world yet again. In many ways, the inherent conflict expressed by the image, as a mere copy of the real, is materializing itself in concrete hybrid forms through the digital entwinement of what we once identified as the factual and the fictitious. The dissolution of former boundaries drawn to distinguish epistemological classes is one striking characteristic of digital technology and its outlets like social media. The digitization of the material world into pure data is akin to an ontological flattening of the real from which, in successive steps, new types of images emerge.

But what is the nature of these images? Are they real or fake? Are these distinctions even operational in the new kind of world they constitute? And if not, how can we assess their value in a meaningful way and benefit from their effects? Before approaching these questions, it will be useful to survey a few key definitions of the "real" and the "image" and understand how they have impacted cultural production and vice versa. Early documentary cinema plays a pivotal role in this survey. By virtue of its own liminal stance between fact and fiction, it forebodes our current state of the real as an analog/digital hybrid. Architecture on the other hand has historically attempted to manifest the real (as truth concepts) through its physical appearance. However, the adoption of certain cinematic techniques via digital technologies has altered architecture's own relationship to the real and the image.

The real image

The Online Etymological Dictionary defines the "real" as "actually existing, having physical existence" and also as "what is belonging to the thing itself." By these two definitions, any field that functions as a medium of representation has an inherently conflicted relationship with the real. Architecture and cinema are, albeit in different ways, ultimately images as they reference ideas beyond their physical selves. On the one hand, they are real as they physically exist but, on the other hand, they are also *not* real as they point to some other content that transcends their physical boundaries and therefore does not belong to themselves.

To define the real solely by its physical presence is often referred to as "Naïve Realism," a dominantly premodern view that our sensual perception of the world is granting us full and unmediated access to the true being of things. All material objects, including images that we can sensibly detect, are by this definition unquestionably real. They exist in the world independent of mind and thought. But to define the real as belonging to the thing itself introduces a rather different take. The real in this case becomes contingent on an implied *self* rather than just being determined by the sheer physical forces of material existence. To presuppose that inanimate objects do have a self in the first place is to imbue them with some sort of essence or ontological root. The real in this scenario becomes a matter of the internal relationship between an object's unique identity, or self, and its physical appearance.

Theories attempting to come to terms with the nature of this type of real reach back to antiquity and have paved the way for centuries of heated debate in western philosophy, religion, and the social sciences.[2] To believe in ideal form or substance or self means to distance the real from the physical object at hand and to split the world into a two-tiered system with essential qualities on the one side and appearances on the other. It also means that the real thing by virtue of not being identical to its own physical appearance has to be immaterial—a spectral quality that anchors objects and thus makes them real without being accessible to direct human inquiry.[3]

This Kantian split of the real into a forever foreclosed "thing-in-itself" and a world of physical phenomena, which can be measured, calculated, classified, and categorized has largely set up the field on which the debates of what constitutes the real have been fought since the Enlightenment. It also deepened the line between those factions who privilege knowledge purely as a scientific means based on empirical facts and those who maintain some metaphysical element in their assessment of the real. Artistic images, in this predicament, are either the only possible way of representing the real or detached from its realm altogether.

In recent years, a number of thinkers have emerged who have specifically targeted this totalitarian divide between two types of real and sought to overcome it.[4] Graham Harman in particular has worked on recovering the thing-in-itself and bringing it back to the table. While he acknowledges the withdrawnness of what he calls the "real object," he does believe that we have the capacity to allude to it.[5] In his object-oriented philosophy, he argues that a beholder and an object together form a third unit, which itself becomes another real object. The basis for this new object is allusion or metaphor, not empirical fact. To characterize our ability to conjure up images, triggered by the things surrounding us, as some form of indirect access to the real has, unsurprisingly, found keen interest in the art and architecture communities.

The consequences of how the real is determined, what we believe it to be at any given time, are far-reaching not only in regard to our understanding of the material world but also in the ways in which the real constructs an ethical scaffold within which our social lives unfold. Ultimately, the real determines the cultural value of all material things that surround us, guides our assessment of what is worthwhile and what is not, and how we are generally to estimate an object's qualities. By associating the real with truthfulness and facts, an opposite "unreal" is defined as well—the realm of ambiguities, fictions, and falsities. While this strict dichotomy is enforced, for instance in the Kantian concept of the real, Harman's ideas allow for a more nuanced approach by including our specie's inherent proclivity to create fictions into the equation. Every act of imagination becomes, ontologically speaking, an element of the real.

The question then of how to best represent the real through images takes on a different angle in object-oriented thought. Older concepts were invested in locating a point of fixity from which to establish universal judgments about the nature of the world. Throughout most of history, the image was in service of representing these principles, or depending on ideological shifts, of breaking them down. But Harman's emphasis on allusion and metaphor as the co-ingredients of the real suggests that the image is neither merely a representation, in the sense that it points to something outside itself, nor reducible to its physical presence as an object. Rather, the image is a fundamental part of a hybrid constellation, and thus a vital constituent of the real.[6]

To speak of a "real image" seems counterintuitive if we recall the dictionary definition of both terms as mutually exclusive. How can "reflections, copies, facsimiles" possibly belong to the "thing itself"? But if images are no longer exclusively viewed as belonging to the domain of perceiving minds but also to real objects, then the image and the real necessarily forge new collaborations. The age-old conflict between the image and the real becomes itself the locus of a betwixt reality. Perhaps no other field in the arts is intrinsically better suited to examine this point further than cinema.

The moving image

One can argue that cinema was born from a desire to image the real as accurately as possible. Early versions of the film camera were not yet considered as tools for artistic expression but as scientific instruments for a closer observation of nature to verify various theses about reality.[7] Film was viewed as the medium to supersede earlier representational formats like drawing, print, and photography in the quest of producing "perfect" copies of objects in the world. In 1896, a famous incident supposedly occurred when a Parisian movie audience panicked and stormed out of the theater at the projected sight of an oncoming locomotive.[8] The separating line between actual life and facsimile had been breached in unprecedented ways, throwing into question, for an instance at least, the prevalent dichotomic dualism of real and copy at the time.

The event in Paris may be viewed today as merely an exaggerated reaction to a then unfamiliar cinematic illusion. But what really had happened was a rather forceful suspension of strongly held beliefs of how reality constitutes itself to us. A momentary glimpse or sensation of the overlap between reality and image had occurred, a seismic shift from the assumptions of what an image is supposed to do, namely, to point at a thing from a safe distance. Even prior to the Lumière brothers' showing off their short film, the distance between the image and the real had already begun to dissolve through earlier motion-photographic techniques like the mounting of successive photographs on rotating discs in order to evoke a higher sense of "realness." But it was on that momentous day in Paris that the space of the projection screen became a truly transgressive device and made cinema the most radical medium to capture the real.

Cinema's hitherto unparalleled ability to make things appear real was, of course, conditioned by a series of modern technological innovations. Building on the chemical and technical achievements of photography and other reproductive machines of the nineteenth century, film combined photorealism with motion to achieve an almost life-like depiction of its subject. By virtue of being a complex mechanical device, the film camera was significantly further removed from the direct influence and control of the human hand than was the case with older, more manual technologies of reproduction like pens, brushes, and printing presses. As such, the camera was viewed by many not only as a superior tool for the production of copies but also as an inherently *objective* device, capable of constituting facts unvarnished by the interference of human agency.[9]

While the problems of this orthodox view of the camera as an incorruptible arbiter of a fact-based truth have been exposed (by pointing to human agency expressed in set-up, framing, and editing, as well as in the construction of film technologies per se), the notion that the real and the image are occupying altogether different planes was put into question. In the opinion of these early film pioneers, cinema, rather than being yet another discernible imitation, had the power to bridge these planes for good. The withdrawn, encapsulated space of the camera obscura and the for the naked eye invisible processes of the cinematic apparatus became the originators of a new type of image—at once captured and invented, real and copy.[10]

The addition of a machinic device to the image/real conflict further complicates the problem at hand, particularly if it is understood not merely as an interface between the image and the real, but as an originator in its own right. Walter Benjamin saw in the camera primarily a device for the destruction of the real. To him, the real was constituted in objects by a natural origin, a root in time and space that determined the thing-itself and granted it a unique aura.[11] Mechanical reproduction on the other hand destroyed the aura of objects by replicating their appearances without capturing the original context in which the object was rooted. Once detached from its spatiotemporal context the object-image is not simply forfeiting the value of being original but becomes a potential weapon in the hands of those who seek to manipulate it for political gain. The aura of an object safeguards it from undue misuse.

Benjamin's position is a reversal of the early documentarians' claims that a better copy is more closely matching reality by erasing visible differences. To him, the "self" of the thing is always foreclosed to any type of mechanical reproduction, making the "better" copy only more susceptible to human exploitation and thus a more deceptive counterfeit. By pitting a pure state of being against a technologically corrupted one, Benjamin largely reinforces the barrier between two value types of the real. The first one is characterized by an existing yet unrepresentable immaterial aura—the thing's natural, contextually constituted self, and the second one by being an artifice with no original context but, nevertheless, a capacity to become a powerful device in asserting agency and remaking the real.

This uncomfortable, mechanically induced, two-sided real is one of the great modern dilemmas: How to understand and represent the world better through advanced technological means without adding more layers of diffusion and distance through said means? The phenomenon of cinema typifies the problem of an "authentic" real subjected to artificial production. What would it take for such artifacts to become truly new originals unburdened by their references or are they intrinsically destined to exist as false projections falling perpetually short of becoming authentic? Is it not perhaps conceivable that Benjamin's judgment notwithstanding, the mechanical image has its own aura, which derives precisely from its distinct hybrid nature rather than from a spatiotemporal root? These questions become even more pertinent once the cinematic image becomes digital and is eventually absorbed into architecture.

Architecture and the digital image

Unlike cinema, architecture's dealings with the real precede the modern technological period and go back to the very beginning of cultural activity. Caught in its own protracted dualism, architecture arose by most accounts from the intersection of shelter and monument. The former serves a practical purpose to house and protect, the latter a representational one to give form to immaterial ideas and to create spaces for social gatherings and contemplation. The question of how each of these architectural types has informed and shaped the discipline, what their points of intersection are, and how they have impacted civilization at large has been the subject of countless spirited debates throughout architecture history and academic discourse.

No matter on which side of these debates one lands, it is incontrovertible that architecture since its inception has performed as a medium for envisaging a given culture's abstract belief systems regarding the real. Along with every functional design innovation, new forms of representation were also integrated into buildings: figurative ornaments developing from structural systems, proportional orders reflecting principles of nature, and specific building sites signaling hallowed ground to name just a few. In fact, our retrospective habit of identifying and ordering history into different artistic classes and styles is made possible to a large degree by architecture's unique way of expressing ideological shifts in society through changes in ornamental detailing, tectonic composition, and the organization of space.

Architecture's ancestral proximity to the monument has over millennia survived as an enduring legacy. We still think of (and value) architecture as a practice imbued with the powers to represent ideas beyond the physical boundaries of a particular building or city. Up until modernity, at around the time leading up to the invention of cinema, architecture deployed mostly mimetic and allegorical language to achieve this. Only with the emergence of modern building materials like steel or reinforced concrete, the construction technologies they spawned, and the establishment of structural engineering as an autonomous professional field in the late eighteenth century, did the question of how to represent the real through architecture begin to radically shift.[12]

This shift is illustrated most formidably by the infamous debates between proponents of the École des Beaux-Arts and the École Polytechnique. In a departure from architecture's long-standing practice of representing the real through abstract or figurative allegories, the then emerging science of engineering privileged an ethics based on a forthright equation of the real with nature. Since buildings already consist of natural materials, "truthful" construction was understood as an act of expressing the various inherent properties and forces of such materials through design. From this vantage point, architecture no longer required conjecture in its effort to represent the real since the laws of nature would directly manifest themselves through the expediencies and performances of a building's structural, mechanical, and construction systems.

This divide between an implicitly naturalistic architecture and one based on representational images came to a head in the politically tumultuous period prior to World War I when the architectural avant-garde rejected most forms of representation as anachronistic signs of oppressive class rule. In this charged climate, the fact-based approach associated with science, technology, and engineering was a better ideological match and also fit well with the abstract formal language promoted by classical modernists. Notwithstanding the immediate appropriation of both technology and nature into new architectural images by said modernists, the idea of machines as "disinterested" depositors of the real has become a foundational ingredient for modern claims of a universally valid, timeless architecture.

With the advent of digital media in architecture and the integration of cinematic techniques like animation into the workflow of design, the competing ideologies between a representational real and a "factual" real aided by technology became further entangled. While the use of digital drawing (computer-aided design) in architecture reaches back to the 1970s, it was first primarily used for utilitarian tasks such as sectioning a building mass, visualizing simple geometrical shapes, and preparing construction drawings with accurate dimensions and labels. Only in the 1990s did digital tools start to play a more vital role in the conceptual and aesthetic realization of architectural design. To consider digital tools as inherently *generative* rather than merely reproductive echoed earlier modernist sentiments and ushered in the era of the "digital project" in architecture. The chief concern of this project was to find novel opportunities in form, structure, material, and space engendered by the specific toolsets of new digital technologies.

The digital project's aim to express novelty was aided by the appropriation of software packages originally developed for fields other than architecture or engineering. Among the programs adopted by architects were those used for film editing and animation.[13] The digitization of film allowed for an easier cross-platform application into architecture. More importantly, with the transfer of sequential and time-based techniques common to film, architectural design took on a more cinematic character. Building projects were often presented as animations highlighting motion and fluid transformations over traditional architectural features such as stasis and objecthood. Techniques stemming from keyframe editing and inverse kinematics became particularly important design tools as they allowed for new workflows, in which the architectural object was no longer restricted inside the three-dimensional grid box of Euclidian space but could expand in time, through motion, and stretch into and over complex topological surface geometries.

During this first phase of the digital project, the avant-garde notions of abstract experimentation and novelty as an expression of progress still weighed in heavily. The real was understood as a thing to be discovered and manufactured through advanced technological equipment. Coming on the heels of postmodern relativism and perpetual disciplinary self-referencing, the digital project invigorated a reemerging sense of can-do. Meaningful progress appeared possible once again for architects, matching the overall positivistic cultural mood of the 1990s in regard to digital technology.

The merging of cinematic time-based techniques into design via digital means fostered two distinct trajectories in architecture in the following years. The first one stresses performance as the guiding principle of design and nature as its north star. Animation and algorithmic simulations are used to generate evolutionary and morphological models which are seen as analogous to natural processes. The architectural images produced by this approach often resemble actual natural phenomena like tree branches, cellular structures, flow patterns, and so forth. This trend is upholding the spirit of the Polytechnique in its commitment to the real as an implicit force of nature that can, and should be, expressed in design. The second trajectory concerns itself not with the processes of digital technique but with its aesthetic consequences. Here, the main focus is the exploration and refinement of the affects generated by the digital artifact's intricate synthesis of form, texture, and color.[14]

The intellectual positions held by these two trajectories are wide apart even though they originated from the same technological source. Both produce very specific images for architecture but differ in their arguments regarding the meaning and value of those images. For those favoring the performance argument, the image is seen as an involuntary but necessary result of deep-seated natural processes, which are unveiled by digital technology. In other words, the real is a material truth exposed by means of design. For those favoring the affect argument, the image becomes an autonomous thing-itself, a sensible artifact shaped by technological estrangement. Here the object of architecture is made unfamiliar by digital means in order to engage the beholder in new ways. This overtly aesthetic approach borrows from Russian Formalism where the estrangement of a perceived normal is used to create tensions and open up new sensible angles from which to perceive the real.[15]

Most recently, the ramifications of digital technology for architecture have expanded into an altogether different realm. Fueled by the unprecedented proliferation of digital images via social media, the most critical questions no longer seem to focus on the digital's capacity to directly advance design methodologies but rather on the effects of the totalizing image-world it has been creating.[16] The familiar routine of using social media as merely an outlet to showcase, curate, and promote architectural work—and to view it thus as separate from the actual act of design—does not cover the full range of influence asserted by image-based social media on contemporary architecture. As we become fully immersed in this collective digital archive, all our actions in the analog world are to some degree impacted by its format and content. In this strange reversal, the real has become contingent on the copy.

The digital archive however is not just a cloud depository for individual copies, which can be accessed and utilized selectively—and deliberately—as is mostly the case with other archives like libraries. Instead, the accumulative effect of image-based social media amounts to a kaleidoscopic experience where context, sequence, and causality are subject to a perplexing mixture of personal preferences, social group dynamics, and algorithmic sorting via artificial intelligence. What we encounter as a result is a bewildering mélange of uprooted images springing from the collaborative minds and actions of individuals, collectives, and machines. This collaboration, be it voluntary or not, is ultimately an act of design. It produces new hybrid objects neither belonging to the real nor to the copy and therefore requires a very different set of criteria through which to assess their relationship to architecture and the world.

Fake architecture

The real, as we have seen through just a few select examples, comes in many guises. It is a term that encapsulates our best knowledge of a material nature but also projects a vision of how we think the world functions as a sociocultural construct. To be "real" is the ultimate reward we bestow upon things that we take to be incontrovertibly true—things on which ideas, value-systems, and societies are built. While the real, as an image itself, has changed over time, its definitive association with qualities such as origin, authenticity, and genuineness has remained steadfast. But given the fundamental restructuring of these concepts through hybrid objects and their multiple constituencies, the real in our day can be described as authentic precisely because it is no longer original.

To further elaborate on this point, let us turn once more to a comparison with cinema. The rise of image-based social media has of course changed the nature of film as well. The motion picture has moved from theaters into handheld devices. What was once the exclusive domain of experimentalists, professionals, and dedicated amateurs has now become a means of expression for anyone with access to a smartphone. The vast majority of "movies" today are shot as brief video clips and shared via cloud services. But the myriads of still images on social media are also consumed in motion, in some kind of vertical zoetrope, animated by the flicking speeds of our tireless thumbs. This new form of cinema has also become the preeminent medium through which we access architecture as a source of education and inspiration.

The animated stream of these individual architectural bits constructs a total image undergirded by disconnected sequencing, abrupt juxtapositions, and unlikely combinations of uprooted artifacts. From this total dynamic image, assembled of parts and wholes alike, new sensibilities emerge that are no longer informed by "real" architecture—based on origin or context—but by *fakes*. With fake, however, I do not refer to its popular definition as the negative of the real or genuine but to its slang meaning for improvisation as used in sports or Jazz music. "Faking" in those contexts is understood as a creative act of bending rules (the "ball-fake" in sports) and deriving new forms of expression from existing archival material (the "fake book" or "fake sheet" in Jazz). In these instances, the fake becomes a productive tactic by which to engage a particular circumstance from within, to take advantage of the existing rules and features of that circumstance, and to discover new performative potentials in it.

Techniques of faking can then be utilized as a way of expanding social media's propensity for producing hybrids directly into design. The digital archive by rejecting traditional value hierarchies based on dichotomies like old/new, mundane/precious, and original/copy opens up new grounds for improvisational design methodologies in architecture. At the core of these methodologies lies an ambition to find design innovation in social media's unique power to conjure up unprecedented collective images and to benefit from its disregard for anachronistic notions of the real. Fake architecture is a collaborative project, where outdated boundaries resolve, and new syntheses are forged. The character of this architecture would thus be heterogenous, combinatorial, and often surprising. It would also be an engaging reflection on contemporary cultural trends and interests rather than a return to an old eclecticism based on symbolic architectural representations.

NOTES

1. For a detailed account on Homo Sapiens aesthetics see; Ellen Dissanayake, *Homo Aestheticus: Where Art Comes from And Why* (Seattle: University of Washington Press, 1992).
2. To divide objects in the world into two distinct categories, material and immaterial, goes back to antiquity and in particular to Plato's theory of forms. Most Western philosophies including eighteenth and nineteeth century Continental philosophy cope in some way with the problems inherent in this divide.
3. This school of thought is largely based on German philosopher Immanuel Kant's (1724–1804) separation of physical objects into sensible phenomena and withdrawn noumena. For Kant,

the "thing-in-itself" is determined by its noumenon, a mind-independent quality, which is inaccessible to human inquiry.

4. For seminal texts on the modern divide see; Bruno Latour, *We Have Never Been Modern* (Cambridge, MA: Harvard University Press, 1993) and the critique of correlationism by the Speculative Realists, in particular; Quentin Meillassoux, *After Finitude: An Essay on the Necessity of Contingency* (London: Continuum, 2010).
5. Graham Harman develops his aesthetic ideas on allusion in multiple texts but most distinctly in: Graham Harman, *Weird Realism: Lovecraft and Philosophy* (UK: Zero Books, 2012).
6. Harman speaks in detail about the mutual relationship of metaphors and objects in art in his book *Object-Oriented Ontology: A New Theory of Everything*. See in particular Chapter 2 page 81, the "Theatricality of Metaphor" (UK: Penguin Random House, 2018).
7. Eadweard Muybridge's use of multiple cameras to understand more accurately the mechanics of a galloping horse or Étienne-Jules Marey's invention of the chronophotographic gun to study bird flight movements are two famous examples of the use of the camera as a device for scientific inquiry. For more detail on this subject, see "History of Film" on Britannica Online (www.britannica.com/art/history-of-the-motion-picture).
8. The short 35mm documentary film *L'Arrivée D'un Train À La Ciotat* was directed and produced by the brothers Auguste and Louis Lumière in 1895 and screened in Paris in 1896.
9. The Soviet filmmaker Dziga Vertov (1896–1954) for instance promoted "Kino-Pravda" (film-truth), as a way of revealing reality by filming everyday scenes without an underlying narrative or deliberate authorial directives. Vertov advanced the notion that the camera could *find* rather than invent or stage the truth. See "Man with a Movie Camera" from 1929.
10. In contrast to Vertov's definition of film-truth as a consequence of an undirected camera, the American filmmaker Robert J. Flaherty took an opposite stance. His documentary "Nanouk of the North" from 1922 deliberately altered and manipulated scenes from the everyday life of Inuit people for dramatic effect. However, Flaherty argued that these distortions were necessary to catch on film the "true spirit" of his subject matter. See: 05-Robert J. Flaherty, "Nanook of the North" (edited by Julian Reboratti) on SCRIBD.
11. Walter Benjamin develops his famous notions on the aura of objects in his essay "The Work of Art in the Age of Mechanical Reproduction" from 1935.
12. The École Polytechnique was founded in Paris in 1794 in the aftermath of the French Revolution and played a significant role in introducing scientific and engineering principles to the field of architecture.
13. In the fall of 1994, the graduate architecture program at Columbia University introduced the first "paperless" design studios to its curriculum. Softimage, a software developed for film/animation, was one of the non-design programs used in these studios. In 2008, the software giant Autodesk acquired the Canadian firm Softimage, Co. and integrated it into its expansive architecture/engineering platform.

14. The exhibition *Matters of Sensation* (2008) curated by Georgina Huljich and Marcelo Spina at the Artists Space in New York, NY, exemplifies the type of work that was explicitly invested in the exploration of a new digital aesthetic and the effects it produced.
15. Russian formalist Viktor Shlovsky (1893–1984) coined the term "defamiliarization" in his essay "Art as Technique" from 1917. In it, Shlovsky argues that art emerges from the act of making common objects unfamiliar and thus more difficult to grasp with the objective to prolong and deepen the beholder's aesthetic experience.
16. In 2021, the number of Facebook users totaled 2.85 billion with over 250 billion uploaded images. Instagram accounts have reached the 1.0 billion mark with 50 billion shared images.

REFERENCES

Benjamin, Walter. "The Work of Art in the Age of Mechanical Reproduction." In *Illuminations*, edited by Hannah Arendt, 217–51. New York, NY: Harcourt, Brace & World, 1968.

Dissanayake, Ellen. *Homo Aestheticus: Where Art Comes from and Why*. Seattle: University of Washington Press, 1992.

Harman, Graham. *Object-Oriented Ontology: A New Theory of Everything*. UK: Penguin Random House, 2018.

Harman, Graham. *Weird Realism: Lovecraft and Philosophy*. UK: Zero Books, 2012.

Kant, Immanuel. *Critique of Pure Reason*. UK: Hackett Publishing Company, Inc., 2002.

Latour, Bruno. *We Have Never Been Modern*. Cambridge, MA: Harvard University Press, 1993.

Lumière, Auguste and Louis Lumière. *L'Arrivée D'un Train À La Ciotat*. New York, NY; Chatsworth, CA: Kino on Video; [Image Entertainment [distributor], 1896.

Meillassoux, Quentin. *After Finitude: An Essay on the Necessity of Contingency*. London: Continuum, 2010.

Reboratti, Julian ed. 05-Robert J. Flaherty "Nanook of the North". https://www.scribd.com/document/266910587/05-Robert-J-Flaherty-Nanook-of-the-North-Edited-by-Reboratti.

Shlovsky, Viktor. *On the Theory of Prose*. London: Dalkey Archive Press, 1990.

11

In-Between Body and Image

Eva Perez de Vega

The unified body

Prior to the possibility of reproducing images photographically or by other technical means, images were often artworks built into the spaces of churches and public buildings, integral to the architecture that houses them;[1] one experiences these images, such as frescos and plastered paintings, just as one experiences a three-dimensional space, one augmenting and enhancing the other. Due to their integration into the space, the conditions for viewing these artworks may not have been optimal—spatial configuration may have impeded a full view, or the lighting conditions might not be equal throughout—which could cause strain in the viewer, but this lack of immediate access to the work also demanded the engagement of senses other than the visual: the sense of smell and tactility provided by the architecture that housed it, as well our sense of balance and orientation—the kinesthetic sense—all contribute to an augmented experience of the artwork images and their communicative capacity. The power of this coupling between image and space became an aesthetic tool used for propagating various agendas, as was made blatant by the work of the influential writer and counter-reformation cardinal, Gabriele Paleotti. A key figure in understanding the critical role that images played prior to the Renaissance in Europe, he set out the church's views on the proper role and content of art in his *Discourse on Sacred and Profane Images*, identifying the capacity images have to communicate more rapidly than text and reaching a much wider audience. Paleotti recognized a powerful tool in art and the architecture that housed it, according to him, these artwork images had the capacity to change people's thoughts and belief systems—they had the power to convert.[2]

In this sense, the images of Christianity were three-dimensional because they were tied to the three-dimensional space that contained them. As soon as images can be reproduced in a two-dimensional form, they lose the dimensionality of the space, and, with that, they eviscerated something very essential to how we experience the world—with our bodies. In other words, the way artwork is displayed and images are appreciated is tightly linked to the architecture that houses them, mediated by our kinesthetic sense. Leaving aside for the moment the important distinction between built space and architecture, our built environment has always played a pivotal role in the way we appreciate artwork, including—as we shall see—cinema.

Another critically important figure to help frame the nuances between image appreciation and architecture that have pervaded in the Western canon is Vitruvius, the first-century BCE Roman architect and author of the influential treatise on architecture, *De Architectura*. Covering a wide range of topics related to the built environment, the treatise focused on the "optimal proportions" of architectural elements based on idealized proportions of the human body. Architecture was understood as a unified body, ordered through an appreciation of the human body as its regulating system. Metaphorically also, Vitruvius claimed repeatedly that he was "writing the body of architecture" and that his work was a "perfectly ordered corpus."[3]

A new life was given to this seminal text by Renaissance architects, such as Leon Battista Alberti, Sebastiano Serlio, and Andrea Palladio, who through their own treatises revitalized Vitruvius's texts and re-envisioned it by producing new versions with images meant to illustrate Vitruvian concepts.[4] These images, however, often embodied their own agenda, distinct from that of the Roman architect. Vitruvius articulates the links between architecture and the human body, discussing proportion and the critical role of the circle and the square geometry as organizers of architectural proportions made analogous to those of a perfectly proportioned male body. Despite the fact that, as far as we know, the original textual description was not accompanied by an illustration,[5] this man is known mostly through the translation into an image drawn by Leonardo da Vinci over a millennium afterwards. Standing in for an idealized humanity, this illustration is ubiquitously known as the "Vitruvian Man."

Da Vinci's Vitruvian Man image and the subsequent versions which have been reproduced so exhaustingly, invariably show a standing naked man actively illustrating the proportional relationship between the body and the geometrical figures of a circle and a square. While this figure is shown standing and is undeniably three-dimensional, it is worth paying closer attention to Vitruvius's original words, who describes the man lying down "placed flat on his back"[6] illustrating the geometric proportions described in a more passive disposition. The man described in the text is a male body with no thickness, an abstract two-dimensional figure used to illustrate proportion and symmetry; a planimetric organizing tool meant to be mapped on a floorplan for the correct layout of its proportions.

The fact that Vitruvius's description had the man lying down indicates a direct correlation between the idealized proportions of the human body and the regulating geometries of the floorplan as generative of architectural organization. It is the square and the circle in plan, not in elevation, that regulated the proportions of the architecture for Vitruvius. Indeed, as eloquently described by Indra Kagis McEwen in her elegant book *Vitruvius: Writing the Body of Architecture,* for the Greeks and Romans of Vitruvius's time, it was the floorplan that was the driver: [7] "Leonardo's figure, like the images that appeared after it in architectural treatises and illustrated editions of Vitruvius, says more about Renaissance humanism than about the geometrical footprints of Roman humanitas."[8]

While the main role of images that accompany texts is to clarify it, in this case the image was produced so many years later that it is imbued with the preoccupations of the time. Curiously, what is obscuring Vitruvius's original words is illuminating the humanistic concepts that motivated image production in the Renaissance, which are a result of the invention of perspective, a technique of drawing that mimics the human cone of vision. With perspective, the subject's particular perception becomes the central and dominant organization of space, elevating the human point of view to a privileged position. This results in a shift away from the floorplan as generative, toward perspective, which emphasizes the projection of a (hu)man-centered point of view.[9]

According to a traditional account by Pliny the Elder, a first century CE Roman writer, the invention of drawing started with the wish of a maiden to capture the figure of her departing lover, which she did by tracing over his shadow being cast on the wall of the space they were in.[10] The image generated embodies in it the memory of the lover having physically been in the space—it is a projected image that nonetheless makes its mark on the space as a drawing. This account also anticipates the projection of moving images in a space, enabled by their reproduction. Indeed, the act of projecting something three-dimensional onto a two-dimensional surface using light as a medium marks a shift in human perception, which underpins the emergence of cinema in the twentieth century.

At the beginning of the century, the loss of dimensionality in the experience of images went hand in hand with a flattening of the space that housed them. Unlike the image of the maiden's lover in the invention of drawing, the projection of a film onto a space is ephemeral, not coupled to the space in which it is projected. As a result, these spaces for the display of images lose a certain three-dimensionality, beyond becoming flatter for the practicalities of accommodating projection. If our experience of things is tightly connected to the architecture that houses those things and allows us to have those experiences, then what occurs when art can be reproduced, severing the connection between it and the space that contains it?

Is there something lacking when—as Walter Benjamin claims—the image is not unique to a particular place and time?[11] As we shall see in the next section, something else is gained by this de-coupling.

Disembodied body

For Vitruvius and the Renaissance masters inspired by his writings, "man" was the unifying body of architecture. This Western canon embodied by da Vinci's image of the Vitruvian Man has been passed down generations and permeated design education and practice, claiming a tight-knit connection between the idealized male human body and the physical spaces that encompass that body. A clear consequence is the exclusivity of these spaces, and the elitist views that discriminate the kinds of bodies that are seen as appropriate to occupy it. This ingrained notion, however, did not remain uncontested. When the threads of idealized convention begin to unravel, a disembodied body emerges.

At the beginning of the twentieth century with the possibility of reproducing images by technical means and the emergence of cinema, the idea of a unifying body of architecture begins to dissipate. While images have always been reproduced by fellow artists, their rapid reproduction, particularly moving images projected on a screen, allowed for almost complete disassociation between the artwork and the space.[12] However, it is not a dual relationship between space and artwork, it is a three-way interrelation that comprises the space, the artwork, and the subject appreciating it; an in-between which in part disembodied, or imaginal, in the words of Chiara Bottici: "It is within this intermediate world -neither material, like the world of pure sensibility, nor immaterial, like that of the intellect—that the so-called acting imagination operates."[13] So, how can a subject be disembodied?

Built space that enables the appreciation of images is the vehicle with which appreciation can occur; it is the intermediary place that enables the subject to be affected by the object.

> As philosopher Emanuele Coccia describes in *Sensible Life*: "There is always an intermediary place between us and objects [...] It is only outside oneself that something becomes capable of being experienced: something becomes sensible only in the intermediate body that lies between the subject and the object."[14]

The intermediary body is what holds the objects of our experience, it is that sensible place that allows the subject to experience the object. Beyond a metaphoric understanding of architecture as a body, here object and subject fuse under the "sensible" or the "imaginal"—a compendium of faculties that enables human and nonhuman animals to be inter-connected with the world, or what Stacy Alaimo calls *trans-corporeality*: the idea that our bodies are already fully enmeshed with the external environment that supports it: "Imagining human corporeality as trans-corporeality, in which the human is always intermeshed with the more-than-human world, underlines the extent to which the substance of the human is ultimately inseparable from 'the environment'".[15] Our senses are the way in which we interface and make sense of the world, and while one tends to think of five main senses—touch, taste, sight, smell, and hearing—with sight as dominant, it is the kinesthetic sense which is key to the appreciation of moving images. Nevertheless, the use of sensory deprivation as a tool for conditioning the experience of appreciating art has gone hand in hand with the typological development of the movie house and the art gallery. It is through these means of control, privileging sight, that these spaces become progressively flatter.

The architecturally integrated artwork up until the sixteenth century gave way to the picture gallery of the eighteenth century where artwork was used to adorn and enhance interior spaces. While full integration was no longer dominant, there was a reciprocal relationship between the space and the image contained in it, insofar as one is used to enhance the other: the picture adorned the spaces, and the space enabled the picture to be contemplated with a particular environment, or aura[16] around it. However, the relationship evolves away from a tight-fit co-dependency. Once the artwork is framed and stripped from the walls and ceilings, there is a dissociation between the space and the artwork. With this separation between image and space, the space itself becomes more two-dimensional. There is a distancing between the spectator and the image, giving way to the typology that is most taken for granted: the white cube. Here, the walls, ceilings, and floors are deprived of any color beyond a neutral white or gray, resulting in a complete dissociation between the artwork and the space. (see Figure 11.1)

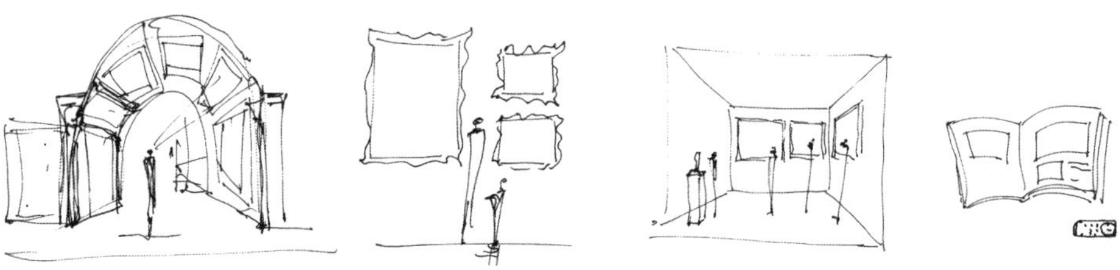

FIGURE 11.1: Evolution of artwork display: full integration (sixteenth century); the Picture Gallery (eighteenth century); the generic white box (twentieth century); individual viewing. Sketches by author.

As we arrive at the white cube as an aesthetic device of modernity, it becomes more specifically about vision, not the complete sensorial experiencing which the architecturally integrated artwork of the sixteenth century demanded. This typology is designed to have a specific ritualistic effect on the viewer: a sense of reverence toward the images on the wall and a complete negation of senses other than sight. There is something controlling about its whiteness and "purity" that makes the spectator behave in a particular way; there is a tendency to leave more distance between the viewer and the artwork, and talking is reduced to a whisper as if it were a place of worship.

In becoming a more specialized experience, focused on sight, there is a sense of disembodiment: the spaces are white, abstract, they entice us, lose our sense of body, and become part of the image itself. This experience is what author and psychoanalyst Gilbert Rose describes as "aesthetic fusion," a sense of fusion with the artwork where "Subject, object, and interaction become interwoven in a dynamic system."[17] This immersive experience weakens the boundary between self and object of observation; the borderline softens, turns penetrable, and allows the world to flow into the viewer and the viewer to flow into the world. The white box is the intermediary space that enables a disembodied appreciation of the image, simultaneously separating us from the space—our sense of self—and joining us to the object of appreciation.

In a parallel with the "white box" for viewing artwork images, the "black box" is still held as the paradigm for optimal viewing of moving images. However, a brief look at the history of this art form will show us that it took between twenty and thirty years of evolution for this particular viewing style to establish itself as the singular way of consuming moving images. In the 1920s, there still was no single viewing style for the film. The "cinema," referred to as "picture house," was where the projector was: in a cafe' or empty garage, under a circus tent, at a fair, or on an improvised vaudeville stage. The picture house emerged as a paradoxical space, in which very different and often opposing functions were brought together. The viewer was not solely focused on the projected image, but rather imbued in a state of "promiscuous distraction" caused by the many parallel events taking place within. One might imagine what the experience was during the first projection of the Lumière brothers at the Café des Capucines in Paris in 1895, or the Winter Garden events at Antwerp as described by cineastes at the turn of the twentieth century.[18] This was a radically different experience from what a contemporary audience associates with movie projection.

There is still a persistent conception that the optimal way of viewing artwork is a white box space and the optimal way of viewing a movie is a black box space. These are understood as neutral backgrounds designed to incite a specific behavior of reverence and ritual in the viewer. When entering such spaces, one tends to know how to behave: lowering one's voice and quietly focusing on that which is meant to be viewed. There is an assumption that there is a singular "correct way" to experience a movie, defined by a particular relationship between the images, the spectator, and the physical environment that houses them. We associate these environments with the artwork without realizing that it took many decades and many variations before we landed on these seemingly stable typologies establishing themselves as the singular way of consuming images.

The art gallery or the auditorium can profoundly influence the viewer's reaction to the content being housed or shown, by imposing precise styles of viewing and of listening.[19] Interestingly, these two typologies have paralleled themselves in time, and what is referred to as the golden age of the "white box" coincided with the most glorious season of the "black box," from the 1920s until the 1970s.[20] Similarly, the crisis that artwork has gone through with its mechanical reproduction is reflected in cinema once the curtain came down on its golden age. Much like artwork, movies can now be experienced without the apparatus of the cinema.

Arriving at the dark identity-less black box space of most contemporary movie-houses took some time, and yet it has persisted. Still today we associate the movie-going experience with: total darkness, separation from the outside world, immobility and silence, and being in a large communal space with other strangers.[21] There is an implicit and socially agreed-upon understanding that as soon as images are projected on the screen, there are certain behavioral norms to follow, a "right way" to experience and behave during the projection of a film, including placing focus on the senses of sight and hearing. This ritualistic behavior emerged with a shift in the kind of spectator provoked by the change in film typology, as well as the architecture of the movie house itself: a new "cinematic architecture" emerged (See Figure 11.2).[22]

In trying to find the optimal architectural typology for projecting movies there was an initial push to assimilate the design of the first movie houses in the 1920s, to known theater typologies which derived from Renaissance conceptions of the

FIGURE 11.2: Evolution of moving images: full integration (nineteenth century); the Picture House (early twentieth century); the generic black box (twentieth century); individual viewing. Sketches by the author.

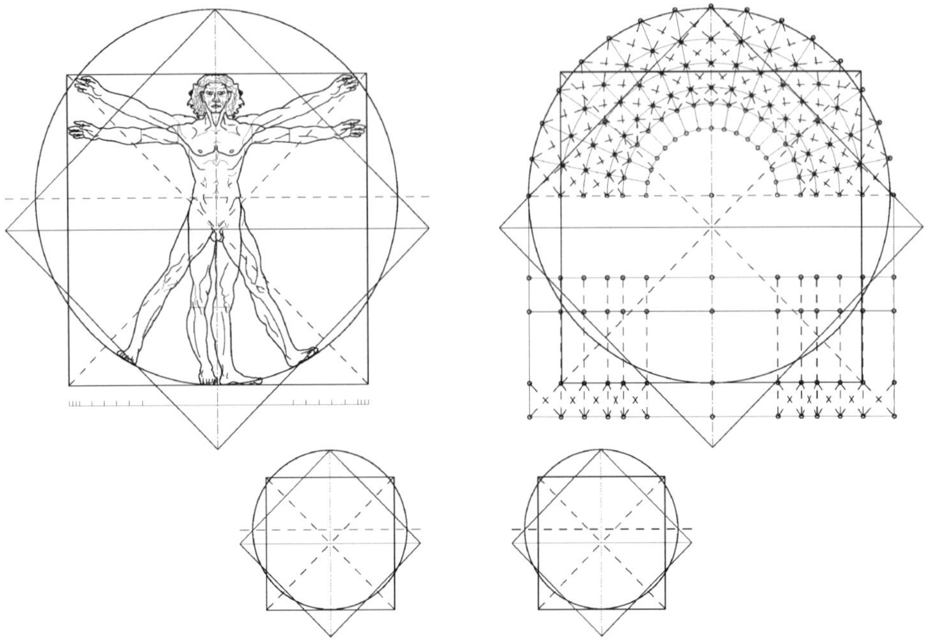

FIGURE 11.3: Vitruvian Man proportions migrating to theatre design. Theater plan: politicworm, 2009.

theater. These conceptions are narrowly focused around the western reference of Vitruvius's writings and the optimal human body exemplified by the aforementioned illustration by Leonardo da Vinci. Applying the "Vitruvian Body" to theater design we can see how the geometric diagram of a circle within a square migrates to the theater typology; with the square rotating inside it around a central point to subdivide and organize the space (see Figure 11.3):

The Renaissance conception of architectural organization was no longer placing religion or notions of God first, it was the idealized human body that became the center. The idealized male-centric unified body discussed earlier permeated most aspects of life in this time period and has its imprints still today. This invites a brief speculation regarding all the alternative forms these designs might have taken had the model for space design not been the Vitruvian body. What if the model for optimal proportions had been given by a giraffe or a woman? Vitruvian Man alternatives abound today, ranging from parody to exquisite representations of more-than-human animals whose presence in the ubiquitous square circle geometry completely revert our inherited ideals.[23] Nonetheless, this is the lineage in accepted western theater design which made its way to the first designs of the space for cinema in the early twentieth century. The goal with this early appropriation was to bring the viewing styles of cinema and theater closer together to elicit equal attention. As Alberti himself claimed, "The architect's only task was to put the spectators in a condition to see and hear effortlessly what was happening on stage."[24]

This lineage gave rise to what Italian writer Gabriele Pedullà calls the "Vitruvian spectator,"[25] defined as someone immersed in the experience of that which is unfolding on the screen, respectful of the physical and communal environment that holds the event and without succumbing to unnecessary distractions. By assimilating the architectural elements of an Italian theater (with the double proscenium arch, the galleries, etc.) the goal was to assimilate the experience of going to the theater and elicit equal attention. Thus, the physical environment was designed to seem familiar, recall behavioral associations, to instill tight control over the behavior of the spectator. "Imitating the theater," Pedullà suggests, "the dark cube in fact aspired to propose itself as a place of absolute aesthetic experience that allowed only one legitimate activity: the contemplation of a film [...]. Suddenly, going to the movies was like going to church."[26]

Certainly, the shift in the type of space was also enabled by the kinds of movies that required more attention and were based on narration. However, they could not have emerged without a concerted effort to control the viewer's perception of space through the careful design and associative power that physical space has on the subject, and the subject's capacity to appreciate the object.

Fragmented body

After decades of aiming to find its place, cinema seemed to have an established location in the black box space. The auditorium's principal objective for the Vitruvian spectator was to impose on the audience a new attitude toward movies. By subjecting spectators to total darkness and voluntarily restricting freedom of movement, they are submitting themselves to the controlled behavior associated with going to the theater. Yet, as any contemporary moviegoer knows, cinema is undergoing a similar crisis that artwork images did once they reached the age of massive reproduction. Given the prevalence of technology that allows the streaming of movies in our own homes, the film is now reproducible, at the level of the individual, who is able to project a film without the apparatus of the cinema. Thus, the ceremonial quality of the cinema and its uniqueness fades. Much like Benjamin recounted the death of artwork without its aura, Susan Sontag eloquently recounts the death of cinephilia without the single screen inside the black box movie house.[27] However, cinema has to evolve despite the nostalgia latent in these accounts and is poised to find itself a new home in a new kind of architectural space.

While movie theaters were initially modeled on the typology of the Vitruvian theater, this assimilation was already being questioned by architects, critics, and filmmakers of the mid twentieth century. Not all designers of these spaces agreed with using the theater as inspiration for the cinema. Frederick Kiesler was one of the architects who criticized this assimilation, claiming the movie house should be something else entirely: "the cinema is a play of surfaces, the theatre is a performance in space, and this difference has not yet been translated concretely into any piece of architecture, neither for the theater nor for the cinema."[28]

Kiesler pointed to some initial practical reasons for this, for instance; in a movie house, the first rows were no longer the best ones, as they are in the theater; the side seating provided by elegant boxes also becomes nonsensical for the viewing of a flat screen which is best viewed frontally; and similarly, the typical fan-shaped seating of the theater house did not provide the best view for the flat screen. As such, some of the unnecessary theatrical elements began to drop away. As can be seen by the design of the Film Guild Cinema in New York City, the assimilation that was taking place was not about it looking like a theater, but rather affording the same behaviors from the spectator that the theater afforded, that of concentrated attention which would allow the spectator to "lose himself in an infinite imaginary space."[29] This quote is worth remarking on briefly and placing into the context of the time: Kiesler was just 34 years younger than Sigmund Freud. Therefore, when he began his professional career as an architect he was already in a fully Freud-imbued Vienna.[30]

The ability to lose oneself into an infinite imaginary space implies that the feeling of containment which a movie house engenders is replaced by a feeling of oneness when the spectator rests his eyes on the screen, putting him in a condition to "lose himself." In a parallel with Freudian psychoanalytic techniques, the consulting room of a psychoanalyst is a very tightly controlled space set up to illicit a certain kind of behavior and response in the patient: the use of the couch, the controlled visual, auditory, and tactile environment is to simultaneously disorient and orient, confuse and enlighten, frighten, and shelter the patient. The space of analysis is not just a passive context for treatment, it is an active participant in the analysis. The room activates daydreaming while protecting and sheltering the daydreamer, functioning as a safe haven and shelter for the patient but also as a stimulant of regression.[31] The aim of the spatial setup of the consultation room is to imbue the patient with a feeling of "the uncanny," a concept developed by Freud in his 1919 paper of the same name.[32] This oscillating movement between opposing states causes a reorientation, or "anamorphosis," of the patient toward the primal oceanic feeling of oneness—toward a state of fusion with the space itself. Similarly, Kiesler is making reference to the ability that the physical environment has to create a palpable effect on the spectator—to put the spectator in a state of oneness with what is occurring in the space.[33]

With our contemporary ability to view film in a variety of modes and at a variety of scales, the sense of fusion is multiplied across scales. This oneness is radically different from the unity experienced by the Vitruvian spectator discussed earlier. The appreciation of film today is multifaceted and fragmented. With the ability to zoom in, slow down, replay, and manipulate through editing, the unity achieved is through fragmentation—similar to the fragmentary nature of film itself. More than mere opposition to unity, the experience emerges from a repetition of different scales of appreciation, which overlap and juxtapose to create a unity of the fragmented. Our appreciation of images with individual media is fragmented through repetition and difference, yet unified through the multiplicity of scales available to us: our screens and access to information allow us to look at the image of artwork by zooming into its pixels—something impossible to see without the mediation of a device—and also remotely experience the way in which the piece is being displayed by literally panning the globe on our screens to understand its context and physical location in the world.

In the era of fragmented modes of viewing, the disembodied nature of the experience shifts. In order to intensify experiences, there have been many attempts to reintroduce bodily three-dimensional sensorial quality back into the experience of viewing images on screens, in order to make it more "real." High-definition technology aims at this sense of "reality," as is the proliferation of 3D movies—or cinema in four dimensions—where there is an uncanny attempt to envelop the spectator in a fully sensorial experience. Enabled by technology, movie houses are aiming to reinvent the experience with immersive cinema, to make it more real, more three-dimensional.

Paradoxically, with this attempt to provide a more realistic experience, we are constantly reminded of its artificiality. In three-dimensional movies, spectators are obliged to wear awkward glasses to perceive the three-dimensional information, which if removed would reveal blurry vision. In aiming to make the experience more bodily by adding the third dimension of space, spectators have to use a device that is external to the body. On the other hand, when we are provided with the added sensorial perks of a shivering seat, or a puff of air suddenly blowing in our face, rather than being immersed in the experience we are reminded of the absurdity of the artifice gone into creating the still awkward effect.

Architecture understood as an aesthetic device does not apply to a world dominated by devices that one must wear to inhabit a mediated version of the physical world. However, there are some interesting developments that acknowledge the diversity of bodies and modes of appreciation. Rather than making us inhabit a reality that is virtual, denying the body, it brings the virtual into our physical world, creating what is known as an "augmented reality." Here, we are not denying the physicality of our bodies. Instead of trying to mimic the physical environment virtually by shutting off the world, there is a reframing of the physical with the introduction of the virtual. We see the physical anew. To some important degree, it signals a return to the appreciation of the physical environment in which our images found themselves prior to their irreproducibility. Images need the physical qualities of the space in order to be understood, there is an inter-dependence between the space and the virtual image that inhabits that space.

By zooming into three moments in history to explore the relationship between architectural space, the image, and the spectator, we have traced how built spaces housing artwork—both still and moving images—have served as aesthetic devices to, either tightly or loosely, control the spectator: going from a "united" conception of images, body, and space, to a "disembodied" conception severing this triad, to a "fragmented" view enabled by the pervasiveness of the digital. The comparison between these three moments is not intended to be exhaustive but rather threaded together by the changing conception of the human body. We have seen how this shifting relationship between modes of appreciating images and the physical space that enables it, has been paralleled by changing attitudes toward the body, and its engagement or depravation of the senses. The advent of the digital in cinema is still very much in development, but by placing the control designers like Kiesler were aiming for, back into the hands of the spectator, it has opened interesting questions. If today, it is mostly through individual screens that we consume images, what does this tell us about our bodies and the spaces we design for them?

Cinema has certainly surpassed the relationship between aesthetic experiences and the moral siphoning advocated by Paleotti's use of imagery. The will to extend control through typological appropriation of aesthetic devices such as the black box might still be latent in film production, but cinema is seeking its own way to navigate the oceans of individual media. Image consumption today is undeniably outside of the black box theater, finding its way through a re-immersion of sensorial experiences that recognizes the body as sensory. It seems that cinema is poised to find a new typology fit for the contemporary spectator.

NOTES

1. The reference to images here is specifically to flat artwork within built spaces, but it is important to recognize the many other types of images that are unrelated to physical space, such as in manuscripts and scrolls, as well as a much broader understanding of images that encompasses non-visual imagery. For an extensive development of the latter, see: Chiara Bottici, *Imaginal Politics. Images Beyond Imagination and the Imaginary* (New York: Columbia University Press, 2014).
2. For Paleotti, images could be transformative; built into the space of churches they become part of the sacredness of the church itself: "painters of sacred images, are like mute theologians" who have the capacity to "delight, teach, and move" Paleotti (2012, 309).

3. Indra Kagis McEwen, *Vitruvius, Writing the Body of Architecture*, 6.
4. In the context of this text, drawings and diagrams are also images. A first example of a treatise that takes Vitruvius's original treatise as a point of departure is Alberti's *De Re Aedificatoria*, illustrated with woodcuts of Alberti's own drawings. Also known as *The Four Books of Architecture*, Alberti's treatise, as well as subsequent ones, does not make explicit reference to Vitruvius's original treatise, but it was the point of departure. For more on this, and a reference to a complete listing of Vitruvius editions, see Kagis McEwen (2003, 306, note 5).
5. It is known that Vitruvius favored words over drawing. Indeed, when he describes the qualities an architect should have, the ability to write comes first, followed by the ability to draw. According to McEwen in the original Ten books, there are a total of four drawings. Indra Kagis McEwen, *Vitruvius: Writing the Body of Architecture*, 17.
6. Vitruvius, *The Ten Books of Architecture, Book 3: On Symmetry*, 73.
7. McEwen describes how starting from the metaphysical framework of the Stoics, to the more explicit Greco-Roman notions by people such as Pythagoras and Cicero, the square and the circle were key organizing principals, including in the origins of the city of Rome: believed to have been initially plowed in a circle—deriving the urbs—but then placed in a square (*quadrata*) for equilibrium and stability. For more information, see McEwen (2003, 156–68).
8. Indra Kagis McEwen, *Vitruvius: Writing the Body of Architecture*, 15.
9. The bracketed content in "(hu)man" is referencing the continued domination of male figures in representations of ideals that are supposed to define all of humanity. Within this text there is an implicit recognition of the perils of erasing differences by continuing to package species into one patriarchal category, but tackling it explicitly will be the part of forthcoming work. For her continued guidance on this matter, I am indebted to anarchafeminist philosopher and mentor Chiara Bottici.
10. For more on this account, see Robin Evans, *Translation from Drawing to Building*, 163.
11. "Even the most perfect reproduction of a work of art is lacking in one element: its presence in time and space, its unique existence at the place where it happens to be." Walter Benjamin, "The Work of Art in the Age of Mechanical Reproduction," 220.
12. In this text, the term "artwork" encompasses film.
13. Chiara Bottici, *Imaginal Politics. Images Beyond Imagination and the Imaginary*, 55.
14. Emanuele Coccia, *Sensible Life*, 14–15.
15. Stacy Alaimo, *Bodily Natures: Science, Environment, and the Material Self* (Indiana University Press, 2010), 2.
16. This is an explicit reference to Walter Benjamin's "*The Work of Art in the Age of Mechanical Reproduction.*" While Benjamin's work is of huge value to the development of this text, there is also a critique embedded in it, by emphasizing a multifaceted understanding of how art can be appreciated.

> Contrary to what Benjamin thought, there is more than one way to appreciate the work of an architect, to go to the theater, or to look at a painting. If this were not the case, there would be no need for aesthetic devices like the dark cube in the first place. (*In Broad Daylight*, 73)

17. Gilbert Rose, *The Power of Form*, 13.
18. For a more detailed account on the writing of Louis Delluc (who describes the picture house as a "promiscuous environment" and "paradoxical place") and others, see Pedullà, (2012, 27–28).
19. Gabriele Pedullà, *In Broad Daylight*, 17–18.
20. Ibid., 17.
21. Pedullà describes how these six elements are key in our conception of movie-going. *In Broad Daylight*, 25–26.
22. "A cinematic architecture and new model of spectator emerged hand-in-hand with a profound change in movies," *In Broad Daylight*, 38.
23. For a more in-depth account on the philosophical repercussions of re-drawing the Vitruvian image, and examples ranging from serious to parody, see: Rosi Braidotti, *The Posthuman* (Oxford: Polity Press, 2013), 21, 63.
24. Leon Battista Alberti, *The Art of Building in Ten Books*. In Latin, *De Re Aedificatoria, c.*1443.
25. This is the title of a chapter in *In Broad Daylight*, 37–60.
26. Gabriele Pedullà, *In Broad Daylight*, 33.
27. This uniqueness is the *aura* that Benjamin refers to when discussing art, although according to him film did not have aura at all. Similarly, in "The Decay of Cinema," Sontag describes a loss for cinema in the era of declining single-screen movie theaters.
28. Frederick Kiesler quoted by Gabriele Pedullà, *In Broad Daylight*, 51–52.
29. Ibid., 52.
30. In *Elastic Architecture*, the author claims that Kiesler had taken an early interest in Freud, with his library showcasing many of Freud's publications, including *The Interpretation of Dreams*, 191.
31. The analogy between psychoanalysis and architecture through the concepts of fusion and regression is further developed in Eva Perez de Vega "Psychoanalysis and Architecture: Effects of Sensuous Space" in *Choreographing Space* (London: Artifice Press, 2021) In particular, the idea that regression is stimulated from a sense of oneness with the environment.
32. Freud's paper "Unheimlich," literally meaning "unhomely" but translated into English as "The Uncanny," deals with the notion of domesticity and familiarity, putting forward the circumstances in which the familiar can become uncanny and frightening. In this paper, Freud explores the psychodynamics of that which arouses dread and horror and is particularly interested in the duality inherent in the meaning of the term. Sigmund Freud, "The Uncanny," in *The Standard Edition of the Complete Psychological Works of Sigmund Freud*, Volume XVII, 219.
33. Gabriele Pedullà, *In Broad Daylight*, 52.

REFERENCES

Alaimo, Stacy. *Bodily Natures: Science, Environment, and the Material Self.* Indiana University Press, 2010.

Alberti, Leon Battista. *On the Art of Building in Ten Books.* Cambridge, MA: MIT Press, 1988.

Benjamin, Walter. "The Work of Art in the Age of Mechanical Reproduction." In *Illuminations.* New York, NY: Schocken, 1968.

Bottici, Chiara, *Imaginal Politics. Images Beyond Imagination and the Imaginary.* New York: Columbia University Press, 2014.

Coccia, Emanuele. *The Sensible Life.* New York, NY: Fordham University Press, 2016.

Braidotti, Rosi. *The Posthuman.* Oxford: Polity Press, 2013.

Evans, Robin. *Translation from Drawing to Building.* Cambridge, MA: MIT Press, 1997.

Freud, Sigmund. "The Uncanny." In *The Standard Edition of the Complete Psychological Works of Sigmund Freud*, vol. XVII, 217–56. *An Infantile Neurosis and Other Works*, 1919.

McEwen, Kagis Inga. *Vitruvius. Writing the Body of Architecture.* Cambridge, MA: MIT Press, 2003.

Paleotti, Gabriele. *Discourse on Sacred and Profane Images.* Los Angeles, CA: Getty Publications, 2012.

Pedullà, Gabriele. *In Broad Daylight: Movies and Spectators After the Cinema.* New York, NY: Verso, 2012.

Perez de Vega, Eva. *Choreographing Space.* London: Artifice Press, 2021.

Phillips, Stephen J. *Elastic Architecture: Frederick Kiesler and Design Research in the First Age of Robotic Culture.* Cambridge, MA: MIT Press, 2017.

Rose, Gilbert J. "The Power of Form." *A Psychoanalytic Approach to Aesthetic Form.* Madison, CT: International Press Inc., 1992.

Sontag, Susan. "The Decay of Cinema." New York Times Magazine, February 25, 1996.

Vitruvius. *The Architecture of M. Vitruvius, Pollio*, vol. 1. Translated by W. Newton. London: Creative Media Partners, LLC, 1791.

12

Projective Environments, Atmospheric Architectures

Giuliana Bruno

> *Geometrical notions [...] are limits of things. But illuminated space implies the attenuation of these limits.*
>
> —Emmanuel Levinas[1]

> *We project our culture, our decipherment of things in the world, as if onto a screen. [...] Projection explains to me the birth of meaning, so in this way I see that the projection modifies the meaning of the object.*
>
> —Fabio Mauri[2]

Light is a medium that travels across space, and as it reverberates in the atmosphere it creates ambiance. From this luminiferous wave of energy the art of projection was born, out of a desire to transform space through luminosity and shadow play. This historical atmospheric transformation of light space into a liminal site by means of technology is the basis of projection.[3] It is its material zero degree: the very materiality that constitutes the illuminated, mutable ambiance of a screening space. Light reflecting on a surface is also the element that makes the screen a transitive, projective architecture. As we watch these surface reflections change on their plane of vision, we can observe an actual process of "becoming screen."[4] A world of moving particles and electromagnetic vibrations is the force that activates screen surface and shapes the atmosphere of projection.

One can sense this precise "elemental" process—screen space becoming an atmosphere—in the work of Tobias Putrih. Interested in visionary concepts of architecture and design, the artist creates architectural modifications of various public spaces, including movie theaters, constructing temporary environments out of such quotidian materials as paper, cardboard, plywood, monofilament, and light. As exemplified in his *(Space for) Total Anastrophes* (2018) (see Figure 12.1), he designs projection spaces that are notably atmospheric. For this work, he created an illuminated space of projection with a structure made of bamboo or arundo, and employed sheer textile materials that hung down from it in the form of drapes, in such a way creating curtain-scrims for projection. Such a display system, which could be reconfigured, was assembled as a performance venue and projection space for video works, which activated the ambiance with their luminous transport of moving images.[5] As is evident here and, as we will see, in other of his works that reinvent the space of cinema, Putrih's installations reimagine the very architecture of projection, recreating its various atmospheric possibilities of liminality. This is an artist who does not conceive of the cinema as a dark room in which our bodies disappear but rather, as he puts it, "as a highly personalized space in which the body comes into direct contact with its surroundings and these surroundings are absorbed" into the very projection space.[6]

The luminiferous architectural nature of Putrih's filmic installations engages the atmospheric genealogy of the act of screening itself. This is because in his work the screen of projection is not simply conceived optically, as a window or a mirror.[7] It is rather understood haptically as a luminous transitional space, and conceived

FIGURE 12.1: Tobias Putrih, *(Space for) Total Anastrophes*, 2018. Arundo poles, fabric, rope, volcanic rocks, projectors, and speakers, approx. 20 × 17 × 4 m. Installation view at Villa Lunatica, Fiorucci Foundation, Stromboli, Italy. Photo: Tobias Putrih. Courtesy of the artist.

materially as an environmental medium. Furthermore, for Putrih the act of screening is architectural, in the sense that it is ambient. His projections foreground the shifting spatial qualities of an atmosphere and often function as sites of passage. They engage access—a form of "dooring"—rather than the pure, fixed geometry of a window or a frame.[8]

As they create this architecture of passage, Putrih's projective screens filter the ambiance, producing transitive atmospheric environments. In this sense, his contemporary projections remind us of the archeology of the medium itself, which at times they even directly engage. The artist is fully aware of the environment in which the cultural history of projection emerged and in which it operates, and works with historical ways of creating what I elsewhere call an "atmospheric screening."[9] By digging into the atmosphere of media archeology, then, we can further flesh out the architectural and ambient elements of the action of screening that are central to Putrih's artistic pursuits. Let us consider aspects of the architectural history of projection that inform his artistic space.

The screen's ambient genealogy

An exploration of the interesting, evolving etymology of the word *screen* can help to illuminate the "elemental" and environmental history of projection that Putrih recreates in his work. As we engage media archeology in a spatial way, we note that the notion of the screen, and its luminous vision, greatly preceded the invention of cinema and even the invention of precinematic devices. The word *screen*, indeed, had long been used in relation to space before it was applied to the art of projection. It took hold during the early Renaissance, after first appearing in the last part of the thirteenth century in Europe. The etymology can be traced back to an earlier, Medieval Germanic root that was also present in Latin languages, as evident in the current French expression *écran* or the Italian *schermo*. The term originally pointed to a variety of mediums, surfaces, and types of screening, a significant portion of which emerged from configurations of material space and, in particular, from the world of architecture. As the media historian Erkki Huhtamo has shown, a screen designated in particular "a floor-standing piece of furniture, consisting of a sheet of lighter, often translucent material (paper, some kind of fabric, etc.) stretched on a wooden frame (or a series of connected, folding frames)."[10]

By the nineteenth century, this fabrication of the screen—its textural materiality—unfolded into a new kind of fabric. Its material state was altered, and a new state of matter emerged on the screen. Transferred from architectural space to the realm of precinematic media, the term came to define a new type of translucent membrane: a light-reflecting fabric for the transmission of luminous images. The term for a material, luminiferous plane of translucency interestingly expanded to encompass a surface of projection. It is significant to note that *The Century Dictionary and Cyclopedia*, published originally in 1889, defines the screen first architecturally, as "a covered framework, partition, or curtain [...]; as, a fire-screen; a folding-screen; a window-screen," but then includes in this form of ambient metamorphosis, "a screen upon which images can be cast by a magic lantern."[11] The architectural fabrication of the screen thus became folded into a projective cultural fabric, retaining its function of making space, transforming sites, and filtering ambiance.

This architectural history of the screen's material evolution is profoundly linked to the environment and to the formation of ambiance. The evolution of the term tells us that what we now call *screen* and understand to be a projective surface originated in the world of objects and in the quotidian materiality of space. The screen was a "thing," a mobile object of furniture that inhabited interiors. It functioned especially as a "cultural technique" to negotiate inside and outside, and materially—atmospherically—to transform space, acting in concert with light.[12] When deployed to divide space in the home, a screen mediated between private and public zones of habitation, creating an ambiance of privacy and intimacy. Such is the spatial function that the screen most powerfully embodied when, at the end of the nineteenth century, it became a feature of the film theater, where spectators could experience the projection of exteriors into interiors in a social atmosphere of "public intimacy."[13]

The architecture and atmosphere of projection

Born as a fabric that served as a translucent filter, the screen lives on in the contemporary visual art of Tobias Putrih as such a piece of material culture. In his installation spaces, screen is always made into an architectural entity, and it has its own materiality. Constructed as a dimensional object, it is at times conceived as a sheer partition or translucent divider, and even fashioned as a curtain-scrim. Furthermore, in all their manifestations, his screens of projection maintain a spatial function that is ambient and transient. They are positioned within a constructed architecture, made of quotidian materials, that plays imaginatively with the filtering of light to create liminality. In this sense, they evoke not only the media-archeological origin of the screen but also its architectural evolution in the space of projection. Hence, in order to underscore how Putrih configures the act of screening as an environment, it is also important to look into the architecture of the historical film theater and consider its various constructions of projective space. This is because the artist himself explores how the architecture of cinema has functioned in history, developing over the course of time.

The phenomenon of projection that we experience in many of Putrih's installations is a film theater reimagined in the public space of the contemporary art gallery. The artist reworks periods of the architectural history of film exhibition as it reinvents them in art spaces. He engages the history of projection itself as an architectural, ambient modality, for this history shows how the screen became a tensile architecture, developing from its etymological origins into a luminous design surface. As his installations remake filmic architectures in this way, they highlight in particular the objecthood of the screen in space. Showing how a screen functions as a fabric of projection, they treat its material consistency as a plastic matter. Putrih sensitizes gallery viewers to the screen's sculptural volume, making them aware of how it is placed volumetrically in the space of projection and how it is activated atmospherically in an exhibition space conceived as a transitive, social environment.

Working in this way, Putrih especially references moments in the pivotal decade of the 1920s, when the architecture of screening developed as a surface for design in ambient ways. The 1920s, in fact, saw the rise of movie palaces: lavishly designed and richly ornamented public spaces of projection.[14] Here, as for Putrih in the contemporary art gallery, the screen is part of a larger space—an element of an "installation"—and participates in the creation of the social atmosphere of the site. Sensitive to this modality of exhibition, Putrih "architects" the space of projection in the public gallery today with this era's specific historical precedent in mind. His work reminds us in particular of the environmental turn that the art of projection took with the design of the "atmospheric theater."

Movie palaces of the modern era underscored the spectator's absorption in the surface environment of projection. Many of them created surface space with simple ornamental lines, curves, and geometries.[15] But John Eberson, the master architect of atmospheric theaters, whose vision is clearly central to Putrih, went further in creating ambiance. He designed film spaces that embodied the nineteenth-century notion of *Stimmung*—that is, affective atmospheres that instill a sentiment, state of mind, mood, or tonality.[16] In these theaters, built as if they were sets, spectators would experience inside and outside as fluid borders, for the surrounding interior décor was often an architectural reproduction of an exterior, and the textures of light and darkness were a featured part of the film show. In describing the Capitol Theater he built in Chicago in 1925, Eberson emphasized the importance of artfully using "paint, brush, and electric light, tree ornament, furnishing, lights and shadows" in atmospheric theater design.[17] The Loew's Paradise Theatre he built in the Bronx in 1929 resembled Italian garden architecture and featured celestial ceiling lights that reproduced the full spectrum of the passage from day to night. This radiant atmosphere resonated with the luminous surface of the screen, conceived as one tiny element of the grand surface design of the immense, ornate theater environment.[18] These atmospheric theaters were stimulating immersive spaces that could surround and engage spectators sensorially, creating an ambiance that was also a tonality of mood.

Attuned to the creation of such ambiance, Putrih has precisely reformulated the elaborate atmosphere that characterized Eberson's design. In 2007, he constructed the Slovenian Pavilion for the Venice Biennale on San Servolo Island, near Venice, with the explicit aim of returning Eberson's design for the Loew's Paradise Theatre back to its roots. The location for the cinematic pavilion was particularly important because that historic theater, redolent of Italian garden atmospheres, was originally called The Venetian. For this reason, Putrih significantly titled his architectural installation, directly inspired by the theater's design, *Venetian, Atmospheric* (see Figure 12.2). In this way, he was gesturing not only to history. He was taking the design of the Loew's Paradise Theatre back to its roots in a way that engaged even more than choosing this perfect name and locating the installation in the very terrain of its cultural origin. His restaging of Eberson's historical atmospherics was a gesture of conceptual reinterpretation: the activation of a philosophy of design. The pavilion was designed with biomorphically curved walls, made of wooden slats that allowed ambient light to transpire within the structure and

FIGURE 12.2: Tobias Putrih, *Venetian, Atmospheric*, 2007. Scaffolding, OSB boards, plywood, PVC curtains, LED lights, approx. 13 × 8 × 6 m. Installation view at San Servolo Island, Slovenian Pavilion, Venice Biennale. Photo: Michele Lamanna. Courtesy of the artist.

enhanced the role of atmosphere, even its affect. In such a way, the very atmosphere of the atmospheric movie palace was reinvented. The temporary structure filtered light during the day and lit up at night, activating an atmospheric play of light and shadows, enabling the formation of color space, and stimulating the diffusion of ambient sensations, tonalities, and moods. At times, the architecture of this filmic space even felt elemental, as when the light turned red and the cinema appeared to be on fire. This particular ambient effect reminds us that celluloid, a fragile substance, is, at its root, a matter of light and fire, and that this material often went up in flames. Igniting such a mutable, luminous ambiance, *Venetian, Atmospheric* thus engaged not only Eberson's atmospheric design but also the genealogy of cinema itself, its "elemental" constituents and material space. Here, experiencing the shifting projections of ambient light that filled the space, we can sense the actual atmosphere, the zero degree, and the very unstable ambiance of the art of projection.

Modernist projections

In the 1920s, when the elaborate atmospheric movie palace was designed, a different kind of perceptual atmosphere emerged as well, and this more minimal form of design also shaped the course of film architecture. The Modernist model of building space created the ambiance of projection with less ornamentation and more purely ambient effects. Attentive to the history of theater design, Putrih has reinvented this ambient philosophy of construction as well in fabricating his perceptual atmospheres. We can see the Modernist structure at work in his more minimal installations of film theaters in gallery spaces, and especially in those works that emphasize simple structures, the mechanics of projection, white planes, and pure surface space. To understand the origin of these configurations and grasp the significance of Modernism for this artist's process of constructing theater space, we need to look more closely at the perceptual filmic atmospheres it engaged.

The perceptual model in question produced a variety of Modernist film theaters, including the Café and Cinéma de l'Aubette, designed in the De Stijl vernacular by Théo van Doesburg, in collaboration with Jean Arp and Sophie Taeuber-Arp, for the city of Strasbourg in 1926–28. In New York, this perceptual modality was embodied in the Film Guild Cinema, designed in Neoplastic style by Frederick Kiesler, a vanguard architect whose mid-century Modernist oeuvre is dear to Putrih.[19] For his cinema, built in New York in 1929, Kiesler conceived of a spectator ideally "projected" from the darkness of the theater into the light of a central screen, which resembled the diaphragm of a camera. With its lack of architectural decoration, ornament here was minimally created by the medium of light and the texture of sound waves. Mechanical panels enabled the screen to expand or contract, and the walls angled toward this flexible, kinetic screen, which Kiesler named a "screen-o-scope." His elastic screen design also called for an unrealized "project-o-scope" that would have extended the projection from the center screen onto the two side walls and ceiling to create multiple, continuous projections and a total, enveloping film environment. The way Kiesler conceptualized projecting light onto these wall screens gave architectural form to the notion of cine-projection as surface space. In envisioning such a surface cinema, the architect stated that "the film is a play on surface, the theatre a play in space. [...] The ideal cinema is the house of silence. [...] The spectator must be able to lose himself in an imaginary, endless space."[20]

This perceptually absorbing model that experimented with the architecture of screening is relevant for Putrih because he explores the formal nature of Modernist experimentation in his own experimental designs, including those of the film theater. In doing so, the artist has particularly mined the visionary work of Kiesler, and even conceived an archival work, *Kiesler vs Fuller* (2003), which reconceived the false dichotomy between the two architects proposed in a 1952 exhibition at the Museum of Modern Art in New York. In architecting cinematic perception in space, Putrih creatively refashions visionary atmospheres of cinema, with a particular penchant for their minimal construction of enveloping ambiance. Modernist experimental design is a significant source of reference especially because the style is radically inscribed in a specific model of the film theater. It informs the cinematheque, as conceived by Kiesler and other architects, whose intimate space of projection Putrih strives to remake in the art gallery.

Cineclub at Thomas Dane (2005) is an example, as even its title suggests.[21] When asked to create a space for projection within an existing London gallery, Putrih researched the formation of the cinematheque, and thought about how a gallery space could serve as such a space, and how best to transform it into this particular site of public intimacy. For this purpose, he delved into the history of the architecture of cinemas of the 1920s and 1930s, particularly as conceived in Britain. He especially found inspiration in the New Victoria Theatre, designed in the Art Deco style by Ernest Wamsley Lewis and William Edward Trent. This design guided him in architecting a contemporary version of this expansive former cinema for a modern cineclub.

Modernist perceptual architecture is thus a generative artistic paradigm for Putrih, who explores its various forms of pure absorption into ambiance. For *Lost Cinema* (2001–02), the artist went so far as to conceive an imaginary movie about the Bauhaus-trained Austrian designer and artist Herbert Bayer, whose notion of an expansive field of vision shaped exhibition design. Putrih's interest in experimentation even extends into spiritual forms of modern design, as seen in *Cinéma*

Attitudes (2008) (see Figure 12.3), whose geometric and organic forms of construction, and play of interior–exterior light, relate to Rudolph Steiner's ideas about the healing powers of architecture. Also perceptually charged is *An Auditorium for "Empty the Pond to Get the Fish"* (2008) (see Figure 12.4). Here, lucent strips of celluloid film were suspended from the ceiling of London's White Cube gallery in order to create the intimate interior of an auditorium for screening the film by artist Runa Islam mentioned in the title. It is significant for Putrih's luminous, minimal design that this film explores an abandoned Modernist building by the postwar Austrian architect Karl Schwanzer, originally built for the 1958 World's Fair in Brussels and later renovated to become the Museum of the Twentieth Century in Vienna. Fashioned into translucent, undulating partitions, the luminescent panels of celluloid strips that curtain the auditorium act as if they were screens, and effectively function to "screen" the space. This effect is reprised in Putrih's *A Room for Four Film Projections* (2008), featuring a scaffolding grid that provides structural support for translucent dividers. Fabricated from simple layers of colored plastic foil, these partitions also perceptually turn into screening devices.

As these works suggest, Putrih considers modern, perceptual experiments with spaces of projection a productive "open form." This is especially visible in *Sequential*, a 2012 projection space inspired by the Open Form concept proposed in 1959 by the Finnish-born Polish architect and artist Oskar Hansen, who

FIGURE 12.3: Tobias Putrih, *Cinéma Attitudes*, 2008. Scaffolding, OSB plates, rope, LCD projector, plywood, zip ties, approx. 16 × 8.5 × 3 m. Installation view at Attitudes, Geneva. Photo: Steeve Luckner. Courtesy of the artist and Gregor Podnar, Berlin.

FIGURE 12.4: Tobias Putrih, *An Auditorium for "Empty the Pond to Get the Fish"*, 2008. Projection screen, film strips, plywood rails, clips, cardboard seats, tape, mirror, scaffolding, 35mm projector, and Runa Islam's film *Empty the Pond to Get the Fish*. Installation view at White Cube, Hoxton Square, London. Photo: Todd-White Art Photography. Courtesy of the artist.

diverged from the orthodoxy of the Modern movement. Putrih's own interest in the formal modality of modern experimentation itself transcends the typical Western European canon. It is rather an open form that extends, in generative ways, both geographically and historically. *Šiška, International*, for example, shown at the Centre Pompidou in 2010, is inspired by two late Modernist cinema spaces of Eastern Europe's socialist era. The architectural form of the Kino International, designed by Josef Kaiser and Heinz Aust in East Berlin in 1963, is here intermingled with Putrih's memory of the Šiška Cinema in Lubljana, Slovenia, his city of origin. The geometric construction of the Kino International's exterior façade is reproduced in the installation's interior, with a design of prismatic walls made of cardboard, plaster, and plywood. The space is further fractured by the LED lights that refract across this geometric surface space. An ambiance redolent of eccentric Constructivist geometry is thus re-architected as a contemporary design construct.

As vital forms of imaginative construction, Modernist configurations are not a thing of the past for Putrih. As he productively explores how a model is transposed into different places and evolves over time, he pays attention to how it has been reincarnated in later experimental forms.[22] In this regard, in the process of reconfiguring modern architectures of cinema he has also turned to the architectural history of Anthology Film Archives, a legendary New York City cinematheque. In 2005, Putrih conceived a project, *Anthology/Maya Deren* and *Anthology/Courthouse*, that is not only informed by but centered on Anthology's previous and current screening spaces.[23] The legacy of an open process of Modernist experimentation lives on in the atmosphere itself of this project, which recreates the intimacy of this cinematheque's spaces in a gallery. Particularly relevant for this project is the history of Anthology's experiment in theater architecture. To see what specifically inspired this work, and how it is connected to others we have been considering, a short detour is necessary.

It is no wonder that Putrih turned his attention to this cinematheque, for Modernist perceptual ambiance deeply informed Austrian filmmaker Peter Kubelka's experimental design for the Invisible Cinema, which was Anthology Film Archive's first space for exhibition.[24] Operating from 1970 to 1974, this theater was a late Modernist architectural expression of a mission to create a museum of film art, a temple especially devoted to avant-garde cinema.[25] The Invisible Cinema seated fewer than 100 people but was visited by more than 14,000 spectators in its first year. In this "interior wholly sheathed in light-absorbing fabric," art and film theorist Annette Michelson found "the architecture of the Velvet Light Trap."[26] To ensure complete perceptual fusion in the environment of the cinema—a total black box—the velvet spectators' seats were outfitted with shell-like partitions that rose on each side and extended above. A screen in its own right, this divider encapsulated the spectator both atmospherically and aurally, with blinders that prevented peripheral vision or distraction from the side. The surroundings were "screened," and one was shielded as well as protected and sheltered in the ambiance. The spectator was thus clearly directed to face a "radiating" screen surface, as Kubelka put it, for "the screen and the film were the only visual points of reference" for the audience.[27] Silence and proper behavior were enforced in this "machine for viewing," though the designer emphasized a possible haptic connection among spectators.[28] "Only your eyes were shaded from your neighbor, approximately from the shoulders on," Kubelka explained, "but you could touch your neighbors, and since this was not a complete partition, you always felt that there was someone on your side."[29] He insisted that, in this way, "a sympathetic community was created," for "architecture has to provide a structure in which one is in a community that is not disturbing to others."[30]

This idea of providing a structure to create, and to sustain, a sense of community, epitomized by Anthology Film Archives, is essential to Putrih, who conceives his installations as social spaces. Fond of Modernist experiments in design such as Kubelka's, he takes particular care in reconceiving the space of the auditorium, which is a focus of his experimental theater design. The seats of his theatrical installations are always architected inventively. His design for *Lost Cinema Lost* (2008) emblematically focuses on spectatorial architecture as a way to provide a structural revision of the Modernist cinema model, and to take modern experiments in public-building into contemporary times. To view projections of Runa Islam's films, here Putrih designed two connected spaces.[31] One auditorium featured a bleacher-like seating unit constructed from metal scaffolding tubes used in the exterior construction of buildings. On the other side of this gridded structure, which has both an abstract and material feel, another, more enclosed projection space is configured. Made of cardboard, styrofoam, monofilament, and colored filters, this temporary structure is reminiscent of De Stijl architecture, and appears to illuminate the space with the ambiance of a Dan Flavin installation. In such a way, Putrih envisions ambient interpretations of the space of projection, and we sense once again a continuation of perceptual experimental histories as well as the longing for reinventing the cinematheque in the gallery. The flexible structures of this "lost cinema" even recall the loss of Kiesler's Film Guild Cinema, long ago destroyed, as well as the loss of Anthology's Invisible Cinema, which also no longer exists. But in this project, as in other installations, the elastic, pliant features for screening film that Kiesler pioneered and the creative seating design that Kubelka promoted have found new life. With temporary filmic structures that are reconfigurable, Putrih remakes a form of experimentation with theater design that focuses on an intimate auditorium and a flexible, adaptable screen architecture, reinventing them for the contemporary gallery's public space.

With regard to this experimental legacy, we should also stress that, within the structure of his spaces, Putrih projects experiential atmospheres with a minimal design of white screen fabric that itself feels Modernist. Several projects presented under the title *Soft Screens* (2001–05) exhibit the pure geometry of the white screen in gallery space, unraveling and twisting it in minimal, folded form. This design is further articulated in the context of *Slight Agitation*, a commissioned project of site-specific works for the Fondazione Prada in Milan.[32] For this occasion, Putrih realized *Corner Set* (2016) (see Figure 12.5), an atmospheric assemblage of translucent white screens that have a sculptural feel and function as architectural partitions to be traversed by the viewers. Reconsider now in this context the 2005 Anthology Film Archives project, which is part of this enterprise of refashioning white screen space. For *Anthology/Maya Deren* and *Anthology/Courthouse*, Putrih recreated projection screens that were sized to match the current screens of Anthology Film Archives, as they exist today in the new incarnation of the cinematheque in New York, located in the former site of the Second Avenue Courthouse. But the artist not only meticulously replicated the size of the projection screens of Anthology's two cinema spaces (the smaller Maya Deren and larger

FIGURE 12.5: Tobias Putrih, *Corner Set*, 2016. Polycarbonate, paint, aluminum. Installation view at Fondazione Prada, Milan. Photo: Delfino Sisto Legnani. Courtesy of the artist.

Courthouse theaters); he reshaped them, installing them sculpturally in an all-white gallery, twisting their sheer white fabric and hanging them from hooks and wires. In twisting Modernist paradigms—so fond of the white wall surface—in this way, a translucent white ambiance was fashioned, in which, as the artist puts it, "the screen materializes and defines its own space" of existence.[33] During the gallery exhibition, no films were projected on the folded white screen fabrics, for they were meant to display their own architectural surface and conceptual texture.

This gesture of creating a minimal white ambiance—a surface environment of projection—reminds us of media theorist Vilém Flusser's claim that "technical images are envisioned surfaces."[34] For Putrih, an artist who envisions the very objecthood of the illuminated white film screen in gallery space, a surface is fundamentally a thing of light. Following the course of *Anthology/Maya Deren* and *Anthology/Courthouse*, this was made even more tangible in the installation *Re-projection: Hoosac*, shown at MASS MoCA in 2010. With minimal means, this work envisions in gallery setting the pure experience of luminous projection activated in a film theater. Without literally exhibiting or reproducing the apparatus of film screening, Putrih recreates its liminal atmosphere. Long lines of monofilament strung horizontally in space are illuminated by spotlights, generating an ambiance of white light. An extended cone of light is formed as waves of luminosity travel through the monofilaments. The effect is that the stream of white light appears to be emitted from some absent film projector, emanating as if it were actually "projected." The viewer of this installation is thus immersed into an enveloping atmosphere that is, in all senses, tangibly projective. Bathed in ambiance, she is absorbed into a surface of light.

For Putrih, then, an architectural surface is ultimately a space of depth. Full of atmospheric nuances, it is dense with ambient effects and layered with strata of architectural history. In working, as we have seen, especially closely with the evolving history of film-theater design, his installations incorporate on their surfaces both the purely perceptual constructions and more elaborate atmospheric forms of these once ubiquitous cinemas. In recreating the social architecture of projection in the art gallery in this way, mutable geometries and variable architectonics come to light. Positioned in tensile sculptural form in temporary, adaptable architectures resembling screen-like partitions, Putrih's envisioned screen surfaces become themselves translucent textural objects. As they filter and veil the light, they too change the tone of the space. Such re-envisioned projective ambiance does not simply remake but translates the illuminated space of filmic projection, transferring it into the social space of a gallery or public site. In doing so, the work also reinforces the architectural genealogy of the screen, a material object that was born as a space of translucency and intended not only to make but also to modify ambiance. Putrih's installations of screen space thus create a transformative "envisioned surface." They construct real ambiance—a material, historically charged atmosphere of projection.

NOTES

1. Emmanuel Levinas, *Totality and Infinity: An Essay on Exteriority*, trans. Alphonso Lingis (The Hague: Martinus Nijhoff, 1979), 190.
2. Interview with Fabio Mauri, *Alfabeta2*, no. 2 (September 2010), cited by Umberto Eco in his preface, "A Convinced Bewilderment," in Fabio Mauri, *Ideology and Memory*, ed. Studio Fabio Mauri (Turin: Bollati Boringhieri, 2012), xiv.
3. See Giuliana Bruno, *Atmospheres of Projection: Environmentality in Art and Screen Media* (Chicago, IL: University of Chicago Press, 2022). This essay expands on the path of research undertaken in that book, which is aimed at defining "atmospheric thinking" and reconfiguring "the projective imagination" as an atmosphere while considering the art of projection, understood as an environment, both in history and in contemporary art.
4. For a previous extended treatment of the role of the screen as haptic, transitional space in art, architecture, and film, see Giuliana Bruno, *Surface: Matters of Aesthetics, Materiality, and Media* (Chicago, IL: University of Chicago Press, 2014). I continued that investigation in more atmospheric and ambient terms in my essay "The Screen as Object: Art and the Atmospheres of Projection," in *Dreamlands: Immersive Cinema and Art, 1905–2016*, ed. Chrissie Iles, exh. cat. (New York, NY: Whitney Museum of American Art, 2016), 156–67.

5. (*Space for*) *Total Anastrophes* was exhibited at Villa Lunatica, in Stromboli, Italy, July 27–29, 2018, and at Dhaka Art Summit, Dhaka, Bangladesh, February 2–10, 2018. The flexible display system was assembled as a performance and projection space for the eighth edition of *Volcano Extravaganza*, a program featuring works by Runa Islam, Cecilia Bengolea, Haroon Mirza, Alex Cecchetti, and Patrizio di Massimo, among others.
6. Putrih's statement appears in *Tobias Putrih 99–07*, ed. Thom Collins and Stuart Krimko, exh. cat. (Zurich: JRP/Ringier, 2008), 16. This publication, produced in conjunction with the exhibition *Tobias Putrih: Quasi-Random* at the Neuberger Museum of Art, is devoted to the first decade of his work, from 1999 to 2007, and includes a discussion of architecture and Modernism.
7. For a review of film theory's association of the screen primarily with visual metaphors, including mirror and window, see Francesco Casetti, *The Lumière Galaxy: Seven Key Words for the Cinema to Come* (New York, NY: Columbia University Press, 2015), 157–60. The optical history of the screen is further treated, along with more environmental aspects, in *Screen Geneaologies: From Optical Device to Environmental Medium*, ed. Craig Buckley, Rüdiger Campe, and Francesco Casetti (Amsterdam: Amsterdam University Press, 2019). See also Dominique Chateau and José Moure, eds., *Screens: From Materiality to Spectatorship* (Amsterdam: Amsterdam University Press, 2016).
8. On the cultural genealogy of the screen as a window, see Anne Friedberg, *The Virtual Window: From Alberti to Microsoft* (Cambridge, MA: MIT Press, 2006); and William John Thomas Mitchell, "Screening Nature (and the Nature of the Screen)," *New Review of Film and Television Studies* 13, no. 3 (2015): 231–46.
9. For further articulation of "atmospheric screening," see my *Atmospheres of Projection.*
10. Erkki Huhtamo, "Elements of Screenology: Toward an Archaeology of the Screen," *ICONICS: International Studies of the Modern Image* 7 (2004): 35.
11. Ibid., 31. Huhtamo cites *The Century Dictionary and Cyclopedia* definition here.
12. On the notion of cultural technique, see Bernhard Siegert, *Cultural Techniques: Grids, Filters, Doors, and Other Articulations of the Real*, trans. Geoffrey Winthrop-Young (New York, NY: Fordham University Press, 2015).
13. On this notion, see Giuliana Bruno, *Public Intimacy: Architecture and the Visual Arts* (Cambridge, MA: MIT Press, 2007).
14. See, among others, Maggie Valentine, *The Show Starts on the Sidewalk: An Architectural History of the Movie Theatre, Starring S. Charles Lee* (New Haven, CT: Yale University Press, 1994).
15. See P. Morton Shand, *Modern Picture-Houses and Theaters* (Philadelphia, PA: J. B. Lippincott, 1930).
16. Eberson built more than 40 atmospheric movie palaces, the majority of which have been destroyed, and altogether about 300 movie theaters, including streamlined, Art Deco versions. In the 1920s, his wife and collaborator, Beatrice Lamb, directed the firm Michael Angelo Studios, which designed the theater interiors. For useful information on Eberson's

atmospheric career, see Richard Stapleford, *Temples of Illusion: The Atmospheric Theaters of John Eberson*, exh. cat. (New York, NY: Bertha and Karl Leubsdorf Art Gallery of Hunter College, 1988).

17. John Eberson, "A Description of the Capitol Theater, Chicago (1925)," in *Moviegoing in America: A Sourcebook in the History of Film Exhibition*, ed. Gregory A. Waller (Oxford: Blackwell, 2002), 106.
18. The Loew's Paradise Theatre, located at 2403 Grand Concourse in Bronx, NY, was subdivided and stripped of features in the 1970s and then closed in 1994. It was renovated and reopened in 2005 as a live theater, and then became a church.
19. On Kiesler, see, among others, Stephen Phillips, *Elastic Architecture: Frederick Kiesler and Design Research in the First Age of Robotic Culture* (Cambridge, MA: MIT Press, 2017); Laura M. McGuire, "A Movie House in Space and Time: Frederick Kiesler's Film Arts Guild Cinema, New York, 1929," *Studies in the Decorative Arts* 14, no. 2 (Spring–Summer 2007): 45–78; and *Frederick Kiesler, Artiste-architecte*, exh. cat. (Paris: Centre Georges Pompidou, 1996). Information on Kiesler's designs also has been drawn from the Kiesler Fund at the Harvard Theatre Collection, Houghton Library, Cambridge, MA.
20. Frederick Kiesler, "Building a Cinema Theater," *New York Evening Post*, February 2, 1929. The Film Guild Cinema, located at 52–54 West Eighth Street in New York City, was short-lived. In 1930, it was renamed, and although it remained opened until 1992, it was stripped of Kiesler's screen-o-scope.
21. Putrih designed the projection space for an exhibition of artists' films curated by Francesco Manacorda, titled *A Certain Tendency in Representation: Cineclub at Thomas Dane*, which was on view September 19–25, 2005.
22. In this regard, I am also thinking of *Majestic* (2007), a projection space that Putrih created for the Wexner Center in Columbus, OH, in which he played with the deconstructivist architectural geometry of Peter Eisenman's building.
23. This work was exhibited at Max Protetch Gallery in New York City, May 6–June 18, 2005.
24. The Invisible Cinema was a part of Joseph Papp's Public Theater at 425 Lafayette Street in New York City, NY. For an oral history of this experimental theater, see Sky Sitney, "The Search for the Invisible Cinema," *Grey Room* 19 (Spring 2005): 102–13.
25. See Kristen Alfaro, "Access and the Experimental Film: New Technologies and Anthology Film Archives' Institutionalization of the Avant-Garde," *Moving Image* 12, no. 1 (Spring 2012): 44–64; P. Adams Sitney, introduction to *The Essential Cinema: Essays on the Films in the Collection of Anthology Film Archives*, ed. P. Adams Sitney with Caroline Sergeant Angell (New York, NY: Anthology Film Archives, 1975), vii–x.
26. Annette Michelson, "Gnosis and Iconoclasm: A Case Study of Cinephilia," *October* 83 (Winter 1998): 5.
27. Peter Kubelka, "The Invisible Cinema," *Design Quarterly* 93 (1974): 32, 34.
28. Ibid., 36.
29. Ibid., 34.

30. Ibid.
31. Installed in Modena, Italy, at Galleria Civica, *Lost Cinema Lost* consisted of two adjoining projection spaces, one constructed to screen Runa Islam's *What is a Thought Experiment, Anyhow?* (2005–06) and the other designed to provide an auditorium structure for her 2007 film *CINEMATOGRAPHY.*
32. The exhibition *Slight Agitation* was curated by the Fondazione Prada Thought Council, whose members are Shumon Basar, Cédric Libert, Elvira Dyangani Ose, and Dieter Roelstraete, and was on view October 20, 2016–January 22, 2017. Putrih realized the first intervention of this four-part artist project, which transformed the Cisterna exhibition space.
33. Putrih's description of this piece appears in *Tobias Putrih 99–07*, 32.
34. Vilém Flusser, *Into the Universe of Technical Images*, trans. Nancy Ann Roth (Minneapolis, MN: University of Minnesota Press, 2011), 33.

REFERENCES

Alfaro, Kristen. "Access and the Experimental Film: New Technologies and Anthology Film Archives' Institutionalization of the Avant-Garde." *Moving Image* 12, no. 1 (Spring 2012): 44–64.

Béret, Chantal, ed. *Frederick Kiesler, Artiste-Architecte.* Paris: Centre Georges Pompidou, 1996. Exhibition catalogue.

Bruno, Giuliana. *Atmospheres of Projection: Environmentality in Art and Screen Media.* Chicago, IL: University of Chicago Press, 2022.

Bruno, Giuliana. *Public Intimacy: Architecture and the Visual Arts.* Cambridge, MA: MIT Press, 2007.

Bruno, Giuliana. *Surface: Matters of Aesthetics, Materiality, and Media.* Chicago, IL: University of Chicago Press, 2014.

Bruno, Giuliana. "The Screen as Object: Art and the Atmospheres of Projection." In *Dreamlands: Immersive Cinema and Art, 1905–2016*, edited by Chrissie Iles, 156–67. New York, NY: Whitney Museum of American Art, 2016. Exhibition catalogue.

Buckley, Craig, Rüdiger Campe, and Francesco Casetti, eds. *Screen Geneaologies: From Optical Device to Environmental Medium.* Amsterdam: Amsterdam University Press, 2019.

Casetti, Francesco. *The Lumière Galaxy: Seven Key Words for the Cinema to Come.* New York, NY: Columbia University Press, 2015.

Collins, Thom, and Stuart Krimko, eds. *Tobias Putrih 99–07.* Zurich: JRP/Ringier, 2008. Exhibition catalogue.

Dominique, Chateau, and José Moure, eds. *Screens: From Materiality to Spectatorship.* Amsterdam: Amsterdam University Press, 2016.

Eberson, John. "A Description of the Capitol Theater, Chicago (1925)." In *Moviegoing in America: A Sourcebook in the History of Film Exhibition*, edited by Gregory A. Waller. Oxford: Blackwell, 2002.

Eco, Umberto. "A Convinced Bewilderment." In *Fabio Mauri: Ideology and Memory*, edited by Studio Fabio Mauri. Turin: Bollati Boringhieri, 2012.

Flusser, Vilém. *Into the Universe of Technical Images*. Translated by Nancy Ann Roth. Minneapolis, MN: University of Minnesota Press, 2011.

Friedberg, Anne. *The Virtual Window: From Alberti to Microsoft*. Cambridge, MA: MIT Press, 2006.

Huhtamo, Erkki. "Elements of Screenology: Toward an Archaeology of the Screen." *ICONICS: International Studies of the Modern Image* 7 (2004): 31–82.

Kiesler, Frederick. "Building a Cinema Theater." *New York Evening Post*, February 2, 1929.

Kubelka, Peter. "The Invisible Cinema." *Design Quarterly* 93 (1974): 32–36.

Levinas, Emmanuel. *Totality and Infinity: An Essay on Exteriority*. Translated by Alphonso Lingis. The Hague: Martinus Nijhoff, 1979.

McGuire, Laura M. "A Movie House in Space and Time: Frederick Kiesler's Film Arts Guild Cinema, New York, 1929." *Studies in the Decorative Arts* 14, no. 2 (Spring–Summer 2007): 45–78.

Michelson, Annette. "Gnosis and Iconoclasm: A Case Study of Cinephilia." *October* 83 (Winter 1998): 3–18.

Mitchell, William John Thomas. "Screening Nature (and the Nature of the Screen)." *New Review of Film and Television Studies* 13, no. 3 (2015): 231–46.

Phillips, Stephen. *Elastic Architecture: Frederick Kiesler and Design Research in the First Age of Robotic Culture*. Cambridge, MA: MIT Press, 2017.

Shand, P. Morton. *Modern Picture-Houses and Theaters*. Philadelphia, PA: J. B. Lippincott, 1930.

Siegert, Bernhard. *Cultural Techniques: Grids, Filters, Doors, and Other Articulations of the Real*. Translated by Geoffrey Winthrop-Young. New York, NY: Fordham University Press, 2015.

Sitney, P. Adams. "Introduction." In *The Essential Cinema: Essays on the Films in the Collection of Anthology Film Archives*, edited by P. Adams Sitney with Caroline Sergeant Angell. New York, NY: Anthology Film Archives, 1975.

Sitney, Sky. "The Search for the Invisible Cinema." *Grey Room* 19 (Spring 2005): 102–13.

Stapleford, Richard. *Temples of Illusion: The Atmospheric Theaters of John Eberson*. New York, NY: Bertha and Karl Leubsdorf Art Gallery of Hunter College, 1988. Exhibition catalogue.

Valentine, Maggie. *The Show Starts on the Sidewalk: An Architectural History of the Movie Theatre, Starring S. Charles Lee*. New Haven, CT: Yale University Press, 1994.

Whitney, William Dwight, and Benjamin E. Smith. *The Century Dictionary and Cyclopedia*. New York, NY: Century, 1889–91.

13

Fictive Ecologies of the In-Between

Jason Vigneri-Beane

Liminal spaces, holoents, and hybrids

Near future scenario narratives and production design in science-fiction cinema have long integrated with each other to comprise a distributed laboratory for experimental design. Science-fiction design is dense with couplings amongst architecture and infrastructures at the macro-scale, tectonic systems and mixed-reality mediums at the meso-scale, and objects of information and industrial design at the micro-scale. These design tropes often explore near-future world building that is made harder, more industrial, and more inorganically technical by world-building around corporate control, military protocol, socioecological degradation, and technocratic infrastructuralism. Yet there are recent explorations in science-fiction, such as *Prospect* (2018)[1] and *Annihilation* (2018)[2] wherein ecological environments produce particularly new kinds of design thinking and, in turn, possibilities for architectural innovation.

The fictive ecologies of these two films, the Green of *Prospect* and the Shimmer of *Annihilation*, are transitional environments for the becoming of characters. Characters enter into their existing states, undergo processes of transformation as they pass through the films' ecological spaces and narrative sequences, and emerge in new, if not indeterminate, states of being. This dynamic is akin to Victor Turner's discussion of "states" and "transitions" in Arnold van Gennep's formulation of the "liminal phase" of rites of passage. Here, there are three phases to a rite of passage: a separation in which an individual is "detached" from their sociocultural conditions, a liminal period during which the individual's attributes are ambiguous as they pass through an unfamiliar space, and a reincorporation (or aggregation) phase wherein the individual returns to their sociocultural condition in a transformed state.[3]

As we will see, both the Green and the Shimmer serve as liminal spaces for the transformation of their respective passengers who are indeed the "liminal *personae*" or "threshold people" that Turner describes as "necessarily ambiguous" in that they "slip through the network of classifications that normally locate states and positions in cultural space." What is more, he begins to refer to threshold people as liminal entities. He writes, "Liminal entities are neither here nor there; they are betwixt and between the positions assigned and arrayed by law, custom, convention, and ceremonial [sic]."[4] Turner prompts us to consider how liminal spaces of passage and transition form and are formed by the entities that inhabit them, thus giving us a dual sense of the betwixt: the mutual formation of ambiguous in-between spaces and entities that elude sociocultural categories of existence. These are spatio-temporal becomings that occur across territories and timelines and their dynamics suffuse the ecological design of *Prospect* and *Annihilation*. Donna Haraway also marshals the word "entity" to transcend categories of being while formulating the neologism "holoent."[5] This term recognizes the organic and inorganic hybridity of organisms and technologies in the more-than-human world. While writing about symbionts or organisms whose existences are in mutually forming relationships with each other (e.g., bobtail squids and bioluminescent bacteria), Lynn Margulis developed the word "holobiont." Margulis, a pioneering biologist of life's hybridity, used holobiont as a term for discussing how organisms in symbiotic assemblages[6] need not be read as separate from each other but, rather, as unified living organisms (*bionts*) that are made whole (*holo*) by virtue of being hybrid: holobionts. Haraway adjusts the term from holobiont to "holoent" (whole entity) such that it is no longer limited to the living. It can therefore stand for hybridizations of organic, inorganic, technical, and informational phenomena. In turn, it also offers a way by which we can briefly zoom in to the kinds of cross-categorical entities that emerge within the urbanized worlds of science-fiction design on the way to more extensively exploring couplings and hybridizations in the immersive liminal ecologies of *Prospect* and *Annihilation*.

For example, the postnatural urban-industrial world of *Ghost in the Shell* (1995 and 2017)[7,8] has no ecological naturalism, no flora, and no fauna. It is, however, populated by augmented human and trans-human characters—holoents and cyborgs—that are organic enough to test bio-technical design strategies sited at sensory organs and network connections. This design is about interconnected entities, their couplings, and how they operate in between conditions. Set in the near future, an elite team of government agents called Section 9 uses their technical prostheses, cyberbrains, and networked connectivity to protect New Port City from hackers, stateless actors, corrupted politicians, and corporate machinations. They operate amongst the mixed-reality spaces of the physical city and ethereal information superhighway and their chief super-agent, Major Kusanagi, is the most hybridized of all of them: her consciousness has been uploaded into a cyberbrain that his housed in a braincase inside her cyborg body. Major Kusanagi's iconic neck jacks are the epidermal transition between her synthetic cyborg body, her biological consciousness, and the information networks to which they are connected. The fine micro-scale of their industrial design connects her to vast flows of information, interactions with spatially distributed agents of Section 9 and visualizations of city grids, architectural infrastructures, and operational targets. At the same time, they signal the hybridity of her existence: she is organic, inorganic, and informational. The hybridity-signaling of her neck jacks is echoed in the synthetic sensory organ upgrading of Batou's ranger-goggle eyes and Saito's Hawkeye—a satellite-enabled prosthetic eye for hyper-accurate sniper scoping. While these ocular implants transition the characters from humans to more-than-humans, they also locate them ontologically in-between human and machine by virtue of their capacity to connect to ethereal information ecologies via electronic networks.

In the similarly postnatural world of *Blade Runner* (1982),[9] we meet more liminal entities. Tyrell Corporation Nexus 6 androids have returned to Los Angeles after having been sent to off-world mines. They are transformed by their experiences in a liminal space outside of earthly society and seek status upon their return to it for the remainder of their programmed life expectancies. They appear as humans but, echoing the cyborgs of *Ghost in the Shell*, their ocular technologies are catalytic features of the narrative. Upon return to earth, they seek out the engineer who designed their eyes and attempt to evade Voight-Kampff diagnostic tests that use iris dilation detection to determine their non-human status for the purposes of termination. In *Blade Runner 2049* (2017),[10] organic and inorganic hybridity is designed around ocular technology once more. Niander Wallace, the visually impaired head of Wallace Corporation, "sees" through a swarm of tiny drone-like artificial eyes that place him somewhere between a human, a machine, and an electronic platform. While this swarm of mobile electronic eyes is physically detached from Wallace's body, its wireless signal receptor is nonetheless snapped into a port in his neck, not unlike the neck jacks of Major Kusanagi.

The notion of bio-technical coupling and its informational augmentation is taken into another territory in *District 9* (2009).[11] Once again, we find ourselves in an ecologically degraded urban environment. In a militarized and xenophobic informal settlement in Johannesburg, insectoid aliens live stranded in captivity below their stalled mothership that hovers overhead. The aliens possess extraordinary military technology that their human governors covet but cannot use because this weaponry only fires when coupled with an alien operator's genetic imprint. The organic–inorganic hybridity of this technology is not connected to vast ethereal networks of data as in *Ghost in the Shell* and *Blade Runner 2049* but, rather, to the hyper-local biological information systems of genetic codes. The protagonist, Wikus, begins the film as a government official who is charged with relocating aliens to a camp outside the city. After becoming contaminated by a spray of alien fuel, he begins to transform. As he is becoming alien, he finds that his genetic mutation gives him access to the use of alien weapons which, in turn, makes him and his limbs the targets of the military arms manufacturers. He is forced to flee into the informal settlement, the liminal space of the film, and become a liminal entity that exists between human and alien as well as government official and enemy of the state. The hand-claw at the end of his arm now couples with all manner of alien technology as it genetically imprints to form holoents with weapons, robotics, and spacecrafts. By the end of the film, the alien state of his transformation is complete.

These preparatory forays into how urbanized science-fiction films explore the hybridization of organic, inorganic, and informational entities suggest that there are particular kinds of cross-categorical design tropes that occur in the context of postnatural liminal spaces. Without immersive organic ecologies, living entities like humans and aliens must themselves provide the biological substrates such as eyes, skins, nervous systems, limbs, tissues, and genes for aesthetic, conceptual, and narrative catalysts. Characters serve as nodes in networks for the cross-categorical transformation of states that carry living matter within them as opposed to it being around them. In contrast, the lush, liminal, and immersively alien ecological spaces of flora, fauna, and atmosphere in *Prospect* and *Annihilation* suggest their own creative capacities to produce new entities that are increasingly ontologically betwixt and between.

Prospect*: Holoents in an allopoietic ecology*

In the film, *Prospect*, we join Cee and Damon on a transport vessel as they prepare to go prospecting for gems on the planet below. This is a last-ditch mission for them to reset their financial and personal lives. The atmospheric objects of a vast outer space drift past the windows of their cramped and worn-down spacecraft. They are a daughter and a father living out on the margins of a near-future world. They are "floaters" on the Fringe and their existence is one of instability and drift, between contracts and places. They are in a small Drop-Pod that is hitched to the Sling, a collective transport structure that travels the inhabited limits of their world. They are going to the planet below to meet mercenaries who have come across a once-in-a-lifetime mining opportunity that they have been contracted to extract. Their craft decouples and they drop. The Sling falls away above them as they plunge from the margins of outer space through the atmosphere of the planet below. There are sunspots, flames, flicker, glare, and racking impact with the surface of the Green Moon of Bakhroma.

As they leave their damaged Drop-Pod, we see them in a forested environment of strangely familiar trees, plants, ground cover, and forest floor. But the atmosphere, the air itself, sparkles with toxic spores. Suspended particulates drift autonomously through the immersive astralized environment. This atmosphere is a visual system through which we read the alien nature of the Green Moon's fictive ecology. It is also the catalytic medium that will provoke a class of distributed sub-architectural envelopes and breathing technologies. For example, death by asphyxiation is imminent without a Level 3 Particle Grade Air Filter.

We will see that this is a world of augmenting-coupling, enveloping-involuting, and embedding-extracting. Prospectors are there to mine for Aurelac gems while the Aurelac spores are always about to enter their lungs and tissues. The Green Moon is inhabited by native Aurelac, rhizomatic networks of organisms that are embedded in the ground. In turn, Aurelac have gems called "root pearls" embedded in them. Prospectors must use special toolkits to perform a double-extraction of Aurelac-from-ground and then root-pearl-from-Aurelac, pulling them out of their biological space of inhabitation and into the financial space of markets and transactional exchange. It is also a world exchanging air, of exhaling and inhaling. The landscape exhales spore-clouds from the Aurelacs embedded within while characters tinker with filters and pant as their fogged-up helmets visualize the invisibility of breath with condensation.

Damon and Cee move slowly and warily through the silent drift of airborne particulates, the rustling of foliage, and the wet sounds of their footsteps on the sodden forest floor. The soft intermittent crackling of low-grade comms and the strained sounds of breathing through broken down air filters present them as technologically augmented organisms in an alien environment. They are liminal people now in a liminal space, referred to in the Green as "floaters." The Green's dense vegetation and thick, toxic air present a smooth and self-consistent space of slow becoming that is intermittently punctuated by narrative intensifications: Cee and Damon pause to mine for gems next to a decomposing prospector; an antagonistic fellow prospector named Ezra appears; Damon dies in a conflict with Ezra that orphans Cee; Cee shoots Ezra in her Drop-Pod; Cee partners with Ezra; Cee flees a religious camp of born-again floaters; Cee and Ezra reconnect; they fail to mine Aurelac for mercenaries; they battle mercenaries; they escape the Green transformed. These transformational moments in Cee and Ezra's arc punctuate their passage through an immersive shimmering space of ecological matter that provokes life support via mediating envelopes and breathing technologies. While this is a living and self-renewing rainforest ecosystem, the creative capacity of this space with regard to the liminal people who pass through it is *allopoietic*. It spawns systems of objects that are neither the ecosystem itself nor its human passengers but, rather, mediators that allow the liminal space and the liminal people to coexist. What is more, these mediating objects couple with liminal people to make them liminal entities (Turner) or holoents (Haraway). The characters will cease to exist without coupling with technical prostheses and vice versa. Neither is whole without the other and a synthetic world of designed objects unfolds out of the presence of toxins in the air of the ecological world and its flora, fauna, and minerals (see Figure 13.1).

While the Green is a space of becoming-characters, it is also a space of co-evolution and trans-individuation. Moving through the ecological space, Cee is dependent on Ezra's violent experience and he is dependent on her air filtration technologies and medical foams. They move together, breathe together, and talk with each other. Toxic dust and airborne gases exhaled by the Aurelac bond them together out of techno-physiological necessity as they inhale and exhale through shared, disembodied, and technical breathing organs. He shoots her father, she shoots him, he saves her, she saves him, he protects her, and, later on, she protects him. Their characters entangle and their states invert as they converge, diverge, and converge again amongst the vegetation, atmospheric particulates, and human floaters that form the Green. Particles and people float through this world with both semi-autonomy from and coupling-potential with each other that are fragilely maintained by what in his book, *Onto-Cartography*, Levi Bryant might call a posthuman ecology of machines and media.[12] In a diverse and heterarchical

FIGURE 13.1: Cee and Ezra: Prosthesis of Envelopes and Technologies. *Prospect*. Earl and Caldwell (2018).

ecology such as the one formulated by Bryant, machines are media for other machines and vice versa. A machine is Bryant's term for an entity and, similar to Haraway's holoent, exists in a state of trans-individuation that does not privilege the human. Bryant's machines form diverse, differential yet mutually reinforcing relationships, or structural couplings with each other. Machines become media when they provide flows (inputs) for other machines that extend, amplify, or modify the activities or becomings (outputs) of the machines to which they are coupled.[13] Cee's air filtration extends the capacity of her and Ezra's lungs in the milieu of airborne Aurelac spores. It amplifies their narrative entanglement with each other. It negatively and positively modifies their capacity to cooperate in the Green and transforms their relationship with each other from adversaries to co-evolutionaries. This machine, which is also media for other machines, does not exist in isolation but rather, specifically emerges in this fictive ecology of bodies, organs, spores, and gem-bearing creatures.

Structural couplings abound in this space and emerge to form inter- and intra-relationships between each other, the floaters, and the ecosystem. The reciprocally alien-making relationship between human floaters and the Green performs a kind of *allopoietic* or other-making operation in generating machines that, in turn, act as media for other machines in structurally coupled relationships: Parcel Class Drop-Pods mediate humans and the Slingback Freighter; Comms mediate mouths and ears; Ralon Crusader Laser Scalpels mediate Prospector hands and Aurelac roots; Level 3 Particle Grade Filters mediate Prospector lungs and Aurelac spores; Prospecting tweezers mediate Prospector hands and Carrom Blisters; Patch-gun foam mediates wounds and Aurelac spores; Visors mediate eyes and spores; Tents and suits mediate individual and collective bodies and atmosphere, and so on. These objects and more are alluded to in the manual, *Aurelac Prospecting: Your Guide to Getting Rich on the Green Moon*.[14]

Design operates as a process of collective and synthetic differential evolution. Across multiple sources and users, objects are upgraded, hacked, swapped in and out, and repurposed into the "painted rust" aesthetic of the filmmakers. There seem to be few, if any, complete or original objects as these human floaters are freelancers without a typical sci-fi state, corporation, or other binding organization that would give them centrally issued or consistently maintained inventories of equipment (all objects are evolved). There are no institutions, headquarters, office blocks, ministries, collective forms, or other "major" architectures of sci-fi world-building. Instead, the architecture is the dense and direct ecological world itself with its atmospheric space, improvised circulation, distributed HVAC infrastructure, extended organs, and individual envelopes. We never see a building but, rather, the atomization and decentralization of architecture into suits, tents, air conditioning, drop-pods, and other crafts, and it is the immediacy of the body without buildings that gives rise to so many disembodied machines and media in the process of structural coupling (see Figure 13.2).

Suits, helmets, tents, hulls, and other envelopes serve as second skins to humans who move through and settle in the Green. When second skins and human skins are breached, gels and creams become further, stranger enveloping technologies toward the critical act of keeping toxic air of the non-human environment out of the tissues and systems of the human body. After Cee shoots Ezra in her Drop-Pod, they leave the safety of that conditioned environment, its enveloping hull, and its mechanical air filtration system. The Drop-Pod is, in a sense, both collective skin and lung for the multiple bodies of Cee and Ezra that occupy it. They leave that meso-scale prosthetic and transition from the collective skin-lung super-organ of the ship to the individualized scale of their suits, helmets, and breathing filters. The "dust" in the air passes into the wound in Ezra's arm and we witness a sci-fi instantiation of what Stacy Alaimo might call "trans-corporeality" or the movement of matter across connected bodies and environments. The toxins in the environment inhabit tissues of the body and, as the outside becomes the inside, the human body is becoming the environment that both envelopes and involutes it, changing it, transforming it, and, in this case, degrading it. But Ezra's degradation subtends Cee's coming of age during a period of mutually reinforcing transformation as they pass through the Green with a system of specially designed and radically decentralized sub-architectural objects.

FIGURE 13.2: Cee and her Drop-Pod: An enveloping organ in the Green. *Prospect*. Earl and Caldwell (2018).

Alaimo's concept of "trans-corporeality" is not only foregrounded in Bryant's *onto-cartography*,[15] but it also seems integral to existence in the Green's environmental ecology and the tandem ecology of machines and media that its allopoietic capacity creates. Per Alaimo, matter and environment have agency and are active—they are neither generic nor passive nor inert. Matter moves across (trans)bodies and environments and "trans-corporeality reveals the interchanges and interconnections between various bodily natures."[16] She argues that "Imagining human corporeality as trans-corporeality, in which the human is always intermeshed with the more-than-human world, underlines the extent to which the substance of the human is ultimately inseparable from 'the environment.'"[17] In *Prospect*, bodies are only separate from the matter of the environment and the environment of the matter insofar as their second skins and prosthetic organs—the machines with which bodies structurally couple—perform.

For architecture, this is not just a problem of matter, space, and technology but also of topology as envelopes create bubbles of human-sustaining micro-environments. Floaters carry a tech-enabled alien extra-territoriality with and around them throughout the Green and crises ensue when outsides and insides are breached by human instruments, Aurelac spores, or alien atmospheres. Involution and exvolution are deeply operative in the Green, triggering character development, physiological crisis, and technological innovation. The trans-corporeality between body and environment, between inside and outside, resonates with Klaus Loenhart's invocation of Tor Nørretranders statement on breathing, during a dialog on atmosphere with Peter Sloterdijk: "When you take a breath, you touch a part of the planet with the inside of your body."[18] Atmosphere is perhaps the medium of our time and *Prospect* is an atomized architectural exploration of the machines and media that emerge in relation to it.

Annihilation: *Hybrids in a sympoietic ecology*

While *Prospect* builds a world around sub-architectural machines and media that operate on the trans-corporeal flows of matter among bodies and environments, *Annihilation* radicalizes categories of existence through the systemic hybridization of all entities that pass through its immersive alien ecology, the Shimmer. A lighthouse has been hit by an alien entity that has plunged into the ground below it. An alien-elsewhere is now embedded deep within the geology of the Southern Reach, under the lighthouse. It roils densely within the cavernous chamber it has created while the radius of its effects grows outward, spreading a quarantine-zone of mutation, hybridization, and ontological confusion across the surface of the earth. The Shimmer envelopes a beach, a swamp, a settlement, a military base, and the flora and fauna that thrive there. It generates an alien-induced liminal space that a multidisciplinary military team must enter and make their way from the human periphery of Area X to the central core of the alien's effects.

The team enters the Shimmer, as if passing through the most ethereal cell membrane. Like the Green Moon of *Prospect*, the atmosphere of this alien environment is cinematically rendered. Yet the atmosphere of the Shimmer is not dense with the sparkle of toxic spores but rather, bright, and subtly prismatic once the team has passed through the soap-filmy and vaporous ether of its envelope (see Figure 13.3). Signals are scrambled, comms are dead, and eerie sounds of an abandoned coastal settlement punctuate the radio silence. Lena, a soldier turned biologist and academic, is drawn into a mission to research the Shimmer after her missing husband emerges from it in an unnervingly transformed state. She and her four team members trans-individuate with the Shimmer, as they move through its transformational space.

Their processes of becoming characters in the context of alien effects are diverse: becoming paranoid, nihilistic, determined, animal, and becoming vegetal. One of the team members, Cass, is attacked and killed by a mutant bear and, as the bear has perhaps ingested part of her, takes on a part of her. In this case, the bear does not take on the form, structure, or physiological features of Cass, but rather her scream: a bear with the scream of a human. Another team member, Josie, remarks that, unlike their team leader and Lena, she neither wants to face nor fight the

FIGURE 13.3: Lena and her team as they approach the Shimmer's envelope. *Annihilation*. Garland (2018).

Shimmer. The scarred skin on her arms begins sprouting foliage as she wanders off to a settled clearing in the forest. This clearing is populated by vegetated human forms. Before Josie herself becomes vegetal, she theorizes to Lena that the vegetation would have human hox genes refracted into them by the Shimmer. They have the matter, pigmentation, and componentry of vegetation but the form, structure, and organization of humans.

Annihilation draws us into a liminal ecology in two senses: it is literally the transformational mission space between our protagonist's departure and destination and, more radically, it is the space in which phenomena exist in-between ontological categories such as organic/inorganic, plant/animal, animal/human–animal, human–animal/plant, plant/mineral, and plant/architecture. Expressions of these ontological in-betweens are both physiological and psychological. They are formal, visual, sonic, and vocal. They are pigmented, floral, crystalline, and intestinal. They occasionally involve mirrorings, duplicates, and mixtures of matter and media. Here, in the Shimmer, an earthly ecosystem undergoes radical transformations as an alien presence creeps across the Southern Reach, scrambling the codes and structures of the entities that comprise it. The Shimmer is a liminal space par excellence. It is an unfamiliar space within which sociocultural categories of existence are destabilized and dissolved and those who pass through it become liminal entities on the way to becoming irrevocably transformed.

It is as if the code-refracting powers of the Shimmer and their differential scrambling of genotypes have generated a commensurate scrambling of phenotypes in this ecology of trans-individuated becoming. Vegetated humans (see Figure 13.4) have become completely transformed, yet there are other instances of partial hybridizations involving material, form, organization, and ontological category. There is an albino alligator with red, lichen-like patches of skin—a continuity of form with a change in material. There are deer-like creatures whose antlers are foliated—a composite body of fauna and flora. Parallel to the comprehensiveness of the fully-vegetated human body plans that Josie joined, there are crystalline trees on the beach—minerals grown to the body-plan of plants and trees. There are single stems blooming different flowers, fungal skeletons, metallic bodies, and flaming structures that take on the explosive conflagration of a phosphorus grenade (in Jeff VanderMeer's original novel, *Annihilation*, these hybridizations even include foliated sentences, vegetating the written word as if from an alien, living illuminated manuscript). The Shimmer is the refractive transformation of a familiar ecology into one that is becoming alien by virtue of the genotypical, phenotypical, and ontological hybridizations that are generated within its space. It is an in-between space for in-between things.

The Green of *Prospect* is a fictive ecology of plants, spores, and imagined organisms that spawns a tandem ecology of envelopes, technologies, machines,

FIGURE 13.4: Mixed ontologies in the Shimmer: Human vegetation. *Annihilation*. Garland (2018).

media, and structural couplings amongst instruments and organs. In contrast, the Shimmer of *Annihilation* is a fictive ecology of scrambled symbiogenesis, blocks-of-becoming, glitched physiology, and ontological confusion. Both are immersive and transformational spaces of narrative and physiological trans-individuation and trans-corporeality among characters, objects, and ecological media. But perhaps their differences fall partially, if not subtly, between *allopoiesis* and *sympoiesis*. The Green (science-fiction meets westerns) is an allopoietic ecosystem that catalyzes a whole other synthetic ecology of artifacts, technologies, manuals, vehicles, breathing tanks, filters, and so on to couple with and mediate among humans, non-humans, and atmospheres. In contrast, the Shimmer (science-fiction meets horror) is fully, if not terrorizingly, a "sympoietic" system that produces new, unpredictable, and hybridized entities by "making-together": plants/minerals, humans/non-humans, animals/plants, and so on. Recall that Josie, the physicist in the team, wants neither to face it nor fight the alien presence but, rather, to become with it. Later, when Lena (or an alien incarnation of herself) returns to society after being transformed by the liminal space of the Shimmer, she is debriefed. Her commander asserts that the Shimmer will destroy everything. She counters that it is in fact making something new. It seems not to make new things alone but, rather, together with other things that pass through its envelope. Regardless of human ontological categories, this more-than-human ecology *sympoietically* scrambles anything and everything that fuses with its space.

Sympoiesis emerged out of a discursive mesh built separately by Humberto Maturana and Francisco Varela, Beth Dempster, and Donna Haraway over the last several decades. In search of a new model for understanding complexity and self-organizing systems, Dempster constructed an alternative to Maturana and Varela's "autopoiesis"[19] (self-making) and coined the term "sympoiesis"[20] (together-making). This is a model that considers ecosystems as opposed (or in addition) to organisms and favors open systems, unpredictability, non-linearity, multiplicity, and diversity. It foregrounds continuity, relationships, and the notion that entities are not separate from their environments, but perhaps, in a fused feedback relationship with them. They are not only energetically open to their environments (like organisms per Maturana and Varela) but also structurally and materially open to them, recalling Bryant's structural coupling or Alaimo's trans-corporeality. The open, relational, distributed, and amorphous nature of sympoietic systems constantly produces liminal entities.

Haraway's work on sympoiesis advances Dempster's work beyond an oppositional approach to autopoiesis and toward a more complex relationship wherein they are not mutually exclusive, but rather, entangled with each other. Haraway suggests that "autopoiesis and sympoiesis, foregrounding and backgrounding systemic aspects of complexity, are in generative friction, or generative enfolding, rather than opposition."[21] Symbiosis and symbiogenesis "make trouble," she writes, for autopoiesis and self-organization. After all, once in the Shimmer, Lena continues to look at cells dividing through her microscope. The cells, she says, are hers but they are the Shimmer's too. And the Shimmer is filled with trouble. It makes trouble. It is trouble. That is, until one decides, as Josie does, neither to face it nor to fight it but to become with it. Lena, who is not simply the prior individual she was before the Shimmer, eventually understands this as well in the realization that an information-scrambling alien phenomenon such as the Shimmer makes something new.

As a liminal space that generates liminal entities, the Shimmer transforms states and relationships of, between, and among multiple entities. It hybridizes entities, placing them out of or in-between ontological categories: mineral plants, vegetal deer, and fungal architecture. It catalyzes processes of becoming: Josie becoming vegetal, Cass becoming bear. Per Dempster's assertion that sympoietic systems induce internal and external structural couplings, the Shimmer's new ontological mixtures induce unexpected media for errant machines (alligator jaw coupling with shark teeth, human hox genes coupling with vegetal tissues). While the Green creates productive holoents by structurally coupling objects, organs, and atmospheres, the Shimmer creates radical hybridizations by mixing ontologies.

Near-futures

The near-future scenarios explored in *Ghost in the Shell*, *Blade Runner*, *Blade Runner 2049*, and *District 9* thrive in the space between and betwixt categories of existence in extremely precise ways. These films generate their liminal power by surgically designing the local, internal, and organic–inorganic couplings that enable connectivity to access global flows of communication, mixed-realities, and bio-technical exchanges of genetic information. This creates new hybrids, holoents, cyborg ecologies, and more-than-human creatures that portend the coming obsolescence of the ways in which we partition the world into culturally defined categories of existence, a partitioning that architecture and its bind with property have almost always upheld in both physical and discursive formats. The agile and augmented beings of these worlds and their mixed-reality existences transcend social states while they also transcend space. They live locally in their physical space as well as globally and fluidly in the networked spaces into which they are jacked. They exist as structural couplings of organic and inorganic material that, in turn, enable them to exist in mixed-realities of physical, virtual, atemporal, and multicentered spaces. While they demand new understandings of space, they also offer micro-cosmic models for a networked architecture of organic–inorganic hybridity.

While the former films speculate on near-future scenarios in the urbanized absence of ecosystems, *Prospect* and *Annihilation* offer immersive models for design thinking in the context of techno-social and socio-ecological change at the transition from the Anthropocene to the post-Anthropocene period. Between these periods ecosystems, information systems, machine intelligence, and human agency increasingly co-evolve in spaces of growing indeterminacy. Indeterminacy may seem at odds with the normative history of architecture and its prodigious creative capacity for clear categories and binary opposites such as private/public, inside/outside, building/landscape, architecture/environment, structure/skin, and so on. In a sense, normative architectures are the built manifestation of humanity's boundaries between categories and conditions, especially the socially constructed boundaries between culture vs. nature, organisms vs. environments, and technologies vs. ecologies. These films accept ecological immersion and cultivate their creative capacities to create hybrids, holoents, and mixed-ontologies for mixed-realities. By deconsolidating architecture, dissolving its boundaries, and allowing events to be directly enveloped by the engaging otherness of ecosystems themselves, these scenarios become densely populated with entities that model how innovative architecture might be in the post-Anthropocene period should the physical and ontological boundaries that are often in tandem with each other be dissolved and reimagined in more open, agile, and speculative ways.

NOTES

1. *Prospect* (2018), directors Christopher Caldwell and Zeek Earl.
2. *Annihilation* (2018), director Alex Garland.
3. Victor Turner, *The Ritual Process: Structure and Anti-Structure* (Abingdon: Routledge, 1995), 94.
4. Turner, *Ritual Process*, 95.
5. Donna Haraway, *Staying with the Trouble: Making Kin in the Chthulucene* (Durham, NC: Duke University Press Books Press, 2016), 60.
6. Lynn Margulis and Dorion Sagan, *What is Life?* (Oakland, CA: University of California Press, 2000), 113–34.
7. *Ghost in the Shell* (2017), director Rupert Sanders.
8. *Ghost in the Shell* (1995), director Mamoru Oshii.
9. *Blade Runner* (1982), director Ridley Scott.
10. *Blade Runner 2049* (2017), director Denis Villeneuve.
11. *District 9* (2009), director Neil Blomkamp.
12. Levi Bryant, *Onto-Cartography: An Ontology of Machines and Media* (Edinburgh: Edinburgh University Press, 2014), 15–36.
13. Ibid. 47.
14. "*Aurelac Prospecting: Your Guide to Getting Rich on the Green Moon*," PROSPECT Wiki. Accessed December 19, 2021. https://imgur.com/a/fGqisra.
15. Bryant, *Onto-Cartography*, 48–49.
16. Stacy Alaimo, *Bodily Natures: Science, Environment and the Material Self* (Bloomington, IN: Indiana University Press, 2010), 2.
17. Alaimo, *Bodily Natures*, 2
18. Klaus K. Loenhart. *Breathe: Investigations into Our Atmospherically Entangled Future* (Basel: Birkhäuser, 2021), 189.
19. Humberto Maturana and Francisco Varela, *Autopoiesis and Cognition: The Realization of the Living* (New York, NY: Springer, 1980), 77–84.
20. Beth Dempster, *Sympoietic and Autopoietic Systems: A New Distinction for Self-Organizing Systems* (Waterloo: School of Planning: University of Waterloo, 2000), 2.
21. Haraway, *Staying with the Trouble*, 61.

REFERENCES

Alaimo, Stacy. *Bodily Natures: Science, Environment and the Material Self*. Bloomington, IN: Indiana University Press, 2010.

Blomkamp, Neill, director. *District 9*. Culver City, CA: Sony Pictures Home Entertainment, 2009.

Bryant, Levi. *Onto-Cartography: An Ontology of Machines and Media*. Edinburgh: Edinburgh University Press, 2014.

Dempster, Beth. *Sympoietic and Autopoietic Systems: A New Distinction for Self-Organizing Systems*. Waterloo: School of Planning, University of Waterloo, 2000. https://www.semanticscholar.org/author/Beth-Dempster/88912464.

Earl, Zeek, and Christopher Caldwell, directors. *Prospect*. Los Angeles, CA: Gunpowder & Sky, 2019. DVD.

Garland, Alex, director. *Annihilation*. Los Angeles, CA: Paramount Pictures, 2018.

Haraway, Donna. *Staying with the Trouble: Making Kin in the Chthulucene*. Durham, NC: Duke University Press Books, 2016.

Loenhart, Klaus K., ed. *Breathe: Investigations into Our Atmospherically Entangled Future*. Basel: Birkhäuser, 2021.

Oshii, Mamoru, director. *Ghost in the Shell*. Santa Monica, CA: Lionsgate Home Entertainment, 2002.

Margulis, Lynn, and Dorion Sagan. *What is Life?* Oakland, CA: University of California Press, 2000.

Maturana, Humberto, and Francisco Varela. *Autopoiesis and Cognition: The Realization of the Living*. New York, NY: Springer, 1980.

PROSPECT Wiki. *Aurelac Prospecting: Your Guide to Getting Rich on the Green Moon*. Accessed December 19, 2021. https://imgur.com/a/fGqisra.

Riekeles, Stefan. *Anime Architecture: Imagined Worlds and Endless Megacities*. London: Thames and Hudson, 2020.

Sanders, Rupert, director. *Ghost in the Shell*. Los Angeles, CA: Paramount Pictures, 2017.

Scott, Ridley, director. *Blade Runner* (The Final Cut). Burbank, CA: Warner Bros. Pictures, 2007.

Turner, Victor. *The Ritual Process: Structure and Anti-Structure*. Abingdon: Routledge, 1995.

VanderMeer, Jeff. *Annihilation*. New York, NY: Farrar, Straus & Giroux, 2014.

Villeneuve, Denis, director. *Blade Runner 2049*. Burbank, CA: Warner Bros. Pictures, 2018.

14

A Realist Conception of Architecture in the Metaverse

Patrik Schumacher

The totality of the human phenomenal world

Architecture, together with the other design disciplines, can claim universal competency and exclusive responsibility for the totality of the designed environment and world of artifacts, both real and virtual, i.e. for the totality of the human phenomenal world. Everything that surrounds us, meets our senses and as interface mediates our communications with the social world was designed by a colleague. The design disciplines include urban design, landscape design, architecture, interior design, furniture design, fashion design, product design, as well as graphic design and web design, and in the near future metaverse design. All the design disciplines together form a single discourse and function system of society with the shared societal function of the spatio-visual framing of all communicative interactions. This discourse revolves around the lead distinction of form (internal reference) vs. function (external reference), which is structured by the persistent binary code of (formally and functionally) "resolved" vs. "unresolved." The criteria for the concrete application of these code values are being programmed and re-programmed by the design disciplines' (or the designer's) historically evolving (adapting) style. To the extent that all designers are plugged into and respond to the global design discourse, this discourse is omnipotent with respect to the spatio-visual and tactile shaping of the phenomenal world, within the economic constraints and social functionality expectations set by (private or public) clients.

The designed spatio-visual frames are themselves communications. All design is communication design. Social life attributes these framing communications to the clients who are the hosts of all communicative interaction events, not to the designers. Within the design discourse however, they are attributed to the designers or design teams as their authors. Designs and the design processes are embedded in the global specialized design discourse demanding explanations and arguments, guided by architectural/design theory.[1]

The design task of the communicative spatio-visual framing of the societal life process must draw on four distinct but interrelated domains of expertise with their respective subtasks as follows: (1) spatiology: organization, (2) phenomenology: articulation, (3) semiology: signification, and (4) dramaturgy: interaction.

"Spatiology" is concerned with spatial organization and plots out the geometric premises, sets the scene as it were, for the other three agendas of phenomenology, semiology, and dramaturgy. Spatiology guides the distribution of places in space with respect to distancing, adjacencies, and connections. To the extent that filmmaking involves set design and the selection of locations, spatiology is also a dimension of filmmaking. The task dimension involves the selection of strategies of spatial organization like axial ordering, grids, stacking, nesting, overlapping, etc.

"Phenomenology," as understood in this chapter (and in the author's theory of architecture in general), is concerned with morphological articulation and addresses the problem of the perceptual tractability of complex spatial/social scenes, i.e. the task of maintaining legibility in the face of complexity. The psychology of perception is a key resource with respect to this task.

"Semiology" is concerned with communication via signification. The meaning of spaces and designs coincides with the social interactions they frame, i.e. meaning is or anticipates use. The semiological project sets out the task of increasing the information-richness of the built environment by means of crafting a spatio-visual language or system of signification that is empowered by the combinatorial potency of grammar. Here linguistics serves as a fertile source domain for conceptual inspiration.

"Dramaturgy" is concerned with patterns and potentials of interaction. In the context of architecture, and in the context of designing for the metaverse, understood as a spatial immersive world wide web, dramaturgy is closely related to what in web design is pursued under the heading of interaction design. Dramaturgy implies environmental action in the time dimension, i.e. the design of a built environment, real or virtual, that is both kinetically responsive to user interaction as well as spontaneously engaging users.

These are the four task dimensions of any architectural design project. It is significant that the related domains of expertise and the respectively related intellectual disciplines have also been reflected and employed within film theory, as resources to address respectively related problems and ambitions.

Genealogy of an insight and project

The author started to think about the relationship between architecture and filmmaking in the late 1990s, in the context of the design research programme "Responsive Environments" at the AADRL, the Design Research Lab at the Architectural Association. Responsive environments are inherently four-dimensional designs. The idea of responsiveness implies that architectural elements respond to or engage with human agents entering the scene. This necessitates that the human agents and their actions, i.e. the social life process, has to be simulated within the architectural model. The ambition quickly expanded from the illustrative animation of isolated interactions between human and architectural agents to the orchestration of elaborate social event scenarios unfolding over several stages of transformation, showing the capacity of the responsive/spontaneous environment to facilitate an unfolding event dynamic that shifted between different social situations to achieve an overall diversity of complementary communicative scenarios. The examples we elaborated were conferences and workshops, as well as social networking gatherings. Such a gathering must provide not only a high number of encounters and conversations but must also maximize the range of types of communications: many quick greetings, short conversations, in-depth one-to-one conversations, in-depth conversations in small groups, larger fluid groups, as well as moments where everybody, the whole party, comes together for a shared experience, etc. An event that produces only a thousand quick greetings and nothing else is as dissatisfying and dysfunctional as getting stuck with a single conversation partner for the whole evening. The spatial organization, its richness of differentiation, as well as the dramaturgy of the interaction dynamics supplied by the architectural agents, can make or break the overall success of the event.

It became clear that the understanding and testing of the design proposals would ideally take the form of mini-movies enacting and playing out the event scenarios envisioned by the designer and called for by the imagined event host and client. It also became clear that—although the idea of kinetic responsiveness had triggered the investment into scenario animations—the point of scenario thinking and the simulation of the social communication processes that were meant to be facilitated by the architectural design was equally pertinent with respect to static environments. Further, we had started to understand the responsive or spontaneous kinetic transformations of the architectural agents, for instance the opening of a door or the rotation of a chair, as gestures and invitations addressed to human agents, i.e. as communications. We then realized that a passive door or chair is equally functioning as invitations, and are also communications in their simple presence. It became clear that the whole built environment was a field of gestures, an array of communications, each functioning as framing premise and definition of the social situation that would or could unfold if the architectural invitation was taken up by human agents. The built environment is like a text, a permanent broadcast.

Framing in architecture and cinema

In the author's general theory of architecture,[2] this insight is expressed in the general formula that the societal function of architecture is the "framing of communicative interactions" and that these frames, static or dynamic, are themselves communications that function as premise and broad situational definition for the communications that can then unfold within this frame. If this focus on the social functionality of the built environment defines architecture in demarcation from the engineering disciplines, and if this framing process becomes increasingly complex and non-trivial, beyond simple stereotypes, then it follows that a design model can only truly be an architectural model if it models the social interaction process together with the architectural agents that are meant to facilitate and shape it. It is also implied here that architectural semiology is an essential ingredient of our discipline's core competency.

The concept of frame and (spatio-visual) framing is central to the author's theory of architecture, as it self-locates within Niklas Luhmann's theory of modern/contemporary society as functionally differentiated society. The concept enters into the formula that defines the societal function of architecture and the design disciplines, namely "the communicative framing of social communication," a formula that explains and justifies the differentiation of design as an autonomous function system. This function of framing is essential for all communications because all communication presupposes that there exists a prior definition of the situation. Only if the social situation is specified (as a selection from the daunting multiplicity of different potential situations that overall society allows for) can encounters be converted into occasions for communication. Luhmann, building in this respect on Parsons, talks about the need to break the indeterminacy of encounters that emerges from the inherent double contingency of every encounter between free agents. On this basis, the author draws the conclusion that this exigency and functional necessity of all societies, and especially in the case of large-scale, anonymous societies, provides the basis for the differentiation and distillation of architecture and the design disciplines as function system, profession, and discourse. This also firmly establishes the semiological project at the heart of the design disciplines, whether pursued only intuitively or consciously and theory-led. Indeed, all societal communication situations are framed by means of design, and this includes the graphic design of the book you are reading now. This too offers a semantic spatio-visual framing and nuanced definition/anticipation of the possible character of the content of the printed communication. Luhmann himself did not see or describe this function system of design. The author thus had to look elsewhere for a pertinent term. A viable point of connection was found in Erwing Goffman's "Frame Analysis,"[3] although Goffman's concept of frame is more abstract and general, in the sense of setting, context, or situation, implying a script, i.e. rules/protocols of interaction that governs a social event. This seemed like a very good match and terminological move: the architectural frame informs about the social framing, the visible informs about and anticipates the invisible, and space denotes script.

There is also a significant, at least non-arbitrary, connection between this concept of architectural frames with the concepts of frames and framing in cinema and film theory. This connection can be brought out via Gilles Deleuze's writings on film. Framing received its own chapter in Deleuze's 1983 book *Cinema I*. Here Deleuze defines "framing" as follows:

> We will call the determination of a closed system, a relatively closed system which includes everything which is present in the image—sets, characters and props—framing. The frame therefore forms a set which has a great number of parts, that is of elements, which themselves form subsets.[4]

Deleuze notes that frames are differentiated in adaptation to social content, for instance "individuals are not framed in the same way as crowds."[5]

Deleuze seems to be interested in the complexity of what can be contained within a cinematic frame. He talks about the possibility of saturation. This coincides with the author's problematic of coping with complexity and delivering information-richness as well as interaction-richness. Deleuze emphasizes the big screen and the depth of field:

> The big screen and depth of field in particular have allowed the multiplication of independent data, to the point where a secondary scene appears in the foreground while the main one happens in the background (Wyler), or where you can no longer even distinguish between the principal and the secondary (Altman).[6]

Deleuze's account emphasizes that filmic frames, like architectural frames, allow for nesting so that

> there are many different frames in the frame. Doors, windows, box office windows, skylights, car windows, mirrors, are all frames in frames. The great directors have

> particular affinities with particular secondary, tertiary, etc. frames. And it is by this dovetailing of frames that the parts of the set or of the closed system are separated, but also converge and are reunited.[7]

Deleuze is also interpreting the visual given semiologically: "the frame teaches us that the image is not just given to be seen. It is legible as well as visible."[8] In Deleuze's account, framing is not only marking out the scene but is also involved with dramaturgy:

> Sometimes the frame is conceived as a dynamic construction in act [en acte], which is closely linked to the scene, the image, the characters and the objects which fill it. The iris method in Griffith, which isolates a face first of all, then opens and shows the surroundings; Eisenstein's researches inspired by Japanese drawing, which adapt the frame to the theme; Gance's variable screen which opens and closes "according to the dramatic necessities," and like a "visual accordion"—from the very beginning attempts were made to test dynamic variations of the frame. In any case framing is limitation.[9]

It also seems as if major film directors used architectural ordering tropes to make their complex (opening) scenes legible, echoing the architects' phenomenologically instrumental compositional stance:

> Eisenstein studied the effects of the golden section on cinematographic imagery; Dreyer explored horizontals and verticals, symmetries, the high and the low, alternations of black and white; the Expressionists developed diagonals and counter-diagonals, diagonals, pyramidal or triangular figures which agglomerate bodies, crowds, places, the collision of these masses, a whole paving of the frame "which takes on a form like the black and white squares of a chess-board" (Lang's *The Nibelungen* and *Metropolis*). Even light is the subject of a geometrical optic, when it is organized with shadows into two halves, or into alternating rays, as is done by one Expressionist tendency (Wiene, Lang).[10]

Cinema must recreate and make legible a spatio-social setting consisting of a non-arbitrary set of parts. Deleuze speaks of closed systems (reminiscent of Luhmann's notion of self-referentially closed social systems) that might further subdivide or are revealed to be a subsystem of an encompassing system. This description indirectly correlates the cinematic framing with the way social situations are differentiated and integrated into systems of situations, and how this is reflected in the spatial order of nesting and subdivision.

> The divisibility of content means that the parts belong to various sets, which constantly subdivide into sub-sets or are themselves the sub-set of a larger set, on to infinity. This is why content is defined both by the tendency to constitute closed systems and by the fact that this tendency never reaches completion. Every closed system also communicates.[11]

Cinematic frames are related to observer positions within the set of parts or reveal an encompassing set. Deleuze insists that angles of framing, i.e. points of view, must make pragmatic sense within the structure of participant positions.

> The frame is related to an angle of framing. This is because the closed set is itself an optical system which refers to a point of view on the set of parts. Of course, the point of view can be—or appear to be—bizarre or paradoxical: the cinema shows extraordinary points of view—at ground level, or from high to low, from low to high, etc. But they seem to be subject to a pragmatic rule which is not just valid for the narrative cinema: to avoid falling into an empty aestheticism they must be explained, they must be revealed as normal and regular—either from the point of view of a more comprehensive set which includes the first, or from the point of view of an initially unseen, not given, element of the first set.[12]

It becomes clear that the legibility of the set must be ascertained for all or several possible observer positions. This is a key aspect of the phenomenological project, especially in the context of complex scenes involving multiple participant positions and audiences.

Architecture as UX/UI design

In recent months the author has increasingly felt compelled to refer to dramaturgy as another key ingredient of our discipline's competency. The context for this is the engagement with the design of virtual communication spaces. In this context it makes sense to interpret the architect's task as UX/UI design. This concept of an interface design and interaction/experience design can be generalized across all architectural design. All architecture and design is UX/UI design, involving organization (spatiology), articulation (phenomenology), signification (semiology), and interaction design (dramaturgy).

In the realm of virtual environment design, the desire for actively self-transforming communicative architectural frames is much easier to realize. On this count, dramaturgy will be much more foregrounded in the metaverse than it ever was in the context of physical architecture. More generally, matters of communication and communicative framing, dynamic or static, are much more distilled here as the essential function of all design.

Reflecting back now on the earlier design explorations within AADRL, it becomes clear that dramaturgy also played a role with respect to understanding and visualizing static environments, in as much as the dramaturgical imagination encompasses both architectural and human agents. The designer must develop a filmmaker's dramaturgical imagination, aided by the life process simulation capacity we find in game engines like Unity and Unreal. The scenarios architects are here called upon to elaborate and visualize are obviously not full-feature films. They are rather like single scenes or episodes of a movie, not whole movies. Their plot is the plot of a social communication event. But then again, there are many such event plots to be considered when designing for large organizations like universities or corporate headquarters.

Complex scenes and unfolding event scenarios can be studied via a totalizing top view. One might also productively use the tool of time compression (acceleration) to gain a perspective on temporally stretched-out dynamics. However, the exploration of first-person perspective "filming" is also important to gauge the participants' perceptual experience and the scene's perceptual tractability from within. This is where the phenomenological project comes in, problematizing navigation, orientation, and perceptual grasp. These are also issues with which filmmakers must grapple, with respect to their audience's spatial orientation, with respect to the legibility of a space or scene. The analogy with filmmaking also reminds us of the fact that the experience of a complex space is always fragmentary and must be mentally synthesized from a sequence of partial experiences.

A successful dramaturgical project presupposes a successful semiological project. Social situations must be identified and deciphered before they can be activated. With respect to developing the semiological project, it is important to elaborate on typical social scenarios that play upon a differentiated, ordered manifold of distinctive settings, and nuanced variants. From the point of view of architecture's societal function, society can be understood as an expansive, richly differentiated, ordered, and connected array of social situations, each with its own interaction protocols and non-arbitrary set of relevant participants. These situations or specific communicative event types are recognizable by means of both spatial (positional) and morphological markers as identifiers so that the relevant participants and contributors to the event can find each other and congregate into a pertinent interaction configuration. The social meanings that the various settings and places acquire are the result of a process of spontaneous semiosis. This might be the spontaneity of an instant discovery of a use potential. Mostly, however, one-time discoveries are as quickly forgotten and lost so that "spontaneous" (unplanned) semiosis is a slow, gradual process of mutation, selection, and reproduction. This can only be very broadly anticipated and predetermined by the client's designations, especially in a world where, like in contemporary business organizations, the tendency for more self-directness and self-organization finds its echo in so-called "agile," "activity-based," or "non-territorial" work environments.

The autocatalytic, path-dependent character of semiosis, whereby selection pressures work on but cannot determine initial spontaneous uses (mutations), implies that the outcome of the bootstrapping of meaning cannot be controlled or precisely predicted. However, broad pattern prediction is possible. In any event, the semiologically informed design can offer a more intricately spatialized, better articulated, more systematically encoded semantic matrix of places for social self-sorting, albeit without being able to guarantee that the intended meanings come to be realized in the actual life process. The semiological project offers a (potentially grammar-empowered) spatio-visual system of significations as a catalyst for a spontaneous social semiosis. However, even if the meanings that the various places, zones, positions, and morphological features acquire are rather different from those intended, the designed spatio-morphological structure will serve this new meaning ensemble as orienting text. The ambition of the semiological project is to give this meaning receptacle a more intricate and nuanced structure, thereby increasing its potential information-richness and interaction-richness.

A successful semiological project presupposes a successful phenomenological project. Semantically codified spatio-morphological signs must become perceptually conspicuous and recognizable before they can trigger semantic associations, i.e., before they can be deciphered or become significant. Complex configurations might require compositional clarification before they become perceptually tractable. Also, the perceptual legibility of a complex ensemble or space will be different from different perspectives, as any photographer and any designer who is setting up renderings knows. The same problematic is faced in movies, perhaps more acutely, due to the imposition of fitting complex narratives into 90 minutes. The movement of the camera, like the scanning glance in real-world orientation situations, can powerfully support the perceptual grasp of a complex scene. It aids 360-degree comprehension as well as depth comprehension. The crafting of vistas and sequences of vistas is an art and effort that has long since been pursued in architecture and urban design, as well as in cinema.

Realism in architecture, cinema, and metaverse

One way to work on and explore this intended layer of meaning is by operationalizing it within the architectural model via agent-based life-process simulations[13] (this is being explored via the research agenda of "agent-based parametric semiology," pursued by a PhD group coached by the author as well as by a dedicated R&D team within Zaha Hadid Architects). Here agents are equipped with decision algorithms based on utility functions that mediate local information about action opportunities with multiple goals and their respective urgency based on internal states in dependence of the cumulative simulation history. Global interaction patterns emerge from heterogeneous agent populations interacting within semantically charged environments.

Another, very different but complementary way would be to develop a method of fictional scenario writing that takes its lesson from (the theory of) the realist novel, aiming to make the typical tangible. Realism in its attempt to capture the historically typical is here—in accordance with Georg Lukacs's literary theory[14]—distinguished from (the seemingly similar) naturalism with its indiscriminate depiction of idiosyncratic individual detail. To be sure, realism is also sharply distinguished from all nostalgia, as well as from all utopian escapism. Realism is historically grounded and situated, and this means bound to contemporary social and technological conditions, possibly extrapolated into the near future.

This realist architectural scenario writing would involve the description of typical event scenarios and typical interaction dynamics in the context of assumed typical goals, i.e. the goals of individual actors and the goals of the host institution. The scenario descriptions would relate the social scenarios to the spatial settings and reveal the semantic encoding of settings with reference to both their formal features and their associated messaging, including connotations and anticipations. The description would switch between overview accounts and first-person experiential accounts, taking up the perspective of multiple participants, each with their own agenda. Realism demands the recognition that participants (for instance employees) and hosts (for instance the corporation) pursue agendas that do not necessarily coincide or dovetail with the brief's ideal intentions.

The "novel" would also reveal that each participant type comes with its particular partial sensitivity to the meanings broadcast within the space, as well as with its particular interpretation of these meanings, attuned to the agenda being pursued. This polycontexturality is something to be reckoned with and built into the design of the semiological system. It does not undermine the system's social functionality, as long as these interpretations are complementary in that they make social cooperation possible despite their divergent underlying agendas. Unity of agenda and motivation does not have to be presupposed.

From here it is easy to imagine that a scenario animation using the repertoire of cinematic narration would be a valuable tool to investigate and home in on the social performance ambitions of the design and to verify the design's potential to facilitate social life. Sketchy attempts toward this have been a tradition at the AADRL for many years. To this extent, architects take up the mantle of filmmakers. These sketches, even as academic avant-garde efforts, indeed precisely as academic avant-garde projects, were always eminently realistic in their ambition, in Lukacs's sense of striving for historical typicality, geared to the progressive aspects of the contemporary conditions and potentials on the near historical horizon. The task was and is to distill the challenges and opportunities of our computationally empowered post-fordist network society.

Although film theory has used semiology to reflect and develop filmmaking's own language of narration, it is clear that a filmmaker must reckon with and work with architectural systems of signification and design semiology in general. Deleuze's account of film, especially of films operating under the paradigm of Realism, recognizes the importance and power of the spatio-social setting in which a depicted (narrated) social action is contextualized. According to Deleuze in realist cinema "milieux assert their independence"[15] and actions are "actualized directly in determinate, geographical, historical and social space-times."[16]

Deleuze even defines realism via the determinate relationship between milieux and modes of behavior. "What constitutes realism is simply this: milieux and modes of behavior, milieux which actualize and modes of behavior which embody."[17] To be sure, the concept of milieu is broader than the spatial environment. It refers to the social setting. However, in film, just like in life, only heightened, it is the furnished spatial setting and the artifact/"fashion" setting that informs, as indexical and/or symbolic sign, about the social setting and situation.

> The milieu always actualises several qualities and powers. It carries out a global synthesis of them, it is itself the Ambiance or the Encompasser [Englobant], whilst the qualities and the powers have become forces in the milieu. The milieu and its forces incurve on themselves, they act on the character, throw him a challenge, and constitute a situation in which he is caught. The character reacts in his turn (action properly speaking) so as to respond to the situation.[18]

The human agent "must acquire a new mode of being (habitus) or raise his mode of being to the demands of the milieu and of the situation."[19]

Reality is determinate, is making demands, delivers resistance and constraints, and requires adaptations. Historical reality poses problems, but it also delivers the concrete resources from which to craft innovative solutions. Innovative architecture has often cherished constraints as engines of invention. Real invention is very different from flights of fancy. Deleuze is certainly describing realism as grounded in historical contexts, as the opposite of untethered, high-flying imagination. The determinate and determinative milieu is opposed to the "any-space-whatevers": "The realism of the action-image is opposed to the idealism of the affection-image. [...] the former is developed in the Any-Space-Whatevers/

Affects pair. The second will be developed in the Determined Milieux/Modes of Behaviour pair."[20]

Deleuze argues that there is a two-way indexicality. If the situation determines (or at least constraints) the action, then the situation can be inferred from the action. Deleuze distinguishes two cinematic movements that essentially both express the dependency between action and situation. The move from situation to action to (modified) situation (SAS), and the move from action to situation leading to further action (ASA). He calls the former the large form and the latter the small form.

> The large form—SAS'—moved from the situation to the action, which modified the situation. But there is another form, which, on the contrary, moves from the action to the situation, towards a new action: ASA'. This time it is the action which discloses the situation, a fragment or an aspect of the situation, which triggers off a new action.[21]

Deleuze explains that these small-form action images communicate via indexical signs, in that the social situation can be inferred from the depicted action: "An action (or an equivalent of action, a simple gesture) discloses a situation which is not given. The situation is thus deduced from the action, by immediate inference, or by relatively complex reasoning."[22] The situation might also be encapsulated and deduced from a fragment or part. This points to the fact that coherently designed settings—within which many items and features correlate in accordance with the laws of integral functionality—allow observers and potential participants to read the situation and make pertinent inferences. This facilitation of inferences is the pragmatic meaning of the information-richness that the semiological project aims to enhance. Parametricism, as well as its most advanced variant tectonism, even without explicitly embracing the semiological project, already embeds this inference facilitation capacity into its designs just through its methodology of weaving dense dependency networks. Everything communicates with everything else.

All the features of realism discussed above could (and should) be brought to bear on the design of metaverses. The metaverse, the author envisages, is not offering an escape into a parallel reality or second life, but is meant to empower productive, integral lives and enhance current social reality. It must be firmly grounded and situated within current social, economic, and technological conditions and can play an important part in advancing these conditions, enhancing social productivity. Social actions and situations are correlated and each situation is framed—distinguished, localized, set up, connected, and configured—by metaverse designers on behalf of clients/entrepreneurs who want to tap into the powerful productivity potentials of realistic virtual worlds.

Realism here also means problem orientation, to quote Georg Lukacs, to "pose questions" and to "always take the most burning problems of the community as starting point."[23] The most potent metaverse conceptions that are about to take off now will not only be realistic but also avant-gardist in spirit. They can and should focus on the typical problematics and nascent opportunities that arise from the current societal transitioning into the new condition of a truly global creative and competitive knowledge economy. This has nothing much in common with video games nor with virtual play worlds for socializing with friends and family like Meta's "Horizon." The metaverse project the author is investing in has more affinity with the project of the realist novel (and indeed realist film) which in Georg Lukacs spirited words is projecting "the hidden fluctuations of society, the intrinsic laws governing its movements, its incipient trends, its invisible growth and its revolutionary upheavals."[24] The metaverse, conceived within this paradigm of realism, can indeed become a harbinger of revolution, not only in architecture but in all that architecture frames.

NOTES

1. This article is an updated contribution to the architectural theory expounded in the author's *Autopoiesis of Architecture.*
2. Patrik Schumacher, *The Autopoiesis of Architecture, Volume 1, A New Framework for Architecture* (London: John Wiley & Sons, 2010) & *The Autopoiesis of Architecture, Volume 2, A New Agenda for Architecture* (London: John Wiley & Sons, 2012).
3. Erving Goffman, *Frame Analysis—An Essay on the Organisation of Experience* (New York, NY: Harper & Row, 1974).
4. Gilles Deleuze, *Cinema I* (UK: Bloomsbury Publishing), 13.
5. Ibid., 15.
6. Ibid., 13.
7. Ibid., 15.
8. Ibid., 14.
9. Ibid., 14.
10. Ibid., 15.
11. Ibid., 17.
12. Ibid., 16.
13. For recent summaries, see Patrik Schumacher, "Operationalising Architecture's Core Competency—Agent-based Parametric Semiology," in *DC I/O 2020, Design Computation Input/Output Conference: Algorithms, Cognitions, Cultures*; also: Patrik Schumacher, "From Intuition to Simulation," in *Positions: Unfolding Architectural Endeavors* (Edition Angewandte, Basel: Birkhaeuser, 2020); also: Patrik Schumacher, "Advancing Social Functionality via Agent Based Parametric Semiology," in *AD Parametricism*

2.0—Rethinking Architecture's Agenda for the 21st Century, ed. H. Castle, Guest-edited by Patrik Schumacher, AD Profile #240, March/April 2016.

14. Georg Lukacs, *Studies in European Realism* (Hong Kong: Hillway Publishing, 1950, republished by Merlin Press, London, 1972).
15. Gilles Deleuze, *Cinema I* (UK: Bloomsbury Publishing), 145.
16. Ibid.
17. Ibid.
18. Ibid., 146.
19. Ibid.
20. Ibid., 127.
21. Ibid., 164.
22. Ibid., 165.
23. Georg Lukacs, *Studies in European Realism* (Hong Kong: Hillway Publishing, 1950, republished by Merlin Press, London 1972), 12.
24. Ibid., 70.

REFERENCES

Deleuze, Gilles. *Cinema I: The Movement-Image*. UK: Bloomsbury Academic, 2013.

Goffman, Erving. *Frame Analysis: An Essay on the Organization of Experience*. New York, NY: Harper & Row, 1974.

Lukács, Georg. *Studies in European Realism: A Sociological Survey of the Writings of Balzac, Stendhal, Zola, Tolstoy, Gorki and Others*. UK: Merlin, 1972.

Schumacher, Patrik. "Advancing Social Functionality via Agent Based Parametric Semiology." *AD Parametricism 2.0: Rethinking Architecture's Agenda for the 21st Century*, AD Profile #240 (March/April 2016).

Schumacher, Patrik. *The Autopoiesis of Architecture: A New Agenda for Architecture, Volume II*. London: John Wiley & Sons, 2012.

Schumacher, Patrik. *The Autopoiesis of Architecture: A New Framework for Architecture, Volume I*. London: John Wiley & Sons, 2010.

Schumacher, Patrik. "From Intuition to Simulation." In *Positions: Unfolding Architectural Endeavors*, edited by Ozvaldič Maja, Pap Bence, and Umbrasaite Indre, 69–75. Germany: Birkhäuser, 2020.

Schumacher, Patrik. "Operationalizing Architecture's Core Competency: Agent-based Parametric Semiology." In *Design Computation Input/Output Conference: Algorithms, Cognitions, Cultures*, London, UK, June 8–9, 2020. https://doi.org/10.47330/DCIO.2020.QPRF9890.

Contributors

MARK FOSTER GAGE is an architect, writer, and theorist. His New York City firm, Mark Foster Gage Architects, has combined philosophical and technological speculation with the assets of a fully licensed architectural practice for clients such as Lady Gaga, Intel, The Biden/Harris Presidential Campaign, and Intel. Gage's work has been exhibited in museums internationally including the Museum of Modern Art (MoMA), the Museum of the Art Institute of Chicago, The Royal Academy of Art in London, and The Royal Danish Academy. In addition to his architectural practice, Gage is a tenured professor at the Yale School of Architecture with academic expertise in the field of aesthetic philosophy.

* * * * *

JUHANI PALLASMAA is arguably Finland's most prolific architect. He has authored or edited more than 70 books. His writings have been translated and published in 36 languages. His books have become a classic of architectural theory worldwide. His writings are being catalogued for the library of the Museum of Finnish Architecture. The subject matters of his writings span from theoretical and critical writings on a multitude of aspects of architecture as well as numerous architects around the world, to essays on the arts artists, photography, and cinema. He is especially interested in the interactions of architecture and cinema as well as the influences of art and artists on cinematic imagination.

* * * * *

JON YODER is a designer and scholar of modern architecture and visual media who received his PhD in architecture from UCLA. He teaches design and theory at Kent State University and taught previously at Syracuse University and SCI-Arc. His designs with Pei Cobb Freed, ZGF Architects, and SPF:architects have been published widely, and his research and teaching have been supported by numerous grants and awards. These include an ARCHITECT Studio Prize for his design studio, "Graphic Novels/Novel Architecture," and a Graham Foundation grant for his forthcoming Getty Research Institute Publications book, *Widescreen Architecture: Immersive Media and John Lautner*.

*****

VAHID VAHDAT is an assistant professor at the School of Design and Construction, Washington State University. His primary field of research is spatial mediation, with an emphasis on virtual reality and film. He is the author of *Occidentalist Perceptions of European Architecture in Nineteenth Century Persian Travel Diaries—Travels in Farangi Space* (Routledge, 2017). His edited volume, *Virtual Interiorities* (Carnegie Mellon University ETC Press, 2022) addresses how virtual media historically frame, filter, and manipulate our perception of the built environment. Dr. Vahdat has held academic positions in the US and abroad, including at the University of Houston and Texas A&M University.

*****

JAMES F. KERESTES is a registered architect who holds a Bachelor of Architecture degree from Syracuse University and a Post-Professional Master of Architecture degree from Pratt Institute. James is currently an associate professor of architecture at Ball State University. Prior to his current position at Ball State, he has taught digital media and emergent technologies at Princeton University and the University of Pennsylvania. His current research focuses on identifying and exploring the latent potential within tools and building typologies to instigate novel architectural design inquiries. This emphasis explores methods for engaging tools as mediums where authorial exchanges lead to new opportunities in design communication, architectural storytelling, user interaction, digital fabrication, and construction.

*****

BEATRIZ COLOMINA is the Howard Crosby Butler Professor of the history of architecture and the co-director of the media and modernity program at Princeton University. Her books include *Sexuality and Space* (1992), *Privacy and Publicity: Modern Architecture as Mass Media* (1994), *Domesticity at War* (2007), *Clip/Stamp/Fold* (2010), and *Are We Human? Notes on an Archaeology of Design* (2016). Her exhibitions include *Clip/Stamp/Fold* (2006), *Playboy Architecture* (2012), *Radical Pedagogies* (2014), and *Sick Architecture* (2022).

In 2016 she was co-curator of the 3rd Istanbul Design Biennial. Her latest books are *X-Ray Architecture* (Lars Muller, 2019) and *Radical Pedagogies* (MIT, 2022).

*****

Maria Sieira was born in Santiago de Compostela, Spain, where she still teaches architecture in the summer program Compostela Architecture. From 2007 to 2017 she coordinated the housing studio, the learning spaces studio, and the history/theory courses in the graduate architecture department. She studied both architecture and theater as an undergraduate at Yale University, a pursuit that led to an interest in architecture narratives. At Pratt, she developed and taught a seminar on film and architecture (architects making space with moving images), with which she further explored this theme of architecture narratives. She worked on the *Cidade da Cultura*, in Santiago de Compostela, Spain, while at Eisenman Architects in New York and on the Philadelphia Airport while at DPK&A in Philadelphia. She is a registered architect in New York State.

*****

Michael Young is an associate professor at The Irwin S. Chanin School of Architecture at the Cooper Union and founding partner at Young & Ayata. Young & Ayata have received the Progressive Architecture Award, Design Vanguard Award, Young Architects Prize, AIA Honor Award, and a first-place prize for the design of the Bauhaus Museum in Dessau, Germany. Michael is the recipient of the Rome Prize from the American Academy of Rome. His book publications include *The Estranged Object* (Graham Foundation, 2015) and *Reality Modeled After Images* (Routledge, 2021).

*****

Mehmet Şahinler is a sociologist teaching at Mimar Sinan Fine Arts University in Istanbul. In his master's thesis, Mehmet looked into "Ideology and Critique of Ideology." After receiving his degree at the Universiteit van Amsterdam, he became a visiting research student at the London School of Economics and Political Science in 2018. He is currently working on his PhD studies at the Department of General Sociology and Methodology. His academic work focuses on the relations between society and ideology, their mutations, and their mechanisms. His articles, interviews, and papers have been published in academic and peer-reviewed journals and presented in several national and international conferences and seminars.

* * * * *

Alican Taylan is an architect and engineer working on his PhD in architecture history at Cornell University. His work was supported by grants from the Architectural League, the New York State Council on the Arts, the Graham Foundation, Pratt Institute SoA Dean's Office, AEFE, and was exhibited at The Cooper Union's Houghton Gallery, the Massachusetts Museum of Contemporary Arts, Pratt Institute's Siegel Gallery, the Venice Architecture Biennale, and the Monaco Yacht Show. Prior to doing doctoral studies, he was a visiting assistant professor at Pratt Institute and worked under architects Peter Eisenman, Shigeru Ban, and Thomas Leeser. He is interested in the role of architectural imagination during the rise of industrialism and is broadly concerned with 19th-century intellectual history from an environmental standpoint.

* * * * *

Graham Harman is Distinguished Professor of Philosophy at the Southern California Institute of Architecture (SCI-Arc) in Los Angeles. His most recent books are *Architecture and Objects* (2022) and *The Graham Harman Reader* (2023). He is a founding member of the Speculative Realism and Object-Oriented Ontology movements, Editor-in-Chief of the journal *Open Philosophy*, and Series Editor of the Speculative Realism series at Edinburgh University Press and the New Metaphysics series at Open Humanities Press. Harman is the recipient of the 2023 Paolo Bozzi Prize for Ontology.

* * * * *

Ferda Kolatan is the founding director of New York based SU11 Architecture + Design and an associate professor at the University of Pennsylvania Weitzman School of Design. He received his architectural diploma from the RWTH Aachen and his MSAAD from Columbia University. SU11's work has been exhibited at such renowned venues as MoMA, FRAC Center, Walker Art Center, Vitra Design Museum, Art Basel, and the Venice, Beijing, and Istanbul Biennales. Ferda has taught, lectured, and written extensively about architecture and co-authored the book *Meander: Variegating Architecture* in 2010. In 2017 his Cairo Research-Studio received the prestigious ARCHITECT Magazine Studio Prize.

* * * * *

EVA PEREZ DE VEGA is an architect, designer, and educator. She is a founding partner at e+i studio, an architecture and design practice based in NYC. She studied architecture at the University of Madrid (ETSAM) specializing in Building Structures and has a master's in philosophy from the New School For Social Research. Prior to establishing e+i studio, Eva was lead design architect at Reiser + Umemoto. She is a professor of architecture at Pratt Institute and at Parsons, having previously taught at the UPenn and Princeton School of Architecture. Originally from Rome, Italy, she has lived in New York City since 2001.

*****

GIULIANA BRUNO is Emmet Blakeney Gleason Professor of visual and environmental studies at Harvard University. Internationally known for her interdisciplinary research on visual arts, architecture and media, she is the author of several award-winning books, including *Atlas of Emotion: Journeys in Art, Architecture and Film* (Verso, 2002), winner of the Kraszna-Krausz prize for best Moving Image Book in the world; *Streetwalking on a Ruined Map* (Princeton University Press, 1993), winner of the Society for Cinema and Media Studies book award; *Public Intimacy: Architecture and the Visual Arts* (MIT, 2007), and *Surface: Matters of Aesthetics, Materiality, and Media* (University of Chicago Press, 2014). Her new book is *Atmospheres of Projection: Environmentality in Art and Screen Media* (University of Chicago Press, forthcoming).

*****

JASON VIGNERI-BEANE is an architect, industrial designer, and associate professor of core design at Pratt Institute's School of Architecture. He has taught, lectured, published, and exhibited in North America, South America, Europe, and Asia, and recently received Pratt Institute's Distinguished Teacher Award, the Institute's highest teaching honor. Jason is the founding principal of Split Studio, a Brooklyn-based practice interested in multi-disciplinary approaches to design with a concentration on working across scales and media that include graphics, video, industrial design, architecture, urbanism, and ecology. His current work focuses on the relationship between ecology, technology, media, and design.

*****

PATRIK SCHUMACHER is principal of Zaha Hadid Architects. He studied philosophy, mathematics, and architecture in Bonn, Stuttgart, and London and received his PhD at the Institute for Cultural Science in Klagenfurt. In 1996 he founded the

Design Research Laboratory at the AA in London where he continues to teach. Since 2007 he is promoting Parametricism as epochal style for the 21st century. His current research interest is focused on the metaverse and the integration of real and virtual communication spaces.

Index

Page numbers in italics indicate black and white figures: color figures are referenced by their figure number.